BAR INTERNATIONAL SERIES 3058 | 2021

Africa, Egypt and the Danubian Provinces of the Roman Empire

Population, Military and Religious Interactions (2nd-3rd centuries AD)

EDITED BY

ŞTEFANA CRISTEA, CĂLIN TIMOC
AND ERIC CHARLES DE SENA

BAR
PUBLISHING

Published in 2021 by
BAR Publishing, Oxford

BAR International Series 3058

Africa, Egypt and the Danubian Provinces of the Roman Empire

ISBN 978 1 4073 5904 5 paperback
ISBN 978 1 4073 5905 2 e-format

DOI https://doi.org/10.30861/9781407359045

A catalogue record for this book is available from the British Library

Cover image *Drawing of clay statuettes with the representation
of the god Osiris from Dierna (Roman Dacia).*

BAR
PUBLISHING

BAR titles are available from:

BAR Publishing
122 Banbury Rd, Oxford, OX2 7BP, UK
  Email info@barpublishing.com
  Phone +44 (0)1865 310431
    Fax +44 (0)1865 316916
www.barpublishing.com

Of Related Interest

The Resilience of the Roman Empire
Regional case studies on the relationship between population and food resources
Edited by Dimitri Van Limbergen, Sadi Maréchal and Wim De Clercq
Oxford, BAR Publishing, 2020

BAR International Series **3000**

Romans in the Middle and Lower Danube Valley, 1st century BC–5th century AD
Case Studies in Archaeology, Epigraphy and History
Edited by Eric C. De Sena and Calin Timoc
Oxford, BAR Publishing, 2017

BAR International Series **2882**

Exercitus Moesiae
The Roman Army in Moesia from Augustus to Severus Alexander
Conor Whately
Oxford, BAR Publishing, 2016

BAR International Series **2825**

Approaches to Healing in Roman Egypt
Jane Draycott
Oxford, BAR Publishing, 2012

BAR International Series **2416**

The Role of Foreigners in Ancient Egypt
A study of non-stereotypical artistic representations
Charlotte Booth
Oxford, BAR Publishing, 2005

BAR International Series **1426**

Ancient Egypt and Antique Europe
*Two parts of the Mediterranean World. Papers from a session held at the European Association
of Archaeologists Seventh Annual Meeting in Esslingen 2001*
Edited by Amanda-Alice Maravelia
Oxford, BAR Publishing, 2002

BAR International Series **1052**

The Impact of Rome on Settlement in the Northwestern and Danube Provinces
Lectures held at the Winckelmann-Institut der Humboldt-Universität zu Berlin in winter 1998/99
Edited by Stefan Altekamp and Alfred Schäfer
Oxford, BAR Publishing, 2001

BAR International Series **921**

In memoriam Prof. Dr. Alexandru Diaconescu

Contents

Abbreviations vi

1. Introduction 1
   Ştefana Cristea, Călin Timoc, Eric Charles De Sena

2. Auxiliary Units from the European Provinces in the Moorish War of Antoninus Pius 5
   Florian Matei-Popescu

3. Militaires de Mésie Inférieure Dans les Maurétanies 17
   Lucreţiu Mihăilescu-Bîrliba

4. Epigraphic Sources on the Movement of People between Egypt and the Provinces of Lower Moesia
   and Thrace (1st - 3rd c. AD) 21
   Ligia Ruscu

5. The Cult of Asclepius in the Roman Empire: A Comparative Analysis of North Africa and Dacia 25
   Jasmin Hangartner

6. The Cults of Serapis and Isis in Roman Serdica 35
   Vessela Atanassova

7. Les Cultes isiaques à Sarmizegetusa 45
   Laurent Bricault, Dan Deac, Ioan Piso

8. Egypt on the Danube. Egyptianizing the Material Agency of Roman Religious Communication in
   Western Illyricum 65
   Csaba Szabó

9. Gods of Egyptian Origin at Dierna (Orşova, Romania): Methodology, Assemblage, Influences and
   Interpretations 75
   Ştefana Cristea, Călin Timoc

Abbreviations

AA: *Archäologischer Anzeiger*. Berlin.

AÉ: L'Année épigraphique (1888 -), Presses Universitaires de France, Paris.

AIIA: *Anuarul Institutului de Istorie și Arheologie*. Cluj.

AISC: *Anuarul Institutului de Studii Clasice*. Cluj.

AMN: *Acta Musei Napocensis*. Cluj-Napoca.

AMP: *Acta Musei Porolissensis*. Zalău.

ANRW: *Aufstieg und Niedergang der römischen Welt*. Berlin.

AntAfr: *Antiquites africaines*. Aix-en-Provence.

Apulum: *Acta Musei Apulensis*. Alba Iulia.

ArchÉrt: *Archaeológiai* Értesitö. Budapest.

ArchHun: *Archaeologia Hungarica. Acta Archaeologica Musei Nationalis Hungarici*. Budapest.

ArchRel: *Archiv für Religionsgeschichte*. Berlin.

CIGD: Ruscu, L., *Corpus Inscriptionum Graecarum Dacicarum*. Hungarian Polis Studies 10. Debrecen (2003).

CIMRM: Vermaseren, M. J., *Corpus inscriptionum et monumentorum religionis Mithriacae I-II*. Den Haag (1956-1960).

CIL: *Corpus Inscriptionum Latinarum*. Berlin.

CRAI: *Comptes rendus des séances de l'Académie des Inscriptions et Belles-Lettres*. Paris.

CSIR: *Corpus Signorum Imperii Romani*. Oxford.

DialHistAnc: *Dialogues d'histoire ancienne*. Besançon.

EphNap: *Ephemeris Napocensis*. Cluj-Napoca.

EPRO: Études *préliminaires aux religions orientales dans l'empire romain*. Leiden.

IAM: *Inscriptions antiques du Maroc*. Paris.

IDR: *Inscriptiones Daciae Romanae*. Bucarest/Paris.

IDRE: Petolescu, C. C., *Inscriptiones Daciae Romanae. Inscriptiones extra fines Daciae repertae*. Bucarest (1996, 2000).

IG: *Inscriptiones Graecae*. Berlin.

IGL: Alexa E. Breccia, *Iscrizioni greche e latine. Catalogue général des antiquités égyptiennes du Musée d'Alexandrie, nos 1-568*. Cairo (1911).

IGLR: E. Popescu, *Inscripțiile grecești și latine din sec. IV-XIII descoperite în România*. Bucharest (1976).

IvPerinthos: M. H. Sayar, *Perinthos-Herakleia (Marmara Ereğlisi) und Umgebung. Geschichte, Testimonien, griechische und lateinische Inschriften*. Vienna (1998).

I. Kyme: Engelmann, H., *Die Inschriften von Kyme*. Bonn (1976).

ILD I: Petolescu, C. C., *Inscripții latine din Dacia*. București (2005).

ILS: *Inscriptiones Latinae Selectae*. Berlin.

ISM II: I. Stoian, *Inscripțiile din Scythia Minor II. Tomis și teritoriul său*. Bucharest (1987).

ISM III: A. Avram, *Inscriptions de Scythie Mineure III. Callatis et son territoire*. Bucharest/Paris (1999).

ISM VI2: A. Avram, *Inscriptions de Scythie Mineure VI. Suppléments. 2. Tomis et son territoire*. Bucharest/Paris (2018).

JRGZ: *Jahrbuch des Römisch-Germanischen Zentralmuseums*. Bonn.

MCDRD: Muzeul Civilizației Dacice și Romane. Deva.

Memnonion: P. Perdrizet, G. Lefebvre, *Les Graffites grecs du Memnonion d'Abydos*. Nancy (1919).

OLA: *Orientalia Lovanensia Analecta*. Leuven.

PIR²: Prosopographia Imperii Romani saec. I. II. III². Berlini et Lipsiae.

PME: Devijver, H., *Prosopographia militiarum equestrium quae fuerunt ab Augusto ad Gallienum*. Louvain (1976).

RE: Realencyclopädie der classischen Altertumswissenschaft. Stuttgart.

RGRW: Religions in the Graeco-Roman World. Leiden.

RGZM: Pferdehirt, B., *Römische Militärdiplome und Entlassungsurkunden in der Sammlung des Römisch-Germanischen Zentralmuseums.* Mainz (2004).

RICIS: Bricault, L., *Recueil des inscriptions concernant les cultes isiaques I-III. Mémoires de l'Académie des Inscriptions et Belles-Lettres XXXI.* Paris (2005).

RIU: Die römischen Inschriften Ungarns. Bonn-Budapest.

RMD: *Roman Military Diplomas.* London.

ROMIS: P. Selem, I. Vilogorac Vilogorac Brčic, J. Osterman, *Religionum Orientalium Monumenta et Inscriptiones Salonitani,* Zagreb (2012).

SCIV(A): Studii şi Cercetări de Istorie Veche (şi Arheologie). Bucureşti.

SEG: *Supplementum Epigraphicum Graecum.*

SHA: *Scriptores Historiae Augustae,* O. Hohl (ed.). Leipzig (1955).

SIRIS: Vidman, L., *Sylloge inscriptionum religionis Isiacae et Sarapiacae.* Berlin (1969).

SYRINGES: J. Baillet, *Inscriptions grecques et latines des tombeaux des rois ou Syringes à Thèbes I-III.* Cairo (1920-1926).

ZPE: Zeitschrift für Papyrologie und Epigraphik. Köln.

The Danubian Provinces of the Roman Empire (2nd-3rd centuries AD)
O. Țentea, Fl. Matei-Popescu, *Frontiers of the Roman Empire between Dacia and Moesia Superior. The Roman Forts in Muntenia under Trajan*. Cluj-Napoca (2016): 3-4.

Introduction

This volume springs from the symposium 'Africa and the Danubian Provinces of the Roman Empire' (July 29-30, 2018), which took place in Timişoara and was organized by the National Museum of Banat, the Center for Middle Eastern and Mediterranean Studies (Babeş-Bolyai University) Cluj-Napoca, and the West University Timişoara. The symposium was attended by well-known specialists along with early career researchers from Romania (Timişoara, Cluj-Napoca, Iaşi, Bucharest, Zalău, Sibiu), France (Toulouse), Bulgaria (Sofia), Austria (Vienna), Italy (Macerata). We had the pleasure to have as keynote speakers Prof. Dr Laurent Bricault (University of Toulouse II Jean Jaurès), Prof. Dr Alexandru Diaconescu (Babeş-Bolyai University Cluj Napoca, Center for Middle Eastern and Mediterranean Studies), Prof. Dr Ioan Piso (Babeş-Bolyai University Cluj-Napoca), Prof. Dr Doina Benea (West University Timişoara), and Dr Florian Matei-Popescu (Vasile Pârvan Institute of Archeology, Romanian Academy, Bucharest). We regret that Prof. Dr Mustafa El Rhaiti (Meknès, Morocco) could not attend the symposium, despite his efforts. His contribution would have given the symposium a different perspective on the common and different elements among the two regions of the Roman Empire and on the population dynamics of the Empire in the 2nd-3rd centuries AD.

The symposium would not have existed without the contribution of the Center for Middle Eastern and Mediterranean Studies (Babeş-Bolyai University) Cluj-Napoca. We had the pleasure to have as keynote speaker the director of this institution, Prof. Dr Alexandru Diaconescu. Unfortunately, he passed away much too soon, during the volume editing process, and this volume is dedicated to his memory. A large number of those present at this symposium, whether or not they contributed to this volume, knew him, either personally or through his work. To some he was professor and to others a colleague or friend. Those who knew him were impressed by his special oratorical talent, by his charismatic personality and by his extensive knowledge of Roman art and architecture, of the Ancient Orient, of the religions of Oriental origin of the Roman Empire, and epigraphy. What gave an even greater depth to the research of Prof. Dr Alexandru Diaconescu, was the fact that he was also an excellent archaeologist. This allowed him to work not only with written sources and discoveries made by other archaeologists, but also to make his own discoveries and interpret the reality in the field, especially in terms of major statuary, minor art, and the architectural structure of a Roman city. He and his teams made important discoveries in many cities of Dacia, including Apulum, Ulpia Traiana Sarmizegetusa and Napoca. His most important work is *Statuaria majoră în Dacia romană* (Monumental Statuary in Roman Dacia), an extremely valuable work for all those who study high Roman art or other related fields.

During the symposium in Timişoara he presented the paper 'Public life in Roman colonies. A parallel between Thamugadi in Numidia and Sarmizegetusa in Dacia'. In this presentation he made an extensive and refined parallel between the municipal organization of these two Roman cities located in such different areas of the empire, emphasizing both the similarities and the differences. The presentation, based mainly on archaeological evidence, was perfectly matched with the theme of the symposium and emphasized once again what the organizers wanted to assert: without ignoring the differences induced by local heritage, the Roman Empire applied the same principles to all its provinces, regardless of the organization of the army, politics, cities or religions (especially of civic religion).

The intention of the symposium was to illustrate the Egyptian and African military and civilian presence in the Danubian provinces, the Egyptian and African influences manifested at the level of material culture, religion and magic, as well as the presence of the inhabitants of the Danubian provinces in the North African region of the Roman Empire, and Egypt through case studies. It is well-known through the study of brick stamps, military diplomas, funerary epitaphs, and other archaeological remains that soldiers from Egypt and North Africa were stationed in Dacia and vice versa. The scholars whose articles are included in this volume have examined literary, historical, epigraphic, archaeological and art historical evidence in order to discuss the cross-pollination of culture and organization within these two regions of the Roman Empire. In the past decade, scholarship has begun to address a broader array of questions pertaining to issues such as the Roman economy, politics and religions, from a more atypical perspective. Topics such as social and individual identity, fear, hope, desire, and how the archaeological evidence can embody them are increasingly discussed. We are dealing with what we can define in a new term as *the archaeology of the imponderable*. This term refers to archaeological evidence that provides us the opportunity to capture, through an unconventional query, very personal aspects of people's lives in antiquity, aspects difficult to measure otherwise.

The symposium was a complex event that included the opening of the exhibition *From Pagan Gods to Christianity*, which was attended by all the specialists involved in the symposium. The exhibition was organized by Dr Ştefana Cristea (Center for Middle Eastern and

Mediterranean Studies, Babeş-Bolyai University Cluj-Napoca and the National Museum of Banat Timişoara) and Dr Călin Timoc (National Museum of Banat Timişoara) and included artefacts belonging to the National Museum of Banat Timişoara, the Museum of Dacian and Roman Civilization Deva, the Museum of the Iron Gates Region Drobeta Turnu Severin, the Buzău County Museum, the Zalău County Art Museum (Vasile Lucăcel History Section), and the Museum of Montane Banat Reşiţa. The exhibition aimed to expose ideas, rituals, and symbols that Christianity adopted from older cults and religions, such as those from Egypt or the Near East (e.g., resurrection, the soul, a happy eternal afterlife for the ones who deserved it, the snake as symbol of chaos), and from the Roman Empire (e.g., displaying the protective deities in specially arranged spaces inside the houses). At the same time, the exhibition aimed to express the materiality of these abstract notions.

During the symposium, the papers were grouped according to general themes, which are followed in this volume: Roman Army. Exchanges of military units between the Danubian provinces, Egypt and North Africa; Public life, romanization, population;   The African and Egyptian influence in the religious life of the Danubian provinces.

The first theme concerns the military connection and the mobility of Roman troops between the two geographical areas of the Roman Empire. This topic was approached by considering both the ancient literary sources, as well as the archaeological record, as in the articles of Florian Matei Popescu and Lucreţiu Mihăilescu-Bîrliba. In the contribution of Dr Florian Matei-Popescu, 'Auxiliary Units from European Provinces in the Moorish War of Antoninus Pius', the author reevaluates the information regarding the participation of the Roman army in the Moorish war, during the reign of the Emperor Antoninus Pius. The current state of research, updated through epigraphic, numismatic, and papyrological discoveries allows a much more accurate view of those involved and the events. The study of military diplomas has greatly enriched our knowledge of the size and composition of combat vexillations that crossed the Mediterranean Sea. The new information brought by Dr Matei-Popescu's work complements that of Prof. Dr Doina Benea, also a participant at the symposium ('Some observations on Maurorum Numerus from the province of Dacia', published in *Sargetia*, IX / 2018, 61-85). Prof. Dr Benea's article focused upon the military relations between the provinces of Dacia and Mauretania (2nd-3rd centuries AD), seen through the perspective of Moors recruited to defend the Roman Danubian limes.

Lucreţiu Mihăilescu-Bîrliba, in his article *Militaires de Mesie Inferieure dans les Mauretanies*, suggests that the conditions in Africa evolved better from the point of view of Romanization, compared to the image of Africa painted by authors such as Marcus Annaeus Lucanus. The inscriptions recall periodic demobilizations of the troops of Lower Moesia who were sent to the African limes, especially in the areas of Mauretania Caesariensis and Tingitana. The conflict between the Romans and the African tribes, which lasted more than 10 years, involved the transfer of military units from the European part of the Roman Empire to the African one. The settling of veterans in the African provinces, where they married local women, might seem a little less common. One explanation could be the political stability of the area, compared to other provinces, and the possibility of owning an extensive piece of land, which would offer prosperous economic prospects for their future descendants.

The social mobility between the Danubian and African provinces of the Roman Empire as well as Egypt's trade relations with the Greek colonies in the Pontic area and Thrace are well demonstrated in the article by Ligia Ruscu: 'Epigraphic Sources on the Movements of People between Egypt and the Provinces of Lower Moesia and Thrace (1st - 3rd century AD)'. Africa's riches attracted merchants who sought the patronage of the Ptolemies to protect their success in business. These relations changed when Rome interfered militarily and administratively in the eastern Mediterranean. In the Roman imperial era, population transfers between Pontus Euxinus and Egypt intensified and became more diverse. Like Lucreţiu Mihăilescu-Bîrliba, Ligia Ruscu noticed that mixed marriages occurred after a long period of not being allowed or not performed, because of cultural traditions. Marriage facilitated the acquisition of Roman citizenship, permitting some African noble families to ascend to the new provincial aristocracy, accumulating wealth and prestige.

The most common theme among the contributions in this volume relates to the religious life of Egypt, the Danubian and African provinces. Most papers address the deities of Egyptian origin Isis, Serapis, Harpocrates, and Osiris, as well as the Sibylline Oracles and the cult of Aesculapius and Hygia.

Jasmin Hangartner offers a comparative study on how the cult of Asclepius was represented in provinces such as Africa Proconsularis, Numidia, Mauretania Caesariensis, Mauretania Tingitana, and Roman Dacia ('The Cult of Asclepius in the Roman Empire: A Comparative Analysis of North Africa and Dacia'). Both the mapping of the places of worship of the god and his competence are taken into account. Based on the existing archaeological evidence, the author concludes that for some of the places of worship attributed to this god there is not enough evidence to support such a claim. Although there are similarities between the way the cult of Asclepius/Aesculapius was perceived in the provinces of North Africa and Dacia (in cities such as Apulum, Ulpia Traiana Sarmizegetusa), there were still many elements characteristic only of the African regions: the association of the god with Punic and Numidian deities and "unlike in North Africa, in Dacia there is no site where the cult is almost exclusively documented through members of the military even though the urban centres of the province are very much influenced by it". Nevertheless, an inscription dedicated by an officer in Roman Dacia (CIL III, 993) mentions the goddess Caelestis together with Asclepius, as well as two *genio*, one African and one Dacian: *Genio Carthaginis* and *Genio Daciarum*. This inscription highlights the idea according to which the provinces of the entire Roman Empire, regardless of the distance between them, were guided towards a military, political, and spiritual uniformity in order to ensure a common language throughout its space. The inhabitants of the empire of course had religious preferences that reflected their uniqueness and helped overcom the fear of death, but recognized the importance of all local gods. They tried to win their goodwill, whether the god was a protective spirit of Carthage or Dacia.

New evidence of the existence of Isiac cults in Thrace (Serdica) is presented by Dr Vessela Atanassova in the article 'Isis and Serapis in Serdica'. The author recalls the stages in which the deities of Egyptian origin arrived in Thrace and groups the material researched by the main deities: Isis and Serapis. The two deities are mentioned in epigraphic material and coins, but also emerge in various representations, including very personal items such as a hair pin and lamps that are present either in temples or tombs. The author concludes that in the 3rd century AD dedications or embodiments of the gods of Egyptian origin came not only from the official environment, but also from the domestic or personal one, inside or outside the cities.

Another Danubian province that benefits from a study discussed in this volume is Illyricum. The focus of this article by Csabo Szabó is on the meaning that the notion of Egyptianism(s) may have had at the general level of the Roman Empire. Another point of interest of the article is the mobility of Egyptian objects inside the empire. The author focuses upon the Western part of the *Publicum Portorium Illyrici* with several case studies (e.g., Savaria, Salona). The methodology and the terms used pertain to the latest approaches in the study of ancient religions and are clearly influenced by the school created by Jörg Rüpke in Erfurt (Lived Ancient Religion). Szabó's study brings into question a problem less discussed in the scientific literature: to what extent can "Africanism" be linked to Roman Egypt, geographically and culturally. To answer this question the author turns to the ancient literary sources. He concludes: "Studying Roman religion today means focusing on individual agency, facets or religious communication, strategies in space sacralization and less prominently, the role of materiality of religion in communication and ritualization. Other important topics however, such as belief, divine agency, and polis religion seem to be marginalized." Even if we agree with him to a large extent, the studies carried out in the last decade show a growing awareness of studying the importance of the ancient human element in all its complexity, being created in this regard new terms and more daring approaches.

Laurent Bricault, Dan Deac, and Ioan Piso discuss the dissemination of the goddess Isis and the other deities associated with her in the Roman Empire, a phenomenon closely related to the local social context. The particular case

they discuss is that of *colonia* Sarmizegetusa. The article summarizes the currently available information related to the adoption of Egyptian deities in the province of Dacia and presents the data in a new light. All the epigraphic and anepigraphic sources available at this moment for *colonia* Ulpia Traiana Sarmizegetusa are analyzed in detail, making this article an invaluable tool for those interested in the subject. The inscriptions are grouped according to the area in which they were discovered, thus, helping to create a more complete picture of the evolution of certain constructions (e.g. the *Serapeum* built in *praetorium procuratoris*, dated by the authors to 213 and continuing to exist during the 3rd century AD) or areas of the *colonia*. A point of great interest is the reading of what the authors consider to be two or three marble plates, extremely fragmented and representing a very important text used in the initiation rituals to the Isiac cult. The text reminds us of the one described by Apuleius, Isis was called here *una quae est omnia*.

Also focusing upon a city in Roman Dacia, the article by Ștefana Cristea and Călin Timoc paints a picture of the proliferation of the Isiac cult in Dierna (Orșova, Mehedinți County). The location of Dierna on the banks of the Danube and the importance of this location in its history are described, based on epigraphic, historiographical and archaeological sources. The first part of the article emphasizes methodology and the use of specific terminology. The authors defend the use of certain terms, while offering their definition. Ancient literary, epigraphic, and archeological sources are considered in the discourse of the article. Moreover, it includes a catalog of artifacts discovered in Dierna and related to the worship of the deities of Egyptian origin. Some of the items are published here for the first time. The authors attempt, as far as possible, an investigation into the social dimension of the motivation for choosing these gods by the inhabitants of the city. Cristea and Timoc have also built a model of the ways in which these deities were introduced into Dierna. Unfortunately, the Roman city is now under the waters of the Danube river, and any further archaeological excavations are limited to the areas adjacent to the ancient city.

We are very happy to have had the chance to collaborate with such an extraordinary group of specialists as those who have chosen to publish in this volume, and we hope that our collaboration does not stop here. We are also grateful for the support of all the institutions involved in the organization of the symposium and the publication of the volume, as well as the publishing house.

The Editors

Auxiliary Units from the European Provinces in the Moorish War of Antoninus Pius*

Florian Matei-Popescu

(Vasile Pârvan Institute of Archaeology, Romanian Academy Bucharest)

Abstract: This paper examines epigraphic sources in order to shed light upon the movement of troops during the Moorish War of the mid-2nd century AD. Relying upon military diplomas, copied after imperial constitutions, funerary stele, and other types of inscriptions, it is possible to accurately trace the deployment of troops from the European provinces into Mauretania. Given the fact that the nomadic tribes in North Africa relied upon horses in their military actions, the Romans often sent cavalry from Pannonia and nearby provinces who were accustomed to fighting against horsemen. Moreover, the paper indicates the transferal of men from Mauretania to the Danubian provinces, in particular to Dacia.

Keywords: Moorish war, European provinces of the Roman empire, epigraphic sources, military diplomas, Mauretania

Introduction

On the occasion of the 1977 Limes Congress in Hungary, M.P. Speidel declared, "The Moorish War of Antoninus Pius was one of the most important wars of the High Empire in Africa."[1] The warfare that occurred in Mauretania in the 140s and early 150s AD involved troops from the Danubian provinces of Pannonia (Speidel's main interest in the Limes Congress),[2] Raetia, Noricum, Moesia Superior and Inferior and, probably, Dacia.[3] As significantly more historical information has come to light since 1977, the aim of this paper is to review all of the known epigraphic sources, and to address questions pertaining to the chronology and the strength of the Danubian contingents sent to Mauretania Caesariensis and Tingitana during that war.

Background

The narrative sources generally praise Antoninus Pius' military victories.[4] Thus, P. Aelius Aristides, in the *To Rome* speech delivered in 143 or 144,[5] declared that some of the contemporary wars were caused by the insanity of the Dacians, the unhappiness of the Libyans, and

the furore of the people residing around the Red Sea.[6] Pausanias discusses the war against the Moorish nomads from Libya, who were considered even more dangerous than the Scythians, and who were forced to retreat to the Atlas Mountains,[7] as well as the war in Britannia.[8] At the beginning of the joint reign of Marcus Aurelius and Lucius Verus, Polyaenus recorded the victories of Antoninus Pius against the Mauri, the Brittones and the Daci.[9] Historia Augusta informs us that Antoninus Pius waged war through his *legati* in some parts of the Empire: Britannia, Mauretania, Dacia, Germania, Iudaea, Achaia, Aegyptus, and the northern shore of the Black Sea.[10] Antoninus Pius'

---

* I wish to thank the editors of this volume for inviting me to attend the conference and having waited so long for me to finish this paper. My gratitude also goes to Dan Dana, Werner Eck, Paul Holder, Yann Le Bohec, Constantin C. Petolescu, and Lluís Pons Pujol for their valuable corrections, comments and suggestions. Needless to say, any remaining mistakes are mine alone.

[1] Speidel 1977.

[2] See the list given by Lőrincz 2001, p. 150.

[3] Christol 1981, with many critical references to the previous publications.

[4] Bénabou 1976, p. 135; Gutsfeld 1989, p. 101-105; Speidel 2017.

[5] PIR[2] A 145; Hund 2017, p. 42-43.

[6] Aelius Aristides *Or.* 26, 70: Πόλεμοι δὲ οὐδ' εἰ πώποτε ἐγένετο ἔτι πιστεύονται, ἀλλ' ὡς ἐν μύθων τάξει τοῖς πολλοῖς ἀκούονται, εἰ δέ που καὶ συμπλακεῖεν ἐπ' ἐσχατιαῖς, οἷα εἰκὸς ἐν ἀρχῇ μεγάλῃ καὶ ἀμετρήτῳ παρανοίᾳ τῶν Γετῶν ἢ δυστυχίᾳ Λιβύων ἢ κακοδαιμονίᾳ τῶν περὶ τὴν Ἐρυθρὰν θάλατταν, ἀγαθοῖς παροῦσι χρήσασθαι μὴ δυναμένων, ἀτεχνῶς ὥσπερ μῦθοι ταχέως αὐτοί τε παρῆλθον καὶ οἱ περὶ αὐτῶν λόγοι; Stroheker 1966, p. 251-253. For the use of Libya for Africa by the Greek authors see Plinius, *NH* 5, 1, 1: *Africam Graeci Libyam appellavere et mare ante eam Libyeum.*

[7] It seems that was a *locus communis* of the ancient literature, since Pliny says that during Claudius' reign some barbarians retreated to the Atlas Mountain, Plinius, *NH* 5, 1, 11: *Romana arma primum Claudio principe in Mauretania bellavere Ptolemaeum regem a Gaio Caesare interemptum ulciscente liberto Aedemone, refugientibusque barbaris ventum constat ad montem Atlantem.*

[8] Pausanias, 8, 43, 3-4: Ὁ δὲ Ἀντωνῖνος ... πόλεμον μὲν Ῥωμαίοις ἐθελοντὴς ἐπηγάγετο οὐδένα, πολέμου δὲ ἄρξαντας Μαύρους, Λιβύων τῶν αὐτονόμων τὴν μεγίστην μοῖραν, νομάδας ὄντας καὶ τοσῷδε ἔτι δυσμαχωτέρους τοῦ Σκυθικοῦ γένους ὅσῳ μὴ ἐπὶ ἁμαξῶν, ἐπὶ ἵππων δὲ αὐτοί τε καὶ αἱ γυναῖκες ἠλῶντο, τούτους μὲν ἐξ ἁπάσης ἐλαύνων τῆς χώρας ἐς τὰ ἔσχατα ἠνάγκασεν ἀναφυγεῖν Λιβύης, ἐπὶ τε Ἄτλαντα τὸ ὄρος καὶ ἐς τοὺς πρὸς τῷ Ἄτλαντι ἀνθρώπους· ἀπετέμετο δὲ καὶ τῶν ἐν Βριττανίᾳ Βριγάντων τὴν πολλήν, ὅτι ἐπεσβαίνειν καὶ οὗτοι σὺν ὅπλοις ἦρξαν ἐς τὴν Γαινουνίαν μοῖραν, ὑπηκόους Ῥωμαίων.

[9] Polyaenus, *Strat.* 6, Praef: ... βουλευσάμενοι καλῶς μετὰ τοῦ πατρός, Μαυρουσίων ἁλόντων, Βρεττανῶν ἁλισκομένων, Γετῶν πεπτωκότων; Hund 2017, p. 74

[10] SHA, *Vita Pii*, 5, 4-6, 1: *Per legatos suos plurima bella gessit. Nam et Britannos pe Lollium Urbicum vicit legatum alio muro caespiticio*

military achievements are also highlighted in an elegiac distich in Rome (AD 150-161): *Germanos Maurosque domas sub Marte Britannos / Antonine tua diceris arte Pius.*[11]

Three serious military engagements are attested during the reign of Antoninus Pius, in Mauretania, Dacia, and Britannia. Scholars have established that the events in North Africa occurred in 145, 150-152, or 144-152.[12] Similar to the situation in Britannia, the borders of the Numidian military district and of Mauretania Caesariensis were shifted further south, and new military installations were built.[13] These actions caused a fierce reaction of the Moorish tribes, leading to three brief wars: the first sometime before 142/143[14] (possibly earlier, in 138, according to the coins),[15] the second around 148-152,[16] and the third in 153-156.[17] The first war broke out in the area of Mauretania Caesariensis, while the last war occurred in Mauretania Tingitana. It is, however, unclear, if these wars were connected, or whether they broke out independently, as the unrest seems to have moved from east to west. As will be demonstrated in this paper, information regarding military activities in Mauretania Tingitana in 144-145 prove that the uprisings were practically contemporary with the ones in Mauretania Caesariensis.

Epigraphic Evidence of Danubian Troops in Mauretania

While epigraphic information referring to the Moorish Wars is scarce, quite a lot can be gleaned from the examples that have come to light.

For instance, we learn that a detachment of the Syrian legion VI Ferrata built a road in the area of Mons Aurasius (Tigaminin) in 145.[18] There is no clear indication whether

the road was built in connection with the military actions of the III Augusta legion in the southern areas of Numidia or Mauretania Caesariensis.[19]

A. Gutsfeld denies that any military action took place under Uttedius Honoratus, *clarissimus vir* in the famous inscription on M. Sulpicius Felix' statue base (AD 144) from Sala (Mauretania Tingitana),[20] or by T. Flavius Priscus, C. Gallonius Fronto, Q. Marcius Turbo, or Publicius Severus' son, Hadrian, *praefectus praetorio*,[21] attested as *pro legato*.[22] In my opinion, their presence is connected with military actions in which legionary detachments took part. Moreover, the two Mauretaniae were probably merged together under Uttedius Honoratus, who could only have been *legatus Augusti pro praetore*,[23] just like Sex. Sentius Caecilianus, attested in 75 as *legatus Augusti pro praetore ordinandae utriusque Mauretaniae.*[24] This could signify the occurrence of a crisis and the need of the governor to command legionary detachments. We must not forget that he was succeeded by T. Flavius Priscus, C. Gallonius Fronto, and Q. Marcius Turbo, *procurator pro legato provinciae Mauretaniae Cesariensis* in 145-147.[25] Interestingly, he was sent to North Africa directly from Dacia Inferior, where, in 142-144, he served as *pro legato et praefectus Daciae Inferioris.*[26] In both cases he commanded legionary detachments.[27]

Probably connected with the logistics and the supply of the army are the possible *horrea* constructed during the reign of Antoninus Pius by the *vexillationes* in the area

summotis barbaris ducto, et Mauros ad pacem postulandam coegit, Germanos et Dacos, et multas gentes atque Iudaeos rebellantes contudit per praesides ac legatos. In Achaia etiam atque Aegypto rebelliones repressit. Alanos molientis saepe refrenavit (see also 9, 9: *Olbiopolitis contra Tauroscythas in Pontum auxilia misit et Tauroscythas usque ad dandos Olbiopolitis obsides vicit*); Stroheker 1966, p. 247-248, 254 (on the coins SCYTHIA from 139, RIC III, p. 106, no. 588); Hund 2017, p. 114-117.
[11] CIL VI 1208 = CLE 881 = AÉ 1952, 160 = 1982, 45; Hund 2017, p. 170; Speidel 2017, p. 266.
[12] Cagnat 1913, p. 47-50; see also Hund 2017, p. 125-136.
[13] Gutsfeld 1989, p. 101-102; Hund 2017, p. 168.
[14] RIC III, p. 122, no. 708; and the Aelius Aristides' testimony (*vide supra*).
[15] RIC III, p. 105, no. 583.
[16] RIC III, p. 136, no. 882; 137, no. 889; 140, no. 911; and the special imperial constitution (*vide infra*).
[17] RIC III, p. 143, no. 941; 145, no. 963; Gutsfeld 1989, p. 105-106; and the special imperial constitution (*vide infra*).
[18] CIL VIII 10230 = ILS 2479 = Saxer 1967, p. 30, no. 56: *Imp(eratore) Caes(are) T(ito) Aelio / Hadriano Antonino / Aug(usto) Pio p(atri) p(atriae) IIII et M(arco) / Aurelio Caesare II / co(n)s(ulibus) per Prastina(m) / Messalinum leg(atum) / Aug(usti) pr(o) pr(aetore) vexil(latio) / leg(ionis) VI Ferr(atae) via(m) / fecit*; Cagnat 1913, p. 111; Cherry 1998, p. 48-50 and 56. See also the altar set by this vexillation at Henchir Sella Uîn, at the western foot of the Mons Aurasius, CIL VIII 2490 = Saxer 1967, p. 30, no. 57: *Herc[uli] / Aug(usto) [sac(rum)] / vex(illatio) [leg(ionis)] VI [Ferr(atae)]*; Rachet 1970, p. 197-198, note 10; Bénabou 1976, p. 141; Le Bohec 1989, p. 378, mentioning that the

name of this legion can be restored on a fragmentary inscription from Lambaesis, CIL VIII 2701 = 18113.
[19] Gutsfeld 1989, p. 106; Hund 2017, p. 134-135.
[20] AÉ 1931, 36, 38 = AÉ 1966, 607 = IAM II/1, 307; PME S 86; Roxan 1973, p. 847, trying to underline that he commanded *cohors II Syrorum milliaria sag.*, attested at Sala during the Severan period (*Genio castrorum, equites cohortis Surorum*, IAM 2, 300 = AE 1989, 913), an elegant way to escape the fact the *ala II Syrorum c. R.*, commanded by M. Sulpicius Felix in his third *militia equestris*, is not otherwise attested in Tingitana, but as M. Euzennat demonstrated, there was no need to have had his third *militia* in Mauretania Tingitana, Euzennat 1989, p. 163-173; Rebuffat 1994; Euzennat 1995. For a fuller discussion and a complete bibliography see Pons Pujol 2013.
[21] Pflaum 1960, p. 199-216, no. 94; Piso 2013, p. 67-109, no. 72.
[22] Pflaum 1960, p. 375-379, no. 157 bis; Gutsfeld 1989, p. 106-107; Piso 2013, p. 151-159, no. 86.
[23] Piso 2013, p. 158; Thomasson 1984, col. 410, no. 12.
[24] AÉ 1941, 79; AE 1969-1970, 747; CIL IX 4194 = ILS 8969; Cagnat 1913, p. 40-41; Benabou 1976, p. 103-104; Thomasson 1984, col. 409, no. 6; Thomasson 2009, p. 170, no. 41:006. Euzennat 1984, p. 375, correctly pointed out that the governor organized both provinces and their frontiers. At the same time, *C. Velius Rufus, tribunus cohortis XIII urbanae* from Carthage, was commissioned *dux exercitus Africi et Mauretanici ad nationes quae sunt in Mauretania comprimendas*, AÉ 1903, 368 = ILS 9200 = IGLS VI 2796 = IPD⁴ 502 = 774a = IDRE II 406 (Heliopolis, Syria); Benabou 1976, p. 109-111; Dobson 1978, p. 216-217, no. 94; Gutsfeld 1989, p. 86-88.
[25] AÉ 1946, 113 = IDRE II 461 (Caesarea); AÉ 1911, 108 = 123 = 1929, 132 (Rapidum); Pflaum 1960, p. 375-379, no. 157 bis; Piso 2013, p. 151-152; Thomasson 1984, col. 410, no. 13 For the date of his tenure, see Piso 2013, p. 158.
[26] For his career, see Piso 2013, p. 151-159, no. 86. See also Hund 2017, p. 111-114. For the title *pro legato* added to the *procuratores* from Mauretania Cesariensis and Mauretania Tingitana see Euzennat 1984, p. 374.
[27] Šašel 1974; Brunt 1983, p. 56-57.

of Iomnium (Tigzirt, Mauretania Caesariensis), located on the coastal road of the province.[28]

In 145-147 or 149,[29] Sex. Flavius Quietus, the former *primus pilus* of the XX Valeria Victrix legion, was sent with a detachment drawn from the army of Britannia to the Mauretanian expedition.[30] The name of the ruling emperor is *Antoninus Augustus*, probably referring to Antoninus Pius. The new information regarding the presence of the detachments of two cohorts from Britannia, sent to Mauretania Tingitana in 152-153 (*vide infra*), strongly supports the assumption that his mission occurred during the reign of Antoninus Pius. After he served as *primus pilus legionis*, he was commissioned to lead the military detachment forces from Britannia dispatched to Mauretania, as *primipilaris*. In addition to a *vexillatio* of this legion, other *vexillationes* were added from the auxiliary units of the *I Batavorum Marsacorum* and *I Baetasiorum* cohorts.

A *vexillatio* of *ala Augusta* from Noricum (probably the *ala I Augusta Thracum*, *vide infra* the imperial constitution issued for the horsemen of the *alae* from Pannonia Superior and Noricum, sent to Mauretania Caesariensis) is attested by an inscription uncovered at Fedjana.[31] Other units are also attested, such as *ala I Cannanefatium* from Pannonia Superior at Tipasa,[32] *ala I Ulpia contariorum*, also from Pannonia Superior, at Tipasa and Portus Magnus[33], and *ala Gallorum Flaviana*, from Moesia Superior, at Caesarea (*praefectus* – since all three equestrian militias are mentioned and a funerary monument was raised by his wife, one can conclude that he was a citizen of Tipasa).[34] Although the chronology is uncertain, at least some of these detachments may

have been in place under Antoninus Pius.[35] Other units that are epigraphically attested are mentioned in special imperial constitutions (*vide infra*), which indicate that their soldiers were released while they were sent to North Africa. Moreover, in order to replace the released soldiers, new recruits joined the detachments. Such was the case of Ulpius Varius from Africa (Proconsularis or Numidia), *veteranus ex statore alae I contariorum*, who remained near the Arrabona fortress after being released from duty.[36] Similarly, C. Iulius Lupercus was from Sala, Mauretania Tingitana and died at Odiavum (Pannonia Superior).[37] His funerary monument was erected by his nephew, C. Iulius Candidianus, the *beneficiarius legati legionis I Adiutricis piae fidelis* (Brigetio, Pannonia Superior) who was probably recruited later. This either suggests that the entire family came to Pannonia Superior, or his uncle convinced him to follow him and join the *I Adiutrix* legion.

Under the command of T. Varius Clemens, Vetustinus' successor as *procurator Mauretaniae Caesariensis* in 151, detachments of auxiliary units from Hispania Taraconensis were sent to Mauretania Tingitana around 145 (*praef(ecto) auxiliariorum tempore / expeditionis in Tingitanam missorum / praef(ecto) eq(uitum) alae II Pannoniorum*; *praef(ecto) auxiliorum in Mauretaniam Tingitanam ex / Hispania missorum*).[38] He had previously been *praefectus alae II Pannoniorum*, which was based in the Roman fort at Gherla in Dacia Porolissensis. Thereafter he received the *honos quartae militiae* as *praefectus alae I (Flaviae Augustae) Britannicae milliariae* stationed in Pannonia Inferior.[39] The area of action was located in the southeastern part of the province.[40] Nothing can ascertain that he received the *honos quartae militiae* while the *ala* was involved in an expedition, as H.-G. Pflaum argued, since it appears that only a detachment, and not the entire unit, was dispatched to Mauretania Caesariensis.

We have more direct information on the involvement of some detachments of the Pannonian *alae* around 148-150, represented by a special constitution issued on 1 August 150 for the horsemen of the following *alae*:[41] *I Hispanorum et Aravacorum*,[42] *III Augusta Thracum sagittariorum*,[43] *I*

[28] AÉ 1957, 176 = 1958, 153: *Imp(erator) Cae[s(ar) T(itus) Aelius] / Hadrianus [Antoninus] / Aug(ustus) Pius p(ater) p(atriae) [horrea fru]/mentaria? [per vexilla]/tiones mil[itum] fieri iussit*; Speidel 2014, p. 84.
[29] Speidel 1977, p. 133.
[30] AÉ 1960, 28 = 1962, 278: *D(is) M(anibus) / Sex(to) Flavio Sex(ti) f(ilio) Quir(ina tribu) Quieto / p(rimo) p(ilo) leg(ionis) XX V(aleriae) V(ictricis) misso cum / exer(citu) in exp(editionem) Maur(etanicam) ab Imp(eratore) / Antonino Aug(usto) praef(ecto) classis / Brit(annicae) Varinia Crispinilla coni(u)g(i) / pientissimo et Fl(avii) Vindex et Qui/etus fil(ii) piissimi*; Pflaum 1960, p. 978-980, no. 156 bis; Dobson 1978, p. 251, no. 130; Gutsfeld 1989, p. 112; Malone 2006, p. 103-104, no. 1.
[31] AÉ 1975, 951 = Benseddik 1979, p. 195, no. 1: *I(ovi) O(ptimo) M(aximo) Victoria/e Noreiae sac(rum) / vexellatio / al(ae) Aug(u)s(tae) Sentius Ex/oratus Spectati/us Viator decurione / exercitus Norici / quibus praeest Iul(ius) / Primus (centurio) leg(ionis) XIIII G(eminae) v(otum) s(olverunt) l(ibentes) m(erito)*; Benseddik 1979, p. 26-27 (23).
[32] AÉ 1951, 265 = 1955, 133: *D(is) M(anibus) / Adiutoris eq(uitis) / al(a)e pri(mae) Can(n)ina/fatium v(ixit) XXXXI mi(litavit) / an(nos) XXIII, pro(curante) l(i)b(erto) ipsi(us) / bene me(renti) Cabanus he(res) / po(suit)* (discovered in the ruins of the amphitheatre of Tipasa); Benseddik 1979, p. 28 (31); Lőrincz 2001, p. 17, no. 7; p. 180, no. 73. For his depiction on a funerary stele, holding a *contus*-lance, see Speidel 2006, p. 118-119, fig. 2.
[33] CIL VIII 9291 = ILS 2519 = AÉ 1955, 133: *D(is) M(anibus) / Ulpius Terti/us curator / alae I contari(orum) / Fl(avius) Tutor emag(inifer) he/res amico pientiss/imo posuit* (Tipasa); CIL VIII 21620: *[- - -] / [- - -] eq(ues) [a]lae Ul/pi(a)e I contar/ioru(m) tur(ma) M[a]/rtini sti(pendiorum) XIX [- - -]*; Benseddik 1979, p. 29-30; Lőrincz 2001, p. 18-19, no. 9; p. 188, no. 97-98
[34] CIL VIII 21037; Benseddik 1979, p. 31-32 (51); Matei-Popescu, Ţentea 2018, p. 22.
[35] Benseddik 1979, p. 149.
[36] CIL III 4379 = RIU 267; Lőrincz 2001, p. 190, no. 104.
[37] CIL III 4321 = RIU 560; Lőrincz 2001, p. 218, no. 197.
[38] CIL III 5211 = ILS 1362 = Saxer 1967, p. 29, no. 53 (this dedication was set by *decuriones alares provinciae Mauretaniae Caesariensis*); CIL III 5212 = ILS 1362a = Saxer 1967, p. 30, no. 54; CIL III 5215 = ILS 1362b = Saxer 1967, p. 30, no. 55; CIL III 15205¹; PIR V 52; Pflaum 1960, p. 368-373, no. 156; Christol 1981, p. 140-141; Šašel 1983; Piso 2013, p. 158.
[39] Lőrincz 2001, p. 16, no. 4. H. Devijver in PME V 52 *s.n.* "praef(ectus) equit(um) al(ae) Britannicae miliar(iae): i.e., militia quarta; ala ex Pannonia Inferiore ad expeditionem Mauretaniae Caesariensis missa." The unit only sent one detachment to North Africa. He probably did not command the unit in North Africa, but in Pannonia Inferior.
[40] Euzennat 1984, p. 382-383.
[41] CIL XVI 99; Christol 1981, p. 134-135; Lőrincz 2001, p. 171, no. 47.
[42] Benseddik 1979, p. 34 (64); Lőrincz 2001, p. 20, no. 13. A copy was given to a former horseman of this unit: *ex gregale Victori Liccai f. Azalo* – since it was a special constitution, the name of the commander was not mentioned, because he had not joined the detachment in expedition.
[43] Lőrincz 2001, p. 25-26, no. 28; p. 218, no. 197.

Flavia Augusta Britannica milliaria (in the area of Tipasa and Portus Magnus, where a detachment of the *ala I civium Romanorum* is also attested on an inscription),[44] *I Thracum veterana sagittariorum*,[45] and *I Augusta Ituraeorum sagittariorum*[46] (Pannonia Inferior). They had been sent to Mauretania Caesariensis, while Porcius Vetustinus was governor (*equit(ibus) qui militaverunt in ali[s] V... quin[is] et vicenis plurib(usve) stip(endiis) emer(itis) dim(issis) honest(a) miss(ione) per Porcium Vetustinum proc(uratorem), cum essent in expedition(e) Mauretan(iae) Caesariens(is)*). Also from Pannonia Inferior, a detachment of the governor's guard attested at Aquae Callidae, *pedites singulares Pannonici Pannoniae Inferioris*, was sent to Mauretania Caesariensis.[47]

It is, however, unclear whether a *vexillatio* of the *cohors III Batavorum milliaria* was also sent to Mauretania Caesariensis, as is presumed.[48] A diploma dated 11 October 146 records it in the third place among the cohorts of Pannonia Inferior, after *cohors I Thracum c. R.* and *cohors I Alpinorum eq.*[49] On two diplomas, copied after an imperial constitution from 9 October 148, the unit appears in the first position among the cohorts of Pannonia Inferior as *cohors III Batavorum (milliaria) vexillatio*.[50] It is also listed on two fragmentary diplomas, copied after an

imperial constitution from 151[51] and 154-156.[52] Although the term *vexillatio* is not directly preserved, it is assumed since the unit is also in the first position among the cohorts. *Vexillatio* is mentioned in the constitution issued on 27 September 154.[53] If we assume that this *vexillatio* was sent to North Africa, we must also imagine that it was first dispatched to Mauretania Caesariensis in 145-146 and, thereafter, to Mauretania Tingitana in 152-153.

A copy of another constitution, also dated to 150-151, is fragmentary. It seems that this constitution was given for the horsemen of the *alae* of the two Pannonian provinces: *I Ulpia contariorum milliaria, [I Thracum victrix c. R.], I Hispanorum et Aravacorum, [I Cannanefatium c. R.], III Augusta Thracum sagittariorum* (Pannonia Superior) and *[I Flavia Augusta Britannica milliaria], I Thracum sagittariorum veterana, [I Augusta Ituraeorum sagittariorum], [I civium Romanorum]* (Pannonia Inferior), probably released while they were dispatched to Mauretania Caesariensis.[54]

Another constitution was issued on 24 September 151 for the horsemen of the cavalry units of Pannonia Superior and Noricum (*I Ulpia contariorum milliaria, I Thracum sagittariorum c. R., I Hispanorum et Aracavorum*. The copy, just like the diploma of 150, was given to a former horseman of this unit, but in this constitution the name of the commander is mentioned: *alae I Hispan(orum) et Arvacor(um), cui prae(e)st M. Antonius Pilatus, ex gregale Octavio Cusonis f. Asalo), I Cannanefatium c. R.* and *III Augusta Thracum sagittariorum* and Noricum (*I Commagenorum sagittariorum milliaria, I Augusta Thracum* and *I Pannoniorum Tampiana*), released *per Varium Clementem cum essent in expeditione Mauretaniae Caesariensis*.[55]

On 31 May 152, horsemen from ten *alae* from Pannonia Superior (*I Ulpia contariorum, I Thracum victrix, I Hispanorum et Aravacorum, I Cannanefatium c. R., III Augusta Thracum*), Pannonia Inferior (*I Flavia Augusta Britannica, I Thracum sag. vet., I praetoria c. R.*), Moesia Superior (*I Claudia nova miscellanea, Gallorum Flaviana*), Moesia Inferior (*I Flavia Gaetulorum* under the governor Q. Fuficius Cornutus[56] and not under T. Flavius Longinus, who probably became governor only in AD 153) and Germania Superior (*felix Moesica*) were released from duty by T. Varius Clemens while they were dispatched to Mauretania Caesariensis.[57] The diploma, copied after this imperial constitution, was discovered during archaeological excavations at Scupi in Moesia Superior. It had been given to a former horseman of the *ala Gallorum Flaviana*, a

---

[44] AÉ 1914, 241 = 1982, 979: *D(is) M(anibus) sacru(m) / (A)elius Publ/ius vetera/nus milita/vit ala Bri/tannica bi/s torquat/a p(ius) v(xit) a(nnis) LV / Numpidia feci/t v(iro) p(ientissimo) et c(arissimo) m(arito) e(ius) / s(it) t(ibi) t(erra) l(evis), v(otum) s(olvit) l(ibens) a(nimo), o(ssa) q(uiescant) b(ene)*; AÉ 1955, 132 (together with *ala I civium Romanorum* – Lőrincz 2001, p. 18, no. 8, or *ala I praetoria c. R.* – P. Holder): *D(is) M(anibus) / [- - -]mi / [dupl(icarii) alae I* vel *I praet(oriae)] c(ivium) R(omanorum) / an(n)or(um) XXXXVII stip(endiorum) / XXVIII, Iul(ius) Martialis / dupl(icarius) alae Britan(n)icae / (milliariae) heres et Primitius / lib(ertus) eius* (Tipasa, near the south gate of the amphitheatre); Benseddik 1979, p. 27-28 (27); Lőrincz 2001, p. 16, no. 4; p. 176, nos. 60-61. Another inscription, CIL VIII 9764, also from Portus Magnus, attests a *librarius* of the *ala I Brittonum c. R.*, also from Pannonia Inferior: *D(is) M(anibus) s(acrum) / Marcus Ulp(ius) Fausti/nus librar(ius) / al(a)e Britt[on(um)] / veteran(orum) [mil(liariae)?] sti(pendiorum) / XII vi[x(it)] a(nnis) XXXII / [s]po(n)s(a)? eiu[s] du[lci] ssi[mo] b(ene) m(erenti) p(osuit)*; Spaul 1994, p. 72; Lőrincz 2001, p. 17, no. 6 (without taking into account this inscription); Eck 2003. Since the date of the funerary monument is not clear, it cannot be connected with Antoninus Pius' reign. A detachment may have been drawn from the *ala I Brittonum c. R.* too. In CIL *milliaria* was read in l. 5, which has no basic ground, since we know that the unit was not a *milliaria*. Based on the facsimile, I propose a different reading of the l. 5: *vet(eranae) Pan(nnoniae) infe(rioris) sti(pendiorum)*.

[45] Benseddik 1979, p. 43 (114); Lőrincz 2001, p. 24-25, no. 26.

[46] AÉ 1955, 131: *D(is) M(anibus) / Iulius Gallianus eq(ues) / alae I Aug(ustae) Itur(aeorum) vix(it) a(nnos) / XXXXV mil(itavit) an(nos) XXIII / C(aius) Beliabo heres et / M(arcus) Anaeus(?)* vel *Intaeius Sec(und)us / her(es) exer(citus) Pan(n)on(iae) Inferior(is)* (Tipasa, reused in the west gate of the amphitheatre); Benseddik 1979, p. 35-36 (72); Lőrincz 2001, p. 21-22, no. 17; p. 202, no. 146.

[47] CIL VIII 21453 = IPD⁴ 280 ("Lectionem huius tituli nuperrime emendavit etiam M. P. Speidel. Vir doctus existimat etiam pedites singulares Pannonicos expeditioni Antonino Pio regnante contra Mauros factae interfuisse"): *D(is) M(anibus) / [Bell?]icus Bel[l]/ici mil(es) ex ped(itibus) sing(ularibus) Pan(n)o(nicis) Pa/nn(oniae) inf(erioris) anno(rum) / XXXVIIII st(i)p(endiorum) XIX / titul(um) pos(uerunt) Calimenus sig(nifer) / et Viator opt(io) / her(edes) / eius h(ic) s(itus) e(st)*.

[48] Saxer 1967, p. 31; Lőrincz 2001, p. 30, no. 9.

[49] Mirković 2008 = AÉ 2008, 1116.

[50] CIL XVI 179 (= AÉ 1944, 102), 180 (= AÉ 1947, 37), both discovered at Regőly. A possible third, fragmentary copy was recently discovered at the *canabae* of Aquincum (information Vámos Péter).

[51] Eck, Pangerl 2018a, p. 34-38, no. 5, part of AÉ 2010, 1272, but probably not listed in the first place, P. Holder.

[52] AÉ 1999, 1267 = RMD V 415; Lőrincz 2001, p. 306, no. 509; this constitution may have been issued on 27 September 154.

[53] AÉ 2004, 1923.

[54] RMD IV 273 = RGZM 36.

[55] RGZM 32.

[56] Fitz 1966, p. 16-17, dated to AD 151/152-153/154; Thomasson 1984, col. 143, no. 85.

[57] Jovanova, Ončevska Todorovska 2018, p. 216-220.

Dardanus whose name was not preserved, under the command of Ulpius Marcellus, also unknown among the equestrian officers.[58] If the other detachments are known from imperial constitutions, the presence of a detachment of the *ala felix Moesica* from Germania Superior is a complete surprise.[59] Another copy of this constitution preserves only the name of the *alae*: *I Hispanorum et Aravacorum, III Augusta Thracum, I Thracum sag., I praetoria c. R., I Claudia nova miscellanea, Gallorum Flaviana* and *I Flavia Gaetulorum*).[60] (see also the appendix).

In 153, horsemen from the two *alae* of Moesia Superior (only *I Gallorum Flaviana* preserved; under Egrilius Plarianus, the governor of the province between 152 and 155/156, after P. Mummius Sissena Rutilianus and before C. Curtius Iustus, or M. Valerius Etruscus, the governor of Numidia in 151-152)[61] were released by T. Varius Clemens, together with horsemen of an unknown *ala* from Moesia Inferior under the governor T. Flavius Longinus. Therefore, the constitution probably dates to 153, since in 152 Q. Fuficius Cornutus was still the attested governor (*vide supra*).[62] This attestation cannot be connected with the inscription from Caesarea (*vide supra*), where a *praefectus* is mentioned. It is likely that only a small detachment was sent (*vide infra* the discussion on the number of horsemen dispatched to the Mauretanian provinces).

In 153, a special constitution was issued for the soldiers of four *alae* from Moesia Inferior: *I Vespasiana Dardanorum, I Flavia Gaetulorum, II Hispanorum et Aravacorum* and *I Gallorum Atectorigiana* as well as two *cohortes* from Britannia: *I Batavorum Marsac(orum)* and *I Baetasiorum*, released by Flavius Flavianus in Mauretania Tingitana.[63]

Finally in 156, horsemen from the same *alae* of Moesia Inferior were also released by Flavius Flavianus in Mauretania Tingitana: *I Gallorum Atectorigiana, I Flavia Gaetulorum, I Vespasiana Dardanorum* and *II Hispanorum et Aravacorum*.[64] Therefore, it is likely that the detachments from Moesia Inferior remained for several years in the area of Mauretania Tingitana. Soldiers of one of these *alae*, if not the entire detachment

of Moesia Inferior, had been previously involved in the military operations in Mauretania Caesariensis. They were later sent to Mauretania Tingitana. If the two cohorts from Britannia, attested together with the Lower Moesian cavalry detachments, had already come to Mauretania together with the *vexillatio* of the XX Valeria Victrix legion in 145-147, then they also remained for several years, having also been moved from Mauretania Caesariensis to Mauretania Tingitana.

Two units, *cohors III Gallorum felix*, were probably added from Hispania, and the *IV Tungrorum vexillatio* from Raetia (demonstrating that, initially, only a part of a unit was brought back to its former strength between 162/163 and 166/167, once again attested as *milliaria*).[65] They remained thereafter among the auxiliary units of Mauretania Tingitana.[66]

The Moorish Uprisings and the Transfer of Mauretanians to the Danubian Provinces

Directly related with the first Moorish War is the transfer of some detachments from the auxiliary units of Numidia and Mauretania Caesariensis, together with *Mauri gentiles*, to Dacia Superior.[67] They are attested in 152 (*vexil(lariis) ex [Afric(a) qui sunt cum] Maur(is) gen[tilib(us) in Dacia super(iore) sub Se]datio Severi[ano]*), 158 (*vex(ilariis) Afric(ae) et Mau[r(etaniae) Caes(ariensis) qui sunt cum Maur(is) gentilib(us) in Dacia super(iore) et sunt sub Statio Prisco leg(ato))*,[68] and 146 (*vexil(lariis) Afric(ae) et [Mauret(aniae) Caes(ariensis) et sunt cum] Mauris genti[lib(us) et numero pedit(um) singular(ium)] Britannicia[nor(um) et sunt in Dacia Superior(e)] sub Orfidio Se[necione]*).[69] It appears that they were transferred in 145 by T. Flavius Priscus in the aftermath of the first war in Mauretania Caesariensis.[70] It is probable that they were recruited outside the province, having served as part of the policy of reducing the warlike potential of the frontier *gentes*. The *honesta missio* was given only to *vexillarii*, members of different units from Numidia and Mauretania Caesariensis, who had built a *vexillatio*[71] (similar to the case of *vexillatio equitum Illyricorum* during the Dacian war,[72] or *vexillationes equitum ex Syria*).[73] For this reason,

---

[58] It is possible that his son was Ulpius Marcellus (cos. 173), the governor of Britannia in 177-180 and 184, identical with L. Ulpius Marcellus, the governor of Pannonia Inferior around 174-176 (Thomasson 1984, col. 119-120, no. 53) and *proconsul Asiae* in 189, Birley 2005, p. 162-170, no. 33; see also Thomasson 1984, col. 76, no. 64; col. 72, no. 30; Thomasson 2009, p. 26-27, no. 14:030.
[59] Spaul 1994, p. 163-164, no. 57.
[60] Eck, Pangerl 2018.
[61] On both governors, see Thomasson 2009, p. 45-46, nos. 20:39 and 41. On C. Valerius Etruscus see Thomasson 1984, col. 127, no. 40, but only tentatively attested by a funerary inscription from Scupi, IMS VI 46: *b(eneficiarii) M(arci) V(aleri) E(trusci) leg(ati) consula(ris)*. For his presence in Numidia see Thomasson 1984, col. 398, no. 35 and Thomasson 2009, p. 165, no. 40:035.
[62] RMD V 405; Eck, Holder, Pangerl 2016, p. 200-201, no. 2; Eck, Pangerl 2018, p. 236.
[63] Eck, Holder, Pangerl 2016 = AÉ 2016, 2021. On the *alae* see Matei-Popescu 2010, p. 169-172, no. 2; 172-178, no. 3; 178-181, no. 4; 188-190, no. 9. On the two cohorts see Holder 1982, p. 113-114.
[64] Chiriac, Mihailescu-Bîrliba, Matei 2006; AÉ 2006, 1213; Eck, Holder, Pangerl 2016, p. 198-200, no. 1.

[65] RMD III 186 = AÉ 1985, 992 = 1992, 1492 (*IV TVNGROR MILL*), dated by the presence of L. Volusius, Thomasson 2009, p. 175, no. 42:041a, the procurator of Dacia Porolissensis between 160 and 162/163, Thomasson 2009, p. 60, no. 21:030a; Piso 2013, p. 123-127, no. 77; AÉ 1966, 606 = IAM 2, 824, AD 232-233; Euzennat 1989, p. 264; 314, no. 9 (Aïn Schkour, in the region of Volubilis); PME C 193; RMD III 186 = AÉ 1985, 992 = 1992, 1492 (*IV TVNGROR MILL*).
[66] Roxan 1973, p. 840-841; 848, nos. 10-11; Labory 1998, p. 87, nos. 10-11.
[67] For an overview of the relations with the *gentes* at the borders of Mauretania Caesariensis, see Christol 2019.
[68] AÉ 2007, 1763; CIL XVI 108.
[69] Eck, Pangerl 2014a, p. 269-272, no. 1.
[70] Petolescu 2014, p. 157-160, no. 7, considering they were the former members of the dispatched detachments to Mauretania Caesariensis, who were sent back to the Danubian provinces, see Wagner 1938, p. 202. The imperial constitution of 146 seems not to confirm this theory.
[71] Speidel 1975, p. 208-211; Hamdoune 1999, p. 150-154.
[72] Nemeth 1997, p. 107, no. 6; Petolescu 2002, p. 131-133, nos. 67-68.
[73] CIL XVI 164; Țentea 2012, p. 77, no. XXIII.

they were no longer listed among their former units (as with the case of the *equites* from the Danubian *alae* sent to Mauretania Caesariensis). It is assumed that the *Mauri gentiles* now formed the core of the various *numeri Maurorum* attested in Dacia,[74] although they are only later attested. Moreover, new recruits joined the units up to the 3rd century. Otherwise, we must accept that their core was represented by the Mauri sent to Dacia and Pannonia in the context of the Marcomannic Wars.[75]

Other *Mauri equites* attested in Moesia Superior received Roman citizenship from Antoninus Pius through a special imperial constitution.[76] Therefore, they had a different status, comparable with the *Mauri gentiles*, and very similar to the *Palmyreni sagittarii* who had received Roman citizenship through special constitutions in 120 and 126.[77] We do not possess any chronological information, since the diploma copied after that constitution is fragmentary; however, they were probably recruited later, in 155-156, from the local communities of Mauretania Tingitana and not from outside the province, like the *Mauri gentiles* from the frontier areas of Numidia and Mauretania Caesariensis.

The causes of the uprisings were probably related to the interference of the Romans in the nomadic way of life of the Moorish tribes.[78] It is possible that the Roman authorities tried to settle them down in order to integrate them into the provincial framework and to use their manpower for the needs of the Roman army. The large number of *Mauri gentiles* sent to Dacia Superior seems to back up such a theory. It is also possible that the development of a new frontier in the desert cut some of the traditional and vital roads used by the nomads. Whatever the answer is, the military effort was important and it is clear that mobile units were needed to travel deep into the area of the nomads. Moreover, the Pannonian units had experience dealing with the nomadic horsemen, given their routine encounters with the Iazyges who inhabited the region between Pannonia Inferior and Dacia. The cavalry units of Moesia Inferior who controlled the Rhoxolani from the Valachian plane had similar experience. Based upon a reading of the special imperial constitutions, it seems that the uprisings began in Mauretania Caesariensis before 146 when the *Mauri gentiles* were first attested in Dacia Superior. Another rebellion broke out in Mauretania Caesariensis around 150. Detachments from the Danubian provinces are epigraphically attested in several places along the coast (Caesarea, Tipasa and Portus Magnus).[79] Between 152-153 and at least 156, the tribes from the southern and

eastern parts of Mauretania Tingitana probably rebelled,[80] or simply raided the towns and forts located there (Sala,[81] Thamusida, Volubilis, and Tocolosida,[82] Sidi Mousa, Aïn Schkour[83] and Sidi Saïd in the area of Volubilis;[84] Tingi, Ad Mercurios, Ad Novas, Oppidum Novum and Souk el Arba). Therefore, military unrest is attested for more than a decade in the two Mauretanian provinces, an important challenge to the Roman imperial command. In this specific context, detachments from the units located in the European provinces were sent to help the garrisons of the two provinces. Since there was no important land route that connected both provinces, they were probably sent from Mauretania Caesariensis by sea (a *classis* is attested in the Mauretanian provinces, their sailors being released both from Mauretania Caesariensis and Mauretania Tingitana).[85] This also occurred with detachments from the Hispanic provinces. Moreover, if we take into account the honorary decree of the *Salenses* for M. Sulpicius Felix and the information from T. Varius Clemens' inscriptions, it seems that the uprisings and associated military activity happened in Mauretania Tingitana in 144-145.

Horsemen from the *alae* of Germania Superior, Noricum, Pannonia Superior and Inferior, and Moesia Superior and Inferior were sent to North Africa during the reign of Antoninus Pius. Foot soldiers and, possibly, horsemen from two cohorts from Britannia were added, as well as cohorts from Raetia and Pannonia Inferior. These were joined by a detachment of the *pedites singulares*. Detachments from the Hispanic provinces were also transferred to Mauretania Tingitana, as the monuments dedicated to T. Varius Clemens attest.[86] The auxiliary units from the provinces of Africa/Numidia (2 *alae* and 9 *cohortes*), Mauretania Caesariensis (2 *alae* and 10 *cohortes*), and Tingintana (5 *alae* and 11 *cohortes*) had proven to be insufficient, since they were stationed in different forts and distributed in different *stationes* along the main roads of the provinces; therefore, reinforcements were required.[87] The emperor

---

[74] Nemeth 1997, p. 103-105, no. 2; Hamdoune 1999, p. 169-186; Petolescu 2002, p. 134-138, nos. 69-74.

[75] AÉ 1956, 124 = IDRE II 445; Hamdoune 1999, p. 167-168; Petolescu 2002, p. 134.

[76] CIL XVI 114 = IDR I 29; Hamdoune 1999, p. 154-155, 166; Petolescu 2002, p. 135; Matei-Popescu, Țentea 2018, p. 76, no. LI.

[77] CIL XVI 17; CIL XVI 27; IDR I 5 = RMD 17; IDR I 8 = RMD I 27; IDR I 9 = RMD I 28; Petolescu 2002, p. 138-139; Țentea 2012, p. 66-71.

[78] Just like in the 1st century AD, Hugoniot 2000, p. 41.

[79] On these ports see Reddé 1986, p. 244-250.

[80] For the tribes within and around Mauretania Tingitana, Euzennat 1984, p. 376-379, comments on Ptolemy's list (4, 1, 5). For an overview of the frontiers and the people living around them, see El Bouzidi, Ouahidi 2014, p. 97-100.

[81] An area protected by a *fossa*, probably set during the Flavian period and intact until approximately 250, with military posts and towers, Euzennat 1989, p. 129-153; an auxiliary fort was located near the *municipium* of Sala, where first *cohors I Lemavorum c. R.* and then *cohors II Syrorum milliaria sag. c. R* were stationed, Euzennat 1989, p. 159-173. See also El Bouzidi, Ouahidi 2014, p. 107-108.

[82] Euzennat 1989, p. 244-245; IAM 2, 815 (= Euzennat 1989, p. 293-294, no. 1); IAM 2, 816 (= Euzennat 1989, p. 294-295, no. 8); IAM 2, 817-818 (= Euzennat 1989, p. 295, no. 9-10)

[83] IAM 2, 826 (= Euzennat 1989, p. 310, no. 2); AÉ 1955, 208 = IAM 2, 820 (= Euzennat 1989, p. 310-311, no. 3), *cohors Asturum et Callaecorum*, PME I 78; AÉ 1966, 606 = IAM 2, 824, AD 232-233; Euzennat 1989, p. 264; 314, no. 9, *cohors IV milliaria Tungrorum*, PME C 193.

[84] On the limes around Volubilis see Euzennat 1989, p. 274-292 and El Bouzidi, Ouahidi 2014, p. 101-106.

[85] Cagnat 1913, p. 275-284; Roxan 1973, p. 841; Reddé 1986, p. 561-567.

[86] Rachet 1970, p. 196-200.

[87] For an overview of the fighting capacity of the North African Roman army see Le Bohec 2000, p. 216-222; for the number of auxiliary units in Mauretania, see Roxan 1973; Labory 1998 and Labory 2009 (Mauretania Tingitana); Benseddik 1979, p. 163-187; Le Bohec 1999 (Mauretania

decided to send horsemen, especially from the Danube area, because they were experienced fighters against the nomadic horsemen of Mauretania. They were probably sent by sea. The detachments from Germania Superior, Raetia, Noricum, and Pannonia would have embarked in Dalmatia (Salonae), while the detachments of Moesia Superior and Moesia Inferior would have travelled south or east and embarked in Thracia (Perinthus) or Asia. If they had crossed the Hellespontus, the detachments from the Moesian provinces could have also used the large port of Ephesus.[88] They would have been dispatched in the various ports of Mauretania Caesariensis.[89] They remained for many years, since the horsemen drawn from Moesia Inferior are attested both in 151-152 in Mauretania Caesariensis and in Mauretania Tingitana in 152-153 and 156. They were probably joined by legionary detachments and at least one *centuria* of the *pedites singulares* from Pannonia Inferior and probably a *vexillatio* of the *III Batavorum milliaria* cohort, two detachments of the *I Batavorum Marsacorum* and *I Baetasiorum* cohorts from Britannia, together with a *vexillatio* of the XX Valeria Victrix legion. The core of the expeditionary forces, however, were the horsemen needed in the specific landscape of the Mauretanian provinces. Interestingly, after the first war, a *vexillatio* was transferred to Dacia Superior. These *vexillarii* looked after and trained the *Mauri gentiles*, recruited and sent abroad.[90]

The *exercitus* from Britannia led by the former *primus pilus* of the XX Valeria Victrix legion, which beside the legionary detachments of the *I Batavorum Marsacorum* and *I Baetasiorum* cohorts, was probably sent immediately after Q. Lollius Urbicus' victory in Britannia in 142.[91] The auxiliary detachments are directly attested in Mauretania Tingitana in 152-152, but we do not have any proof that the legionary detachment remained for a longer period of time there.

Conclusions

In the end, the information at our disposal allows us to raise questions about the building of the auxiliary *vexillationes* in the middle of the 2nd century AD.[92] First of all, how large were the *vexillationes* sent to the Mauretanian provinces? W. Eck and A. Pangerl assume that perhaps half of an *ala quingenaria* was sent, increasing the number of horsemen to almost 5000.[93] However, some epigraphic information seems to indicate that such a number is too high.

The *vexillatio* of the *ala (I) Augusta (Thracum)* from Noricum was commanded by a *decurio*; therefore, it was not larger than a *turma* (32 horsemen for an *ala quingenaria*).[94] At the head of the *exercitus Noricus* was a legionary centurion from the *XIIII Gemina* legion, which was stationed at Carnuntum. One can, thus, conclude that the entire detachment from Noricum was not very large. It consisted of three *vexillationes alarum* of 32 horsemen each, if we consider that three *alae quingenariae* are mentioned in the imperial constitution. To these forces, a small legionary *vexillatio*, not larger than a *centuria*, of the *XIIII Gemina* legion was added. Since the *centurio legionis* was higher in command than the three *decuriones* from the *alae*,[95] he was commissioned at the head of the *exercitus Noricus*, even though he was based in Pannonia Superior.

From *ala I Flavia Augusta Britannica milliaria* there is a *duplicarius* attested (probably an *evocatus*, since he was still serving after 28 years of service), a charge under *decurio alae*.[96] Since the unit was *milliaria*, it may have sent two *turmae* (out of 24 *turmae* of 42 horsemen each)[97] or even more. The presence of the *duplicarii*, possibly attested in the same inscription as *ala I civium Romanorum*, suggests that detachments were formed in a *turma* type, commanded by a *decurio* and helped by a *duplicarius*.

From the *ala I contariorum milliaria* there are an *imaginifer* and a *curator* attested,[98] which suggests that the *vexillatio* was larger, since the unit was also *milliaria*, like *I Flavia Augusta Britannica milliaria*. This is inferred from the indication of the name of the *decurio* of the *turma* in the funerary inscription from Portus Magnus. It is possible that the *vexillatio*, after the model of the *turma*, had an *imaginifer*, or the entire *turma* may have been sent.[99] Therefore, the *exercitus Pannoniae Inferioris* was larger, since detachments of two *alae milliariae* and three *alae quingenariae* were sent ($42 \times 4 + 32 \times 3 = 264$ horsemen) together with a detachment of the *pedites singulares* and

---

Caesariensis); Eck, Pangerl 2005. For the auxiliary units of Africa/Numidia see Le Bohec 1989a, p. 27-157 (*alae, cohortes* and *numeri*) and Le Bohec 2007, p. 499-502.

[88] Reddé 1986, p. 391-392. The *classis Perinthica* (IGR I 781) is attested in military diplomas in AD 88 (Eck, Pangerl 2014, p. 251-253, no. 1 = AÉ 2014, 1654). Reddé 1986, p. 560-511, raised doubts regarding its survival after Nero's reign.

[89] Baradez 1954; Reddé 1986, p. 248-250.

[90] Piso 2013, p. 159: "Der Grund dafür wird wohl nicht die Lage in Dakien gewesen sein, die friedlich war, sondern der Wunsch, die Mauren zu schwächen und einen künftigen Aufstand zu vermeiden."

[91] SHA, *Ant.*, 5, 4 (*vide supra*); Birley 2005, p. 136-140, no. 24; Speidel 2017, p. 259; Hund 2017, p. 95-105.

[92] See Domaszewski 1967, p. 35-36 and Saxer 1967, p. 118-123.

[93] Eck, Pangerl 2018, p. 235: "Doch auch wenn jeweils nur die Hälfte einer Einheit dort eingesetzt wurde, waren dies wohl weit mehr als 5000

Mann, die über lange Jahre nötig waren, um des Aufstandes Herr zu werden. Dass es fast nur berittene Einheiten waren, zeigt zudem, dass es sich bei den revoltierenden Mauren vor allem um nomadisch lebende Stämme gehandelt hat, gegen die wegen ihrer Beweglichkeit Alen wirkungsvoller waren, als die Kohorten zu Fuß".

[94] An *ala quingenaria* was divided in 16 *turmae*, Hyginus, *De mun. cas.* 16: *ala quingenaria turmas habet XVI*; CIL III 6581 (AD 199, in the area of a former Roman fort near Alexandria, Egypt), which records 16 *decuriones* of each *ala veterana Gallica* and *I Thracum Mauretana*; Arrian, *Tactica* 18, mentions that the *ala quingenaria* has 512 *equites*, which was divided into 16 *turmae*, giving a strength of 32 *equites* in a *turma*, officers included; Dixon, Southern 1992, p. 23; Bartoloni 1995, p. 147-148.

[95] Domaszewski 1967, p. 53, no. 2

[96] Domaszewski 1967, p. 53-54, no. 3.

[97] Hyginus, *De mun. cas.* 16: *nunc, ut suo referam loco, ad alam miliariam. Turmas habet XXIIII, in eis decuriones, duplicarii, sesquiplicarii*; Dixon, Southern 1992, p. 23-24 (considering that the strength of a *turma* was 32 *equites*, just like the *turmae* of an *ala quingenaria*); Bartoloni 1995, p. 147-148.

[98] Domaszewski 1967, p. 55, nos. 5 and 9.

[99] Domaszewski 1967, p. 58, no. 15, CIL III 3256 = ILS 2581 (Acumincum, Pannonia Inferior): *eq(ues) imag(inifer) coh(ortis) /I Brit(annicae) tur(ma) Monta(ni)*; Lőrincz 2001, p. 240, no. 277; see also AE 2004, 1524 = IK 61 (Perge), no. 469.

a *vexillatio* of the *cohors III Batavorum milliaria*. Each of these units probably sent a *centuria*.

For the other provinces, we do not have direct information, but it is possible that the detachments were not as large as previously thought. Every *ala quingenaria* probably sent a *turma* and every *ala milliaria* probably sent two *turmae*. The *pedites singulares* from Pannonia Inferior probably sent a *centuria*, the same as the XIIII Gemina legion from Carnuntum. The size of the *vexillationes* from Britannia is not known, but they probably did not exceed one *centuria* each. The Hispanic *vexillatio*, active around 145, consisted of about 1000 soldiers, since T. Varius Clemens' command was equated with his *secunda militia equestris*.

On which criteria was a *vexillatio* of a unit built? The large number of horsemen released and the funerary inscriptions which mention how many years the deceased soldier had served give us the impression that experienced soldiers were chosen. We do not know if entire *turmae* or *centuriae* (in the case of *pedites singulares Pannoniae inferioris*) were used to build a *vexillatio*. The *vexillatio* of the *ala* from Noricum was not larger than a *turma*, but the *vexillatio* was one of the *turmae* of the *ala*, or was built with horsemen from many *turmae*.[100] The presence of the *decurio* may be a strong argument against this view and a valid argument that an entire *turma* was drawn from the unit, but the cited inscription from Coptus indicates that six *decuriones* commanded 424 horsemen, divided into six *turmae* from three different *alae*. They were helped by a *duplicarius* and four *sesquiplicarii*. Unfortunately, the list of the auxiliary horsemen is lost, so we do not know if they belonged to entire *turmae* or if they were drawn from all *turmae* of the three *alae*. The unusually high number of horsemen in their last years of service, among the horsemen sent to the Mauretanian provinces, could prove that entire *turmae* were taken from the units, instead of building detachments. The same conclusion can be drawn, based on the funerary inscription from Portus Magnus, where the name of the *decurio* of the *turma* was given. If the Roman high command had decided to build special detachments, it would not have been practical to send horsemen who would be released a few months after their reassignment. We can thus conclude, that entire *turmae* were chosen, together with their *principales*, and sent to North Africa.

Ancient literary sources

Aelius Aristides: Elio Aristide, *A Roma*, traduzione e commento a cura di Francesca Fontanella, introduzione di Paolo Desideri. Pisa (2007).

Pausanias: *Pausaniae Graeciae descriptio*, vol. II, libri V-VIII, edidit Maria Helena Rocha-Pereira. Leipzig (1977).

Pausanias: Pausanias, *Description de la Grèce*, tome VIII, libre VIII, *L'Arcadie*, texte établi par Michel Casevitz, traduit et commenté par Madeleine Jost, avec la collaboration de Jean Marcadé. Paris (2002, reprint).

Plinius: Pliny, *Natural History*, volume II, libri III-VII, by H. Rackham. Cambridge MA-London (1961).

Polyaenus: *Polyaeni Strategematon libri octo ex recensione Eduardi Woelfflin*, iterum recensuit, excerpta Polyaeni e codice tacticorum Florentino addidit, Leonis imperatoris strategamata e Rud. Schoellii apographo subiunxit Ioannes Melber. Leipzig (1887).

SHA: *The Scriptores Historiae Augustae with an English translation by David Magie*, volume I. Cambridge MA-London (1991, reprint).

Bibliography

Baradez 1954: Baradez, J., "Les nouvelles fouilles de Tipasa et les opérations d'Antonin le Pieux en Maurétanie", *Libyca (archéologie, épigraphie)* 2 (1954): 89-147.

Bartoloni 1995: Bartoloni, R., "Alcune ipotesi sulla composizione e la sulla forza numerica dei reparti ausiliari dell'esercito altoimperiale". In *La hiérarchie (Rangordnung) de l'armée romaine sous le Haut-Empire. Actes du Congres de Lyon (15-18 septembre 1994)*, Y. Le Bohec (ed.). Paris (1995): 147-150.

Benseddik 1979: Benseddik, N., *Les troupes auxiliaires de l'armée romaine en Maurétanie Césarienne sous le Haut-Empire*. Alger (1979).

Bénabou 1976: Bénabou, M., *La résistance africaine à la romanisation*. Paris (1976) (= Paris (2005) preface inédite de Michel Christol).

Birley 2005: Birley, A. R., *The Roman Government of Britain*. Oxford (2005).

Brunt 1983: Brunt, P. A., "Princeps and Equites". *JRS* 73 (1983): 42-75.

Cagnat 1913: Cagnat, R., *L'armée romaine d'Afrique et l'occupation militaire de l'Afrique sous les empereurs*. Paris (1913).

Cherry 1998: Cherry, D., *Frontier and Society in Roman North Africa*. Oxford (1998).

Chiriac, Mihailescu-Bîrliba, Matei 2006: Chiriac, C., Mihailescu-Bîrliba, L., Matei, I., "Un nouveau diplôme militaire de Mésie Inférieure". In *Pontos Euxeinos. Beiträge zur Archäologie und Geschichte des antiken Schwarzmeer- und Balkanraumes. Manfred Oppermann zum 65. Geburtstag von Kollegen, Freunden und Schülern*, S. Conrad, R. Einicke, A. E. Furtwängler, H. Löhr, A. Slawisch, (eds) (Schriften des Zentrums für Archäologie und Kulturgeschichte des Schwarzmeerraumes 10). Langenweißbach, (2006): 383-390.

---

[100] 2 × 16 *turmae*, after the attested model of the legionary *vexillationes* formed by soldiers drawn from different *centuriae*, like the case of the *Bauvexillation* from Coptus, where every *centuria* gave a soldier. CIL III 6627+14147 = ILS 2483; Domaszewski 1967, p. 35; Saxer 1967, p. 97-99, no. 294.

Christol 1981: Christol, M., L'armée des provinces pannoniennes et la pacification des révoltes maures sous Antonin le Pieux. *Antiquités africaines* 17 (1981): 133-141.

Christol 2019: Christol, M., "Le pouvoir romain et les tribus de Maurétanie Césarienne". In *Les sociétés tribales en Afrique du Nord. IXe Journée d'études nord-africaines. Actes du colloque*, J. Scheid, M. Zink (eds.). Paris (2019): 45-57.

Dixon, Southern 1992: Dixon, K. R., Southern, P., *The Roman Cavalry. From the First to the Third Century AD*. London (1992).

Dobson 1978: Dobson, B., *Die Primipilares. Entwicklung und Bedeutung, Laufbahnen und Persönlichkeiten eines römischen Offiziersranges*. Cologne (1978).

Domaszewski 1967: von Domaszewski, A., *Die Rangordnung des römischen Heeres. 2. Durchgesehene Auflage. Einführung, Berichtigungen und Nachträge von Brian Dobson*. Cologne-Graz (1967).

Eck 2003: Eck, W., "Eine Bürgerrechtskonstitution Vespasians aus dem Jahr 71 n. Chr. und die Aushebung von brittonischen Auxiliareinheiten". *ZPE* 143 (2003): 220-228.

Eck, Pangerl 2005: Eck, W., Pangerl, A., "Neue Militätdiplome für die Truppen der mauretanischen Provinzen". *ZPE* 153 (2005): 187-206.

Eck, Pangerl 2014: Eck, W., Pangerl, A., "Zwei Diplome für die Truppen der Provinz Thracia, darunter das früheste unter Kaiser Domitian". *ZPE* 188 (2014): 250-254.

Eck, Pangerl 2014a: Eck, W., Pangerl, A., "Zwei neue Diplome für die Truppen von Dacia Superior und Dacia Porolissensis". *ZPE* 191 (2014): 269-277.

Eck, Pangerl 2015: Eck, W., Pangerl, A., "Neue diplomata militaria aus der Zeit von Hadrian und Antoninus Pius". *ActaMN* 52/I (2015): 73-84.

Eck, Pangerl 2018: Eck, W., Pangerl, A., "Eine Konstitution für abgeordnete Truppen aus vier Provinzen aus dem Jahr 152". *ZPE* 208 (2018): 229-236.

Eck, Pangerl 2018a: Eck, W., Pangerl, A., "Neue Diplomzeugnisse für die Truppen in den Donauprovinzen aus dem 2. Jh.". *AMN* 55/I (2018): 25-42.

Eck, Holder, Pangerl 2016: Eck, W., Holder, P., Pangerl, A., "Eine Konstitution aus dem Jahr 152 oder 153 für niedermösische und britannische Truppen, abgeordnet nach Mauretania Tingitana. Mit einer Appendix von Paul Holder". *ZPE* 199 (2016): 187-201.

El Bouzidi, Ouahidi 2014: El Bouzidi, S., Ouahidi, A., "La frontière méridionale de la Maurétanie Tingintane: contribution à la carte archéologique de la région de Volubilis". *DHA* 40/1 (2014): 97-108.

Euzennat 1984: Euzennat, M., "Les troubles de Maurétanie". *CRAI* 128 (1984): 372-393.

Euzennat 1989: Euzennat, M., *Le limes de Tingitane. La frontière méridionale*. Paris (1989) (Études d'antiquités africaines).

Euzennat 1995: Euzennat, M., "*Praefecti equitum* adjoints au gouverneur de province". In *La hiérarchie (Rangordnung) de l'armée romaine sous le Haut-Empire. Actes du Congrès de Lyon (15-18 septembre 1994)*, Y. Le Bohec (ed.): 201-207.

Fitz 1966: Fitz, J., *Die Laufbahn der Statthalter in der römischen Provinz Moesia Inferior*. Weimar (1966).

Gutsfeld 1989: Gutsfeld, A., *Römische Heerschaft und einheimischer Widerstand in Nordafrika. Militärische Auseinandersetzugen Roms mit den Nomaden*. Stuttgart (1989).

Hamdoune 1999: Hamdoune, C., *Les* auxilia externa *africains des armées romaines IIIe siècle av. J.-C. - IVe siècle ap. J.-C.*. Montpellier (1999).

Holder 1982: Holder, P. A., *The Roman Army in Britain*. New York (1982).

Hugoniot 2000: Hugoniot, C, *Rome en Afrique. De la chute de Carthage aux débuts de la conquête arabe*. Paris (2000).

Hund 2017: Hund, R., *Studien zur Außenpolitik der Kaiser Antoninus Pius und Marc Aurel im Schatten der Markomannenkriege*. Rahden/Westf (2017) (Pharos. Studien zur griechisch-römischen Antike 40).

Jovanova, Ončevska Todorovska 2018: Jovanova, L., Ončevska Todorovska, M., *Scupi. Sector Southeastern Defensive Wall and the Thermae – Atrium Basilica Complex*. Skopje (2018).

Labory 1998: Labory, N., "L'ordre des unités dans les diplômes militaires de Maurétanie tingitane à partir de 122 ap. J.-C.". *AntAfr* 34 (1998): 83-92.

Labory 2009: Labory, N., "Quelques remarques sur les listes de troupes auxiliaires de Maurétanie tingitane mentionnées dans les diplômes après 122", *AntAfr* 45 (2009): 37-49.

Le Bohec 1989: Le Bohec, Y., *La troisième légion Auguste*. Paris (1989) (Études d'Antiquités Africaines).

Le Bohec 1989a: Le Bohec, *Les unités auxiliaires de l'armée romaine en Afrique Proconsulaire et Numidie sous le Haut-Empire romain*. Paris (1989).

Le Bohec 1999: Le Bohec, Y., "Frontières et limites militaires de la Maurétanie Césarienned sous le Haut-Empire". In *Frontières et limites géographiques de l'Afrique du nord antique. Hommage à Pierre Salama*, Cl. Lepelley, X. Dupuis (eds.). Paris (1999): 111-127 (= "L'armée romaine en Afrique et Gaule". *Mavors* 14. Stuttgart (2007): 255-271).

Le Bohec 2000: Le Bohec, Y., "Le rôle social et politique de l'armée romaine dans les provinces d'Afrique". In *Kaiser, Heer und Gesellschaft in der Römischen Kaiserzeit. Gedenkschrift für Eric Birley*, G. Alföldy, B. Dobson, W. Eck (eds.). Stuttgart (2000): 207-226 (= "L'armée romaine en Afrique et Gaule". *Mavors* 14. Stuttgart (2007): 221-240).

Le Bohec 2007: Le Bohec, Y., "L'armée romaine d'Afrique dans l'épigraphie de 1984 à 2004". In *L'armée romaine en Afrique et Gaule*, Y. Le Bohec (ed.). *Mavors* 14. Stuttgart (2007): 478-502.

Malone 2006: Malone, S. J., *Legio XX Valeria Victrix. Prosopography, Archaeology and History*. Oxford (2006) (BAR IntSer 1491).

Matei-Popescu 2010: Matei-Popescu, F., *The Roman Army in Moesia Inferior*. Bucharest (2010) (The Centre for Roman Military Studies 7).

Matei-Popescu, Țentea 2018: Matei-Popescu, F., Țentea, O., *Auxilia Moesiae Superioris*. Cluj-Napoca (2018) (The Centre for Roman Military Studies 9).

Mirković 2008: Mirković, M., "Ein neues Diplom aus Pannonia Inferior und RMD V 401: Wo sind die übrigen fünf Kohorten geblieben?". *ZPE* 166 (2008): 285-290.

Nemeth 1997: Nemeth, E., "Die Numeri im römischen Heer Dakiens". *Ephemeris Napocensis* 7 (1997): 101-116.

Petolescu 2002: Petolescu, C. C., *Auxilia Daciae. Contribuție la istoria militară a Daciei romane*. Bucharest (2002).

Petolescu 2014: Petolescu, C. C., "Noi contribuții epigrafice privitoare la organizarea militară şi administrativă a Daciei romane". In *Influențe, contacte şi schimburi culturale între civilizațiile spațiului carpato-dunărean, din preistorie până în antichitate. Lucrările colocviului național desfăşurat la Cumpăna, 2-4 octombrie 2013*, D. Măndescu (ed.). Piteşti (2014): 149-162.

Pflaum 1960: Pflaum, H.G., *Les carrières procuratoriennes équestres sous le Haut-Empire romain, I-III*. Paris (1960-1961).

Pons Pujol 2013: Pons Pujol, L., "Omnia a Sulpicio Felice optumo rarissimoq(ue) praefecto Salenses habere (I. A. M. lat., 307, 3). Historiografía e interpretaciones sobre la actuación de Marcus Sulpicius Felix en Sala". In *La société de l'Afrique romaine*, Y. Le Bohec (ed.). Paris (2013): 103-114 (Bulletin Archéologique 37).

Rachet 1970: Rachet, M., *Rome et les Berbères: un problème militaire d'Auguste à Dioclétien*. Bruxelles (1970) (Collection Latomus 110).

Rebuffat 1994: Rebuffat, R., "M. Sulpicius Felix à Sala". In *L'Africa romana. Atti del X convegno di studio Oristano, 11-13 dicembre 1992*, A. Mastino, P. Ruggeri (eds.). Sassari (1994): 182-215.

Reddé 1986: Reddé, M., *Mare Nostrum. Les infrastructures, le dispositif et l'histoire de la marine militaire sous l'Empire Romain*. Rome (1986).

Roxan 1973: Roxan, M. M., "The Auxilia of Mauretania Tingitana". *Latomus* 32 (1973): 838-855.

Šašel 1974: Šašel, J., "Pro legato". *Chiron* 4 (1974): 467-477.

Šašel 1983: Šašel, J., "Zu T. Varius Clemens aus Celeia". *ZPE* 51 (1983): 295-300 (= *Opera selecta*. Ljubljana (1992): 206-211).

Spaul 1994: Spaul, J. E. H., *Ala². The Auxiliary Cavalry Units of the Pre-Diocletianic Imperial Roman Army*. Andover (1994).

Speidel 1975: Speidel, M. P., "The Rise of Ethnic Units in the Roman Imperial Army". *ANRW* II/3 (1975): 202-231 (= *Roman Army Papers I*. Amsterdam (1984): 117-148).

Speidel 1977: Speidel, M. P., "Pannonian Troops in the Moorish War of Antoninus Pius". In *Akten des XI Internationalen Limeskongresses. Székesfehérvár 30.8-6.9 1976*, J. Fitz (ed.). Budapest (1977): 129-135 (= *Roman Army Papers I*. Amsterdam (1984): 211-215).

Speidel 2006: Speidel, M. P., "Hadrian's Lancers". *AntAfr* 42 (2006): 117-124.

Speidel 2014: Speidel, M. A., "Herrschaft durch Vorsorge und Beweglichkeit. Zu den Infrastrukturanlagen des kaiserzeitlichen römischen Heeres im Reichsinneren". In *Infrastruktur und Herrschaftsorganisation im Imperium Romanum. Herrschaftsstrukturen und Herrschaftspraxis III Akten der Tagung in Zürich 19.-20. 10. 2012*, A. Kolb (ed.). Berlin (2014): 80-99.

Speidel 2017: Speidel, M. A., "Antoninus Pius, das Militär und der Krieg. Epigraphische Korrekturen zur literarischen Überlieferung". In *Jenseits der Narrativs. Antoninus Pius in den nicht-literarischen Quellen*, C. Michels, P. F. Mittag (eds.). Stuttgart (2017): 255-268.

Stroheker 1966: Stroheker, K. F., "Die Aussenpolitik des Antoninus Pius nach der Historia Augusta". In *Bonner Historia-Augusta-Colloquium 1964/1965*, J. Straub (ed.). Bonn (1966): 241-256.

Thomasson 1984: Thomasson, B. E., *Laterculi praesidum. Volumen I*. Göteborg (1984).

Thomasson 2009: Thomasson, B. E., *Laterculi praesidum. Vol. I ex parte retractatum*. Göteborg (2009) (http://www.isvroma.it/public/Publications/laterculi.pdf).

Țentea 2012: Țentea, O., *Ex oriente ad Danubium. The Syrian Units on the Danube Frontier of the Roman Empire*. Cluj-Napoca (2012).

Wagner 1938: Wagner, W., *Die Dislokation der römischen Auxiliarformationen in den Provinzen Noricum, Pannonien, Moesien und Dakien von Augustus bis Gallienus*. Berlin (1938).

Synoptic Table

Unit	Province	Attestation
cohors I Batavorum Marsacorum	Britannia	Eck, Holder, Pangerl 2016 = AE 2016, 2021 (AD 152-153, MT)
cohors I Baetasiorum	Britannia	Eck, Holder, Pangerl 2016 = AE 2016, 2021 (AD 152-153, MT)
ala felix Moesica	Germania superior	Jovanova, Ončevska Todorovska 2018, p. 216-220 (AD 152, MC)
cohors IV Tungrorum vexillatio	Raetia	MT, starting with AD 153 – after 162/163, again *milliaria* (RMD III 186), before only *vexillatio*
ala I Commagenorum sag. milliaria	Noricum	RGZM 32 (PS; AD 151, MC)
ala I Augusta Thracum = ala Augusta?	Noricum	AE 1975, 951 (Fedjana, MC); RGZM 32 (PS; AD 151, MC)
ala I Pannoniorum Tampiana	Noricum	RGZM 32 (PS; AD 151, MC)
ala I Ulpia contariorum milliaria	Pannonia superior	CIL VIII 9291 = ILS 2519 = AE 1955, 133 (Tipasa, MC); CIL VIII 21620 (Portus Magnus, MC); CIL III 4379 = RIU 267 (Arrabona, PS); CIL III 4321 = RIU 560 (Odiavum, PS); RGZM 32 (PS; AD 151, MC); RMD IV 273 = RGZM 36 (AD 150-151, MC); Jovanova, Ončevska Todorovska 2018, p. 216-220 (AD 152, MC)
ala I Thracum sag. c. R.	Pannonia superior	RGZM 32 (PS; AD 151, MC)
ala I Hispanorum et Aravacorum	Pannonia superior	CIL XVI 99 (Szőny, PS; AD 150, MC); RGZM 32 (PS; AD 151, MC); RMD IV 273 = RGZM 36 (AD 150-151, MC); Jovanova, Ončevska Todorovska 2018, p. 216-220; Eck, Pangerl 2018 (AD 152, MC)
ala I Cannanefatium c. R.	Pannonia superior	AE 1951, 265 (Tipasa, MC); RGZM 32 (PS; AD 151, MC); RMD IV 273 = RGZM 36? (AD 150-151, MC); Jovanova, Ončevska Todorovska 2018, p. 216-220 (AD 152, MC)
ala III Augusta Thracum sag.	Pannonia superior	CIL XVI 99 (Szőny, PS; AD 150, MC); RMD IV 273 = RGZM 36 (AD 150-151, MC); Jovanova, Ončevska Todorovska 2018, p. 216-220; Eck, Pangerl 2018 (AD 152, MC)
ala I Thracum victrix	Pannonia superior	RMD IV 273 = RGZM 36 (AD 150-151, MC); Jovanova, Ončevska Todorovska 2018, p. 216-220 (AD 152, MC)
ala I Flavia Augusta Britannica milliaria	Pannonia inferior	CIL XVI 99 (Szőny, PS; AD 150, MC); RMD IV 273 = RGZM 36? (AD 150-151, MC); Jovanova, Ončevska Todorovska 2018, p. 216-220 (AD 152, MC)
ala I Thracum vet. sag.	Pannonia inferior	CIL XVI 99 (Szőny, PS; AD 150, MC); RMD IV 273 = RGZM 36 (AD 150-151, MC); Jovanova, Ončevska Todorovska 2018, p. 216-220; Eck, Pangerl 2018 (AD 152, MC)
ala I Augusta Ituraeorum sag.	Pannonia inferior	CIL XVI 99 (Szőny, PS; AD 150, MC); RMD IV 273 = RGZM 36? (AD 150-151, MC)
ala I praetoria c. R.	Pannonia inferior	CIL XVI 99 (Szőny, PS; AD 150, MC); Jovanova, Ončevska Todorovska 2018, p. 216-220 (AD 152, MC); Eck, Pangerl 2018 (AD 152, MC).
ala I civium Romanorum	Pannonia inferior	AE 1955, 132 (Tipasa, MC); RGZM 36? (AD 150-151, MC)
pedites singulares Pannonici	Pannonia inferior	CIL VIII 21453 = IPD⁴ 280 (Aquae Calidae, MC)
cohors III Batavorum milliaria vexillatio	Pannonia inferior	CIL XVI 179, 180 (AD 148, MC?); Eck, Pangerl 2018a, p. 34-38, no. 5 (AD 151, MC?); RMD V 145 (AD 154-156, MT?)
ala I Claudia nova miscellanea	Moesia superior	RMD V 405; Eck, Holder, Pangerl 2016, p. 200-201, no. 2; Eck, Pangerl 2018, p. 236? (AD 151, MC); Jovanova, Ončevska Todorovska 2018, p. 216-220 (AD 152, MC); Eck, Pangerl 2018 (AD 152, MC)
ala I Gallorum Flaviana	Moesia superior	RMD V 405; Eck, Holder, Pangerl 2016, p. 200-201, no. 2; Eck, Pangerl 2018, p. 236 (AD 151, MC); Jovanova, Ončevska Todorovska 2018, p. 216-220; Eck, Pangerl 2018 (AD 152, MC)
ala I Gallorum Atectorigiana	Moesia inferior	Eck, Holder, Pangerl 2016 = AE 2016, 2021 (AD 152-153, MT); Chiriac, Mihailescu-Bîrliba, Matei 2006; AE 2006, 1213; Eck, Holder, Pangerl 2016, p. 198-200, no. 1 (AD 156, MT)
ala I Flavia Gaetulorum	Moesia inferior	Jovanova, Ončevska Todorovska 2018, p. 216-220; Eck, Pangerl 2018 (AD 152, MC); Eck, Holder, Pangerl 2016 = AE 2016, 2021 (AD 152-153, MT); Chiriac, Mihailescu-Bîrliba, Matei 2006; AE 2006, 1213; Eck, Holder, Pangerl 2016, p. 198-200, no. 1 (AD 156, MT)
ala I Vespasiana Dardanorum	Moesia inferior	Eck, Holder, Pangerl 2016 = AE 2016, 2021 (AD 152-153, MT); Chiriac, Mihailescu-Bîrliba, Matei 2006; AE 2006, 1213; Eck, Holder, Pangerl 2016, p. 198-200, no. 1 (AD 156, MT)
ala II Hispanorum et Aravacorum	Moesia inferior	Eck, Holder, Pangerl 2016 = AE 2016, 2021 (AD 152-153, MT); Chiriac, Mihailescu-Bîrliba, Matei 2006; AE 2006, 1213; Eck, Holder, Pangerl 2016, p. 198-200, no. 1 (AD 156, MT)

Appendix – The Imperial Decree of 31 May 152

Tabella I of a military diploma discovered at Scupi, Moesia Superior, during the archaeological excavations in the bath-house ("Large Thermae"), Jovanova, Ončevska Todorovska 2018, 216-220 (my transcription after the photo of the *extrinsecus*); see also Eck, Pangerl 2018, a fragment of military diploma, copied after the same imperial constitution.

Imp(erator) Caes(ar) divi Hadriani f(ilius) divi Traiani
Parthici n(epos) divi Nervae pron(epos) T(itus) Aelius
Hadrianus Antoninus Aug(ustus) Pius pont(ifex)
max(imus) trib(unicia) pot(estate) XV imp(erator) II co(n)s(ul) III p(ater) [p(atriae)]
equitib(us) qui mili(taverunt) [i]n al(is) X appell(antur) I [101]
Ulp(ia) conta(riorum) ∞ et I Thrac(um) victr(ix) et I Hisp(anorum)
Aravac(orum) et I Cannanef(atium) et III Aug(usta) Thrac(um),
quae est in Pann(onia) Super(iore) sub Claudio Ma-
ximo, item I Fl(avia) Aug(usta) Britt(anica) ∞ et I Thrac(um)
sag(ittaria) vet(erana) et I praet(oria) c(ivium) R(omanorum), quae sunt in Pann(onia)
infer(iore) sub Nonio Macrino et I Claud(ia)
nova misc(ellanea) et Gall(orum) Fl(aviana), quae est in Moes(ia)
sup(eriore) sub Egrilio Plariano et I Fl(avia) Gaet(ulorum), [102]
quae est in Moes(ia) infer(iore) sub Fuficio
Cornuto et Felix Moes(ica) quae est Ger-
  ●   ●
man(ia) sup(eriore) sub Popilio Pedone leg(atis), quin(is)
et vicen(is) plurib(us)ve stip(endiis) emer(itis) dim(issis) hon(esta)
miss(ione) per Varium Clementem proc(uratorem) cum
essent in expedit(ione) Maur(etaniae) Caes(ariensis), quor(um) nom(ina)
subscr(ipta) sunt civit(atem) Rom(anam), qui eor(um) non
hab(erunt), dedit et con(ubium) cum uxor(ibus) quas tunc
hab(uissent) cum est civit(as) [iis data] aut cum i(i)s
quas post(ea) dux(issent) dum[taxat singuli sin]gul(as), pr(idie) k(alendas) Iun(ias)
P(ublio) Sufenate Severo et Tullio Tusco co(n)s(ulibus).
Alae Gall(orum) Fl(avianae) cui praeest
Ulpius Marcellus
ex gr[egale]
[- - -]co? Pedica[e]? f(ilio) Dard(ano) [103]
[Des]criptum et recognitum ex tabula aerea,
[qu]ae fixa est Romae in mur(o) post
[tem]pl(um) divi August(i) ad Minervam.

---

[101] There are eleven *alae*.
[102] On the table *GAES*
[103] The surface of the diploma is badly damaged here.

Militaires de Mésie Inférieure Dans les Maurétanies

Lucrețiu Mihăilescu-Bîrliba
(Université "Alexandru Ioan Cuza" de Iași)

Abstract: Many epigraphic texts, especially military diplomas, mention soldiers from Moesia Inferior who were stationed in the Mauretanian provinces. The majority of the inscriptions date to the time of Antoninus Pius with many referring specifically to Flavius Flavianus, *procurator* of Tingitana in 152(153)-156. The auxiliary soldiers and cavalry units from Moesia Inferior and other Danubian provinces were detached to Tingitana at this time in order to fight against the local tribes. The conflicts between the Romans and the local tribes in Mauretania were not rare, and in fact, lasted for more than 10 years. Several inscriptions attest that some veterans from Moesia Inferior settled in Africa and married local women. In my opinion, there are two reasons why the troops of Moesia Inferior came to fight in the Mauretania provinces: the relative stability of the region and the fighting capacity of the auxiliary units.

Keywords: Moesia Inferior, Mauretania, epigraphic sources, military diplomas

Il y a plus de dix ans, j'avais publié avec Costel Chiriac et Ionel Matei un diplôme militaire trouvé sur le territoire de l'actuelle Dobroudja (nord de la province de Mésie Inférieure).[1] La *constitutio* avait été promulguée en 156 par Antonin le Pieux pour les troupes de cette province, qui avaient participé à une *expeditio* en Maurétanie Tingitane. Le procurateur de Tingintane, Flavius Flavianus, est connu seulement par l'intermédiaire des diplômes militaires.[2] Une autre *constitutio* de Tingitane, datée du 26 octobre 153, le mentionne Flavius Flavianus en tant que *procurator* de cette province.[3] L'activité de ce personnage en Tingitane est liée à une expédition militaire à laquelle ont participé les vexillations des ailes venues de Mésie Inférieure. Un autre diplôme, daté 152-153, atteste la liberation des troupes appartenant aux *exercitus* de Mésie Inférieure et de Bretagne par le même procuratuer de la Tingitane, Flavius Flavianus.[4] Le conflit avec les populations locales de Maurétanie n'était pas à ses débuts pendant la procuratèle de Flavianus.

Ces documents font allusion, à mon avis, à des conflits successifs qui ont opposé les Romains aux populations indigènes des provinces nord-africaines. Je vais reprendre en bref ce dossier, afin de remarquer le role des unites de Mésie Inférieure dans ces combats.

Même si peu nombreuses, les sources littéraires et épigraphiques fournissent certaines informations importantes concernant les luttes entre les Romains et les indigènes. Ainsi, une inscription de Sala, datant de 144 et érigée en l'honneur du préfet Sulpicius Felix, mentionne ses activités afin de protéger la cité menacée d'un danger extérieur.[5] Cette inscription a généré plusieurs interprétations. M. Rachet[6] et M. Sigman[7] estiment que le texte fait allusion aux attaques de certaines tribus locales sur la cité et met en évidence un état permanent d'insécurité dans cette zone. Pour M. Bénabou, ces attaques seraient des phénomènes isolés dans la province,[8] tandis que pour Ed. Frézouls, lequel cherche à réduire au minimum le rôle de ces attaques, il s'agirait de mesures habituelles prises contre les insurgents locaux.[9] E. Gozalbes Cravioto pense que le texte doit être mis en relation avec les travaux de renouvellement du *limes* à 10 km au sud de Sala, qui était menacé par les attaques de brigands et de tribus locales.[10] Cette hypothèse nous semble plus probable, à juger à la fois d'après le texte de l'inscription et les fouilles effectuées, lesquelles ont confirmé la reconstruction du *limes* vers le milieu du IIe siècle.[11] A. Rhorfi, en réalisant un bilan des conflits en Maurétanie, concentre son analyse sur le IIIe siècle et estime qu'au IIe siècle les disputes entre Rome et les tribus indigènes étaient moins dignes d'intérêt.[12] Il tient tous ces conflits armés pour des actes isolés de brigandage plutôt que pour des rébellions.[13] Ce qui est infirmé par

[1] Chiriac, Mihailescu-Bîrliba, Matei 2006, 383-390.
[2] Pour la carrière de Flavius Flavianus, voir surtout Mihailescu-Bîrliba, Dumitrache 2016, 67-74.
[3] Plusieurs copies: RMD V, 409, 410 (AE 1997, 1767; 2005, 1727), 411 (AE 2003, 1547); RGZM 34; Eck, Pangerl 2005, 199, 202; Eck, Pangerl 2007, 244-245; Chiriac, Mihailescu-Bîrliba, Matei 2006, 383-390. Weiß 2007, 251, 255; Weiß 2009, 246. Voir un petit recueil chez Mihailescu-Bîrliba, Dumitrache 2016, 67-68 (le commentaire), 70-73 (les textes).
[4] Eck, Holder, Pangerl 2016, 187-201.

[5] IAM 307.
[6] Rachet 1970, 195.
[7] Sigman 1977, 428.
[8] Bénabou 1976, 136-137.
[9] Frézouls 1957, 70; Frézouls 1980, 77.
[10] Gozalbes Cravioto 2002, 476.
[11] Euzennat 1989, 129.
[12] Rhorfi 2005, 557-558, 560.
[13] Rhorfi 2004, 556.

nos diplômes: car le terme *expeditio* indique une action organisée de l'armée romaine.[14] En ce qui concerne les sources littéraires, un passage de l'Histoire Auguste nous informe qu'Antonin contraignit les Maures à demander la paix.[15] Pausanias affirme à son tour qu'Antonin n'avait pas déclenché la guerre, mais qu'il vainquit les Maures qui s'étaient insurgés contre lui. Pour Pausanias, la victoire d'Antonin était prestigieuse, puisque les Maures étaient d'excellents cavaliers.[16] Les autres sources épigraphiques de ces expeditions sont représentées d'abord par un diplôme attestant les troupes des Pannonies en Césarienne (en 150),[17] ensuite par une autre *constitutio* qui évoque des troupes de la Pannonie Supérieure dans la même province, étant procurateur T. Varius Clemens[18] et enfin par six inscriptions de Celeia (Norique) érigées en l'honneur de T. Varius Clemens, ancien procurateur de cette province.[19]

T. Varius Clemens a été *praefectus auxiliariorum tempore expeditionis in Tingitaniam missorum* (ou, comme il est mentionné dans un autre texte, *praefectus auxiliorum in Mauretaniam Tingitanam ex Hispania missorum*). Dans deux cas, les dédicants étaient de Maurétanie Césarienne (deux *decuriones alarum proviniciae Mauretaniae Caesarensis* et deux *patroni causarum provinciae Mauretaniae Caesarensis*). Nous n'insisterons pas sur le *cursus honorum* de T. Varius Clemens, analysé déjà par H.-G. Pflaum,[20] H. Devijver,[21] B. E. Thomasson,[22] A. Mastino,[23] J. Šašel,[24] C. C. Petolescu[25] et I. Piso.[26] On peut admettre que T. Varius Clemens est devenu procurateur de la Maurétanie Césarienne en 150 ou 151. Nous reprenons en ordre chronologique les données fournies par les sources épigraphiques: en 144, à Sala, une inscription mentionne des travaux afin d'assurer la protection de la cité, suite à un état d'insécurité; en 150, des vexillations des ailes envoyées des Pannonies participent à une expédition en Maurétanie Césarienne; vers 151/152, et probablement dans les années suivantes, des détachements des unités auxiliaires des Espagnes sont envoyés en Tingitane; enfin, en 156, Antonin promulgue une autre *constitutio*, qui atteste la libération des militaires appartenant aux ailes de Mésie Inférieure et qui avaient lutté toujours en Tingitane. Ces données, corroborées par les informations fournies par l'Histoire Auguste et Pausanias, confirment l'existence d'un conflit assez long entre les tribus locales et l'autorité romaine. Selon Pausanias, le conflit a représenté une rébellion des autochtones contre le Romains, ce qui est accepté par M. Bénabou.[27] Pausanias écrit que les Romains

se sont imposes difficilement. Nous ne connaissons pas exactement l'acharnement de ces combats, mais on constate que les armées des Maurétanies ont eu besoin de renforts venus des Espagnes, des Pannonies et de Mésie Inférieure. Si les Espagnes ne sont pas loin des Maurétanies, il n'en va pas de même pour les Pannonies et la Mésie Inférieure. Il faut également remarquer que les unités envoyées en Afrique sont toujours des ailes et parfois des cohortes; les militaires pouvaient se déplacer plus rapidement et étaient capables d'intervenir avec plus d'efficacité au cours des combats que les soldats des cohortes. Les ailes de Mésie Inférieure sont *I Gallorum Atectorigiana, I Flavia Gaetulorum, I Vespasiana Dardanorum* et *II Hispanorum Aravacorum* (mentionnées toutes en deux diplômes – dans le texte de 151, les noms des trois ailes n'est pas conservé, mais il est à supposer qu'il s'agit de mêmes ailes).

À tout ce dossier il convient d'ajouter quelques textes. En Tingitane, il y a deux textes (malheureusement fragmentaires) attestant des *equites ex Moesia*.[28] À Rome, C. Valerius Maximus, *decurio* de l'*ala Atectorigiana* (en fait, *I Gallorum Atectorigiana*) fait ériger l'épitaphe à Ulpia Danae, originaire de Maurétanie Césarienne.[29] En texte, le militaire indique que l'aile appartient à l'*exercitus Moesiae Inferioris*. Probablement il a connu sa femme pendant l'expédition effectué sous Antonin (d'ailleurs, le gentilice de sa femme suggère une datation post-Trajan).

Je n'évoquerai pas maintenant les diplômes de Mésie Inférieure attestant des soldats enrôlés dans les unités de Tingitana qui rentrent chez eux (comme le Dace Damanaeus en 144, un soldat dont le nom n'est pas conservé et le Thrace Cu[..]is, fils de Titus, les derniers textes datant de 153).

Par consequent, effectifs des quatre ailes de Mésie Inférieure ont été déplacées dans les Maurétanies dans les années 150, afin de combattre contre les tribus indigènes. Les témoignages épigraphiques indiquent que ces conflits ont été sérieux et les Romains ont eu des difficultés pour surmonter les forces des Maures. Pourquoi les ailes de Mésie Inférieure? Je suppose deux raisons: la première, une relative stabilité dans la province danubienne; la deuxième, la force montrée par ces unités à d'autre occasions. En tout cas, les soldats de Mésie Inférieure envoyés en Maurétanie sont restés une certaine période de temps: le mariage du décurion C. Valerius Maximus avec une femme originaire de la Césarienne représente une preuve dans ce sens.

Remerciements

Cet article a été réalisé dans le cadre du projet PN-III-IDP4-PCE-2020-0383.

[14] Voir aussi Rebuffat 1998, 193-242.
[15] SHA, *Antonius Pius* 5.
[16] Pausanias 8, 43.
[17] CIL XVI 99.
[18] RGZM 32.
[19] CIL III 5211-5212, 5214-5216, 15205. Sur les troupes des provinces danubiennes détachées dans les Maurétanies, voir surtout Farkas 2011, 189-195.
[20] Pflaum 1960, 370-371; Pflaum 1982, 143.
[21] PME 52.
[22] Thomasson 1984, 411; Thomasson 1996, 202–203.
[23] Mastino 1987, 363.
[24] Šašel 1983, 295–300 (= AE 1987, 795); AE 1988, 905.
[25] IDRE II, 254, *sub numero*.
[26] Piso 2013, 151-159.
[27] Bénabou 1976, 135-144.

[28] AE 1992, 1939; IAM 818.
[29] CIL VI 33032.

Bibliographie

Bénabou 1975: Bénabou, M., *La Résistance africaine à la romanisation*. Paris (1975).

Chiriac, Mihailescu-Bîrliba, Matei 2006: Chiriac, C., Mihailescu-Bîrliba, I., Matei, I., "Un nouveau diplôme militaire de Mésie Inférieure". In *Pontos Euxeinos. Beiträge zur Archäologie und Geschichte des antiken Schwarzmeer und Balkanraumes*, S. Conrad, R. Einicke, A. E. Furtwängler, H. Löhr, A. Slawisch (eds.). Langenweißbach (2006): 383-390.

Eck, Holder, Pangerl 2016: Eck, W., Holder, P., Pangerl, A., "Eine Konstitution aus dem Jahr 152, oder 153 für Niedermösische und Britannische Truppen, abgeordnet nach Mauretania Tingitana". *ZPE* 199 (2016): 187-201.

Eck, Pangerl 2005: Eck, W., Pangerl, A., "Neue Militärdiplome für die Truppen der mauretanischen Provinzen". *ZPE* 153 (2005): 187-206.

Eck, Pangerl 2007: Eck, W. and Pangerl, A., "Weitere Militärdiplome für die mauretanischen Provinzen". *ZPE* 162 (2007): 243-247.

Euzennat 1989: Euzennat, M., *Le limes de Tingitane. La frontière méridionale*. Paris (1989).

Farkas 2011: Farkas, I. G., "La paertecipazione delle truppe del *limes* danubiano nella spedizione di Antonino Pio contro i mauri". *Quaderni Friulani di Archeologia* 21 (2011): 189-195.

Frézouls 1957: Frézouls, Ed., "Les Baquates et la province romaine de Tingitane". *Bulletin d'Archéologie Marocaine* 2 (1957): 65–116.

Frézouls 1980: Frézouls, Ed., "Tome et la Maurétanie tingitane: un constat d'echec". *Antiquités Africaines* 16 (1980): 65–94.

Gozalbes Cravioto 2002: Gozalbes Cravioto, E., "Tumultos y resistencia indigena en Mauretania Tingitana (siglo II)". *Gerion* 20 (2002): 451–485.

Mastino 1987: Mastino, A., "La ricerca epigrafica in Marocco (1973–1986)". In *L'Africa romana 4, Atti del IV convegno di studio, Sassari 13–15 dicembre 1985*, A. Mastino (ed.). Sassari (1987): 337-384.

Mihailescu-Bîrliba, Dumitrache 2016: Mihailescu-Bîrliba, L. and Dumitrache, I., *Diplômes militaires-carrières équestres: le cas de Flavius Flavianus*. In *Moesica et Christiana. Studies in Honour of Professor Alexandru Barnea*, A. Panaite, R. Cîrjan, C. Căpiţă (eds.). Brăila (2016): 67-74.

Pausanias: Pausanias, *Descriptioon of Greece*, W. H. S. Jones (éd.). Harvard (1935).

Pflaum 1960: Pflaum, H.-G., *Les carrièes procuratoriennes équestres sous le Haut-Empire romain*, I–III. Paris (1960).

Pflaum 1982: Pflaum, H.-G. *Les carrièes procuratoriennes équestres sous le Haut-Empire romain. Supplément.* Paris (1982).

Piso 2013: Piso, I. *Fasti provinciae Daciae II. Die ritterlichen Amtsträger*. Bonn (2013).

Rachet 1970: Rachet, M. *Rome et les Berbères. Un problème militaire d'Auguste à Dioclétien*. Bruxelles (1970).

Rebuffat 1998: Rebuffat, R., "L'armée de Maurétanie Tingitane", *Mélanges de l'École Française de Rome. Antiquité* 109 (1998): 193–242.

Rhorfi 2004: Rhorfi, A., "La Pax Romana en Tingitane et les conditions de sa permanence aux trois premiers siècles ap. J.-C.". In *L'Africa romana 15. Ai confine dell'Impero: contatti, scambi, conflitti*, M. Khanoussi, P. Ruggieri, C. Vismara (eds.). Rome (2004): 547-566.

Šašel 1983: Šašel, J., "Zu T. Varius Clemens aus Celeia". *ZPE* 51 (1983): 295–300.

Sigman 1977: Sigman, M., "The Romans and the indigenous tribes of Mauretania Tingitana". *Historia* 26 (1977): 415–439.

Thomasson 1984: Thomasson, B. E., *Laterculi praesidum* I. Göteborg (1984).

Thomasson 1996: Thomasson, B. E., *Fasti Africani. Senatorische und ritterliche Amtsträger in den römischen Provinzen Nordafrikas von Augustus bis Diokletian*. Stockholm (1996).

Weiß 2007: Weiß, P., "Weitere Militärdiplome in Mauretania Tingitana aus dem Balkanraum". *ZPE* 162 (2007): 249-256.

Weiß 2009: Weiß, P., "Statthalter und Konsulndaten in neuen Militärdiplomen". *ZPE* 171 (2009): 231-252.

Epigraphic Sources on the Movement of People between Egypt and the Provinces of Lower Moesia and Thrace (1st - 3rd c. AD)

Ligia Ruscu

(Babeș-Bolyai University Cluj-Napoca)

Abstract. This paper investigates the connections between Egypt and the cities of Lower Moesia and Thrace in the 2nd and 3rd centuries AD. While the paper presents an overview of the commercial and cultural connections that began in the Hellenistic period, the bulk of the analysis is based upon an assessment of five inscriptions from Perinthos and Tomis. These inscriptions indicate that during the Principate people moved predominantly from Egypt to the Greek cities of Lower Moesia and Thrace, reversing the Hellenistic trend.

Keywords: Egypt, Lower Moesia, Thrace, prosopography, epigraphic sources

Introduction

The connections between Egypt and the regions of Lower Moesia and Thrace during the Principate generally follow patterns established in the Hellenistic period.[1] The regions were linked socially and economically via routes through the Aegean Sea. Given the economic importance of both regions in the Roman period, contact was somewhat heightened and the religious and cultural attractions of Egypt clearly influenced the frequency and intimacy of contact. The prosopographic aspect of these relations has been explored from various standpoints.[2] This paper examines five examples of epigraphy which provide information concerning the movement of people between the Greek cities of Lower Moesia and Thrace and the province of Egypt. The study focuses upon people from Egypt who are attested in the Moesian and Thracian cities and vice versa.

Overview of the Inscriptions

Two inscriptions from Perinthos, dated to the 2nd century AD beginning with the reign of Hadrian, document an association of businessmen from Alexandria, Ἀλεξανδρεῖς οἱ πραγματευόμενοι ἐν Περίνθῳ.[3] The association honoured P. Aelius Harpokration, no doubt one of their own, for benefactions such as building a Tychaion and a wall.

An association called the οἶκος τῶν Ἀλεξανδρέων is mentioned in an inscription from Tomis dated by Roman and Egyptian calendars, precisely, to 26 March 160.[4]

The purpose of this association is not explicitly stated. It may have been affiliated with the cult of the Egyptian deities, to which the altar is dedicated along with the emperor Antoninus Pius and his designated successor. In all likelihood, however, the association was comprised of businessmen[5] whose interests were similar to the association attested at Perinthos. However, the men from Tomis appear to have held a lower social standing than those in Perinthos, since none of the three individuals mentioned in the inscription of Tomis had the franchise. Their names, in the peregrine formula, are either theophoric names derived from Egyptian deities (e.g., Sarapion or Anubion), or common Greek or Roman names (e.g., Karpion, Polymnos, Cornutus, or Longinus).

Two other inscriptions from Tomis mention two more individuals. A funerary inscription in verse (late 2nd - early 3rd c. AD) refers to a man named Kantharos who died at Alexandria,[6] while a fragmentary inscription mentions ---πιος / Σέππονος, a wine merchant from Alexandria (οἰνέμπορος Ἀλεξανδρίας).[7]

Discussion

This evidence, however slight, allows us to gain some insight into the dynamics of the connections between these areas of the Roman Empire. A comparison with the trends of the Hellenistic period is instructive. From the late 4th to the 1st century BC, a number of people from Greek cities in Thrace made their way to Egypt. Epigraphic and literary evidence indicates that people from Istros,[8]

[1] Dana 2001, esp. 297-307; Avram 2003; Avram 2004; Archibald 2004; Archibald 2007a; Bingen 2007; Bricault 2007; Ruscu 2014, 102-103.
[2] La'da 2002; Avram 2007; Avram 2013.
[3] IvPerinthos 27 (= IGR I 800) and 28.
[4] ISM II 153 = ISM VI2, 153 = IGR I 604 = SIRIS 708 = RICIS 618/1005.

[5] For communities of Roman citizens in Greek cities, see Brélaz 2016 and Ramgopal 2017. For communities of *cives Romani consistentes* in Greek cities see, van Andringa 2003, Avram 2007b, Bourigault 2011.
[6] ISM II 285 = ISM VI2, 285.
[7] ISM II 463 = ISM VI2, 463 = IGLR 28.
[8] Μοσχιάδης Ἰστριανός, mercenary (Syrinx: Syringes 1202; Avram 2013, 2159; Hellenistic period); Ἀσία Ἴστρα (Alexandria: Preisigke

Tomis,[9] Kallatis,[10] Odessos,[11] and Mesambria[12] journeyed to Egypt, while only one person made the reverse voyage from Egypt to Kallatis.[13] The differences to the situation in the Roman period are obvious. In the Hellenistic period, there were no associations of any sort involved, just isolated individuals. Also, the direction of travel was reversed: predominantly from Thrace towards Egypt in the Hellenistic period, predominantly from Egypt towards Thrace in the Roman period. The explanations for these changes are connected with evolutions in Thrace as well as in Egypt. The coming of Rome in Lower Moesia and Thrace was one of the most important turning points in the history of the Greek cities in this area.[14] Previously, especially in the case of the Western Pontic cities, the *poleis* were caught in a losing fight against the increasing pressure of their barbarian neighbours. There were certainly many forms of interaction between Greeks and non-Greeks, not all of them involving violence. However, over the long period between the late 4th and the 1st century BC, the balance of political and military power changed slowly but inexorably to the disadvantage of the Greek cities. Instances of raids, plundering, sudden attacks on the cities' territories and their crops, the capture of prisoners, ransom payments, tribute payments, and payments for protection are recorded in a multitude of sources.[15] The whole process culminated around the mid-1st century BC with the attack of the Getae, led by king Burebista, against the Western Pontic cities. Many cities fell to the Getae at this time.[16]

Under the Romans the climate ultimately changed for the better. Roman armies now stood between the Greek cities and their enemies, repulsing most of the attacks. It took a while, but Rome managed to eradicate piracy in the Black Sea. Rome built a network of roads across the Balkans, connecting the cities along the Black Sea and the Thracian part of the Aegean Sea to the inland regions of the empire. Trajan established, after his conquest of Dacia and the comprehensive administrative overhaul of the Balkan provinces, ten or eleven new Greek *poleis* in inner Thrace, where there had not previously been any cities (in

the Roman or Greek sense).[17] As a result of Romanisation, the Greek *poleis* in Thrace experienced a lasting period of peace and prosperity, which rendered them interesting as long-distance trade partners. This explains the presence of merchants from Alexandria, numerous enough to form their own associations.

There are, however, no merchants from the Greek cities of Lower Moesia and Thrace attested in Egypt. This may be due to two facts. On the one hand, Alexandria had been, from its inception, and still was, a global city and its merchants had a similar outlook. The Thracian *poleis* on the other hand were midsize to small provincial cities, whose merchants had a much narrower vision. A more comprehensive explanation is connected to a supra-regional phenomenon. During the Hellenistic period, the Western Pontic shore was connected to Egypt via a major navigational route through the straits, the Aegean, and along the western coast of Asia Minor. Most epigraphic examples concerning the movement of people to and from the Western Pontic *poleis* were discovered along this route. This route did not cease to function during the Roman period; however, as far as these cities are concerned, it lost much of its importance. The Aegean route was supplanted by another, which connected the *poleis* in Thrace with those in Asia Minor, in particular with Bithynia, but also with areas in inland Anatolia. Beginning in the reign of Trajan, this axis was elongated westward towards inland Thrace and along the Danube.[18]

This leads to the other reason why Egypt was less attractive during the Principate for people coming from the Greek cities in Lower Moesia and Thrace. The coming of Rome into Egypt, accompanied as it was by political and military upheaval, proceeded smoothly from the point of view of social and institutional structures.[19] Change generally came gradually. There was, however, one area in which change was sudden, which explains the loss of interest for Egypt by the Greeks in Thrace: the disappearance of the royal house of the Ptolemies and the royal court. All known individuals from Thrace with connections to Egypt had enjoyed royal patronage. They were either mercenaries serving in the armies of the Ptolemies or scholars and writers attracted to the stimulating and congenial environment of Alexandria.[20] With the disappearance of royal patronage, the motivation of Greeks in Thrace to travel all the way to Egypt dwindled.

Finally, of all the Greek cities in Lower Moesia and Thrace, there were only two with direct connections to Egypt in the Roman period: Tomis and Perinthos. Prior to the Roman period, Tomis had been a small and rather unimportant city, despite the fact that it had the largest

1915, I 4990 = IGLAlexa 234, 3rd c. BC).

[9] Μελάνιππος Τομίτης, mercenary (Syrinx: Syringes 1202; Avram 2013, 3153; Hellenistic period).

[10] Σάτυρος, peripatetic philosopher from Kallatis (Oxyrynchos: Kind 1921; Peremans/Dack 1968, 16948 = 16949; Heichelheim 1925, 50; Avram 2013, 2220; second half 3rd c. BC); Ἡρακλείδης Λέμβος Σαραπίωνος, epitomator from Kallatis (Oxyrynchos: Daebritz 1912; Peremans/Dack 1968, 16922; Heichelheim 1925, 50; Avram 2013, 2218; under Ptolemy VI). On the cultural and intellectual connections between the Black Sea cities and the rest of the Greek world, see Dana 2011.

[11] Ἁρμόδιος Ὀδησίτης, mercenary (Abydos: Preisigke 1915, I 3782; Memnonion 382; La'da 2002, E1959; Avram 2013, 2559; late 4th – first half 3rd c. BC).

[12] Δωρίων Κρατέρου Μεσημβριανός (Herakleopolis or Oxyrynchos: Turner/Lenger 1955, 267; Peremans/Dack 1975, 3900a; La'da 2002, E1840; Avram 2013, 2525; ca. 230 BC).

[13] Θέων Ποτάμωνος Ἀλεξανδρεύς (ISM III 155,3[rd] c. BC).

[14] Haynes 2011; Ivanov 2012; Lozanov 2015.

[15] For the fate of the Western Pontic cities in the Hellenistic period, see Pippidi 1984a, Munteanu 2013, Ruscu 2013.

[16] For Burebista, see Crişan 1977, Pippidi 1984b, Vinogradov 1989, 266-272, Dobesch 1994.

[17] Boteva 2014, with further literature.

[18] Ruscu 2014.

[19] Haensch 2008, with further literature.

[20] For scholars from the Black Sea area in Egypt, see Dana 2011, esp. 297-307.

harbour on the Western Pontic coast.[21] Under Roman rule, however, the city benefited from the *pax Romana*, whereby piracy was eliminated in the Black Sea. Moreover, of all the Greek cities in this area, Tomis was situated at the end of the shortest cross-country road to the Danube. Thus, by the 2nd century AD Tomis had become the largest and most prosperous city along the Western Pontic shore. It was attractive for and welcoming to foreigners, boasting of the title μητρόπολις τοῦ Εὐξείνου Πόντου. Moreover, it probably served as the residence of the governor of Lower Moesia.[22] Perinthos[23] was another prosperous harbour city which benefited from the opening up of the Thracian inland and was probably the seat of the governor of Thrace.[24] As such, Tomis and Perinthos were among the most attractive cities for merchants from far-away Egypt.

Conclusion

The epigraphic sources for the period of the Principate indicate that people moved predominantly from Egypt to the Greek cities of Lower Moesia and Thrace, reversing the Hellenistic trend. This was due to the disappearance of royal patronage in Egypt and the enhanced economic attraction of Thrace in the Roman period. This is as far as the epigraphic evidence concerning the movement of people will take us. Other types of evidence will no doubt add to or modify this picture.

Bibliography

van Andringa 2003: van Andringa, W., "Cités et communautés d'expatriés installées dans l'Empire romain: le cas des *cives Romani consistentes*". In *Les communautés religieuses dans le monde gréco–romain. Essais de définition,* N. Belayche, S. C. Mimouni (eds.). Turnhout (2003): 49–60.

Archibald 2004: Archibald, Z. H., "In-groups and out-groups in the Pontic cities of the Hellenistic Age", In *Pontus and the outside world. Studies in Black Sea History, Historiography and Archaeology (Colloquia Pontica 9),* C. J. Tuplin (ed.). Leiden (2004): 1-15.

Archibald 2007: Archibald, Z. H., "Contacts between the Ptolemaic Kingdom and the Black Sea in the Early Hellenistic Age". In *The Black Sea in Antiquity. Regional and Interregional Economic Exchanges,* V. Gabrielsen, J. Lund (eds.). Aarhus (2007): 253-271.

Avram 2003: Avram, A., "Antiochos II Théos, Ptolémée II Philadelphe et la mer Noire". *CRAI* (2003): 1181-1213.

Avram 2004: Avram, A., "Sur la date de la divinisation de Ptolémée II Philadelphe à Byzance". In *Orbis antiquus.*

Studia in honorem Ioannis Pisonis, C. Găzdac, C. Roman (eds.). Cluj (2004): 828-833.

Avram 2007a: Avram, A., "L'Égypte lagide et la mer Noire: approche prosopographique". In *Colloque La Méditerranée d'une rive à l'autre: culture classique et cultures périphériques,* A. Laronde, J. Leclant (eds.). Paris (2007): 127-153.

Avram 2007b: Avram, A., "Les *cives Romani consistentes* de Scythie Mineure: état de la question". In *Étrangers dans la cite romaine. Actes du colloque de Valenciennes (14–15 octobre 2005) "Habiter une autre patrie": des incolae de la République aux peuples fédérés du Bas–Empire,* R. Compatangelo–Soussignan, Ch.– G. Schwentzel (eds.). Rennes (2007): 91–109.

Avram 2013: Avram, A., *Prosopographia Ponti Euxini Externa* (Colloquia Antiqua 8). Leuven (2013).

Bingen 2007: Bingen, J., "The Thracians in Ptolemaic Egypt". In *Hellenistic Egypt: Monarchy, Society, Economy, Culture,* J. Bingen, R. S. Bagnall (eds.). Berkeley (2007): 83–93.

Boteva 2014: Boteva, D., "Trajan and His Cities in Thrace: Focusing on the Two Nico*poleis*". In *Trajan und seine Städte. Colloquium Cluj-Napoca, 29. September – 2. Oktober 2013,* I. Piso, R. Varga (eds.). Cluj (2014): 195-204.

Bourigault 2011: Bourigault, M., "Le droit des autres: les *cives Romani consistentes*". In *I diritti degli altri in Grecia e a Roma,* A. Maffi, L. Gagliardi, (eds.). Sankt Augustin (2011): 78–87.

Brélaz 2016: Brélaz, C., "Des communautés de citoyens romains sur le territoire des cités grecques: statut politico–administratif et régime des terres". In *Propriétaires et citoyens dans l'Orient romain,* Fr. Lerouxel, A.- V. Pont (eds.). Bordeaux (2016): 69–85.

Bricault 2007: Bricault, L., "La diffusion isiaque en Mésie Inférieure et en Thrace: Politique, commerce et religion". In *Nile into Tiber. Egypt in the Roman World. Proceedings of the Third International Conference of Isis Studies, Leiden, May 11-14, 2005,* L. Bricault, M. J. Versluys, P. G. P. Meyboom (eds.). Leiden (2007): 245-266.

Buzoianu, Bărbulescu 2007: Buzoianu, L. and Bărbulescu, M., "Tomis". In *Ancient Greek Colonies in the Black Sea 2 (BAR IS 1675),* D. V. Grammenos, E. K. Petropoulos (eds.). Oxford (2007): 287-336.

Buzoianu, Bărbulescu 2012: Buzoianu, L. and Bărbulescu, M., *Tomis. Comentariu istoric şi arheologic / Historical and Archaeological Commentary.* Constanţa (2012).

Crişan 1977:: Crişan, I. H., *Burebista şi epoca sa (Burebista and His Times).* Bucharest (1977).

Daebritz 1912: Daebritz, R., "Herakleides" no. 51. *RE* VIII (1912): 488-491.

---

[21] On Tomis, see Buzoianu/Bărbulescu 2007 and Buzoianu/Bărbulescu 2012.
[22] Haensch 1997, 333-336; for a different opinion, see Piso 2014.
[23] Sayar 1998.
[24] Haensch 1997, 329-332. For arguments in favour of Philippopolis, see Sharankov 2007, 185.

Dana 2011: M. Dana, *Culture et mobilité dans le Pont–Euxin. Approche régionale de la vie culturelle des cités grecques (Scripta antiqua 37)*. Bordeaux (2011).

Dobesch 1994: Dobesch, G., "Zur Datierung des Dakerkönigs Burebista". In *Die Hexadrachmenprägung der Groß-Boier. Ablauf, Chronologie und historische Relevanz für Noricum und Nachbargebiete*, R. Göbl (ed.). Vienna (1994): 51-68.

Haensch 1997: Haensch, R., "Capita provinciarum. Statthaltersitze und Provinzialverwaltung in der römischen Kaiserzeit". *Kölner Forschungen 7*. Mainz (1997).

Haensch 2008: Haensch, R., "Die Provinz Aegyptus: Kontinuitäten und Brüche zum ptolemäischen Ägypten. Das Beispiel des administrativen Personals". In *Die römischen Provinzen. Begriff und Gründung (Colloquium Cluj-Napoca, 28. September – 1. Oktober 2006)*, I. Piso (ed.). Cluj (2008): 81-106.

Haynes 2011: Haynes, I. P. (ed.), *Early Roman Thrace. New Evidence from Bulgaria (JRA Suppl. 82)*. Portsmouth RI (2011).

Heichelheim 1925: Heichelheim, F., *Die auswärtige Bevölkerung im Ptolemäerreich*. Leipzig (1925).
Ivanov 2012: Ivanov, R. (ed.), *Roman Cities in Bulgaria*. Sofia (2012).

Kind 1921: Kind, F. E., "Satyros", no. 16 (and 17?). *RE* II A1 (1921): 228-235.

La'da 2002: La'da, Cs. A., *Prosopographia Ptolemaica X. Foreign Ethnics in Hellenistic Egypt*. Leuven (2002).

Lozanov 2015: Lozanov, I., "Roman Thrace". In *A Companion to Ancient Thrace*, J. Valeva, E. Nankov, D. Graninger (eds.). Oxford (2015): 75-90.

Munteanu 2013: Munteanu, L., "Legăturile oraşelor vest-pontice cu populaţiile "barbare" în epoca elenistică. Evidenţa numismatică (The Relations of the Western Pontic Cities with the "Barbarian" Populations in the Hellenistic Period. The Numismatic Evidence)". In *Poleis în Marea Neagră: Relaţii interpontice şi producţii locale / Poleis in the Black Sea area: Inter-Pontic relations and local productions*, F. Panait Bîrzescu, I. Bîrzescu, F. Matei-Popescu, A. Robu (eds.). Bucharest (2013): 358-392.

Peremans, Dack 1968: Peremans, W. and Dack, E. van't, *Prosopographia Ptolemaica VI*. Louvain (1968).

Peremans, Dack 1975: Peremans, W. and Dack, E. van't, *Prosopographia Ptolemaica VIII. Addenda et corrigenda aux volumes I (1950) et II (1952)*. Louvain (1975).

Pippidi 1984a: Pippidi, D. M., "Les villes grecques de Scythie Mineure à l'époque hellénistique". In *Parerga. Écrits de philologie, d'épigraphie et d'histoire ancienne*, D. M. Pippidi (ed.). Paris/Bucarest (1984): 118-134.

Pippidi 1984b: Pippidi, D. M., "Gètes et Grecs dans l'histoire de la Scythie Mineure à l'époque de Byrebistas". In *Parerga. Écrits de philologie, d'épigraphie et d'histoire ancienne*, D. M. Pippidi (ed.). Bucureşti/Paris (1984): 175-188.

Piso 2014: Piso, I., "Le siège du gouverneur de Mésie Inférieure". In *Interconnectivity in the Mediterranean and Pontic World during the Hellenistic and Roman Periods (Pontica et Mediterranea III)*, V. Cojocaru, A. Coşkun, M. Dana (eds.). Cluj (2014): 489-504.

Preisigke 1915: Preisigke, Fr., *Sammelbuch griechischer Urkunden aus Ägypten*. Straßburg (1915).

Ramgopal 2017: Ramgopal, S., "One and Many: Associations of Roman Citizens in Greece". In *Social Dynamics under Roman Rule. Mobility and Status Change in the Provinces of Achaia and Macedonia. Proceedings of a Conference Held at the French School of Athens, 30–31 May 2014 (Meletemata 74)*, A. D. Rizakis, F. Camia, S. Zoumbaki (eds.). Athens (2017): 407–425.

Ruscu 2013: Ruscu, L., "Relaţiile apoikiilor vest-pontice cu vecinii lor greci şi barbari în epocile elenistică şi romană (The relations of the Western Pontic Greek cities with their Greek and Barbarian neighbours in the Hellenistic and Roman periods)". In *Poleis în Marea Neagră: Relaţii interpontice şi producţii locale / Poleis in the Black Sea area: Inter-Pontic relations and local productions*, F. Panait Bîrzescu, I. Bîrzescu, F. Matei-Popescu, A. Robu (eds.). Bucharest (2013): 11-44.

Ruscu 2014: Ruscu, L., "Die Beziehungen privaten und offiziellen Charakters zwischen Einzelpersonen und Staaten in Bezug auf die westpontischen Griechenstädte in hellenistischer und römischer Zeit". In *Die Außenbeziehungen pontischer und kleinasiatischer Städte in hellenistischer und römischer Zeit. Akten einer deutsch-rumänischen Tagung in Constanţa, 20.-24. September 2010*, V. Cojocaru, Chr. Schuler (eds.). Stuttgart (2014): 87-120.

Sayar 1998: Sayar, M. H., *Perinthos-Herakleia (Marmara Ereğlisi) und Umgebung. Geschichte, Testimonien, griechische und lateinische Inschriften*. Wien (1998).

Sharankov 2007: Sharankov, N., "Stratura praesidis Thraciae". In *The Lower Danube in Antiquity (6th c. BC – 6th c. AD). International Archaeological Conference Bulgaria – Tutrakan, 6.- 7. October 2005*, L. F. Vagalinski (ed.). Sofia (2007): 181-187.

Turner, Lenger 1955: Turner, E. G. and Lenger, M. T., *The Hibeh Papyri II*. London (1955).

Vinogradov 1989: Vinogradov, J. G., *Političeskaja istorija Olbijskovo polisa, VII.- I. vv. do n. e. Istoriko-epigrafičeskoje issledovanje (Political History of the City of Olbia, 7th- 1st c. BC. Historical and Epigraphic Study)*. Moscow (1989).

5

The Cult of Asclepius in the Roman Empire: A Comparative Analysis of North Africa and Dacia

Jasmin Hangartner (University of Vienna)

Abstract: A thorough study of the cult of Asclepius in Roman North Africa for my master's thesis, revealed similarities to the cult in the Danubian provinces, especially in Dacia. The cult of Asclepius in North Africa was complex, given its association with local Punic or Numidian cults. There were also similarities to Greek practices in terms of ritual and architecture. Furthermore, there was a strong military influence and adherence to the Roman imperial cult. The same principles seem relevant with regard to the cult of Asclepius in Dacia. In both regions, Asclepius was worshipped in temples with a *porticus* and three *cellae*, together with gods that were not typically worshipped together with Asclepius. Additionally, the sacrifice of statues of the god in wells at the sanctuary of Sarmigezetusa has analogies in several locations in North Africa. Another connection between Dacia and North Africa is given by an inscription (CIL III,993), dedicated by an officer in Dacia which mentions Caelestis and Asclepius, as well as the *Genio Carthaginis* and the *Genio Daciarum*. Through an interdisciplinary approach, using methods of epigraphy and archaeology, the reasons for these similarities are investigated.

Keywords: Asclepius/Aesculapius cult, North Africa, Roman Dacia, temples, epigraphy

Introduction

This paper compares the cult of Asclepius in the North African provinces (Africa Proconsularis, Numidia, Mauretania Caesariensis and Mauretania Tingitana) and Dacia. In a previous study, the cult of Asclepius in Roman North Africa was analysed in terms of attribution, architecture, the distribution of sanctuaries, and the rituals of the cult.[1] In some cases, there was not enough evidence to attribute particular sanctuaries to Asclepius. However, through the analysis of inscriptions and the architecture of the known sanctuaries, it was demonstrated that some cult sites in North Africa shared characteristics of the cult of Asclepius in the Balkan region. There were also elements only found in North Africa that can be attributed to the *interpretatio romana* or syncretism of the cult.

By comparing the cult of Asclepius in North Africa to the practice of the cult in Dacia, new information can be gained about the practice of the cult throughout the Roman provinces, its distribution, and the organisation of the religious landscape of the provinces in question. Healing gods are found in many religions and, therefore, were part of the *interpretatio romana* in many provinces. Comparing information pertaining to religion from North Africa with that of Dacia will provide insights into the wider practice of this adaptation of gods.

The first section of this paper summarises the results of my previous research about the cult of Asclepius in North Africa. The second section presents an overview of the cult in Dacia with a focus on the sanctuaries at Apulum and Ulpia Traiana Sarmizegetusa, the cities with the most evidence of the cult in Roman Dacia. Finally, the attributes and practices of the cult in these two geographic locations will be compared.

The Cult of Asclepius in North Africa

A considerable amount of research was conducted in the North African provinces in the late 19th and the early 20th centuries, resulting in a wealth of evidence referring to Asclepius, including statues and inscriptions, primarily from baths and temples. Unfortunately, many finds lack a specific provenance. Due to the unscientific excavation methods of the time, there is no information concerning the small finds from the temples that may have been dedicated to Asclepius. After an intense review of archaeological literature, I concluded that there are only seventeen sites with clear evidence of temples dedicated to Asclepius.[2]

---

[1] Hangartner 2018.

[2] Hangartner 2018, 137: Althiburos, Aradi, Auzia (not discussed and only documented for Valetudo), Bulla Regia, Bordj abd el Malek Hr Chett, Caesarea, Karthago, Lambaesis, Maxula, Musti, Thibicaae, Thignica, Thisiduo, Thugga, Thuburbo Maius, Vazi Sarra, Uchi Maius. In contrary to Benseddik 2010a, I, 86 which lists 27 temples. Temples with architectural remains: Africa Proconsularis: Althiburos, Ammaedara, Aradi, Bulla Regia, Djebel Oust, Gigthis, Tebessa Khalia, Thibicaae, Thuburbo Maius, Uchi Maius; Numidia: Lambaesis, Castellum Tidditanorum, Timgad; Mauretania Caesarensis: Rapidum, Rusazus (only Hygieia). Temples attested epigraphically according to Benseddik:

Only three of these have been excavated in detail,[3] while the others are only known through epigraphy mentioning a temple or through architectural elements found on the surface.

In total, more than 100 inscriptions mention Asclepius or his priests. Several sites exist where the cult is attested by statues or inscriptions, but lack the epigraphic or architectural elements of a temple.[4] This has resulted in reconstructions of presumed temples of Asclepius at sites where they cannot be proven.[5] The majority of the archaeological evidence of the cult of Asclepius in North Africa dates to the second half of the 2nd and the 3rd centuries AD. Most objects were dedicated by members of the local elite.[6] There is a concentration of evidence in Africa Proconsularis, especially in the cities within the hinterland of Carthage. In the military locations of Numidia, most dedications were installed by high-ranking members of the army, such as *legatus* or *vir perfectissimus*. N. Benseddik divides the cult places into three categories: the old Berber-Punic cities, settlements along important transportation routes, and thermal baths.[7] She also shows the importance of the cult for the military.[8] Considering the inscriptions and the other sources, such as architectural components of temples, statues, and the references to gods Asclepius is accompanied by, it seems the attributes of the cult in North Africa were diverse from one location to another. Greek, Roman, and Punic characteristics can be observed, at times resulting in syncretism.

An important question is whether there was an *interpretatio romana* of a local healing deity in the form of the Graeco-Roman Asclepius or an *interpretatio africana* of Asclepius.[9] The result of this discussion has been to divide the cult into an Asclepius-Eshmun cult and a Graeco-Roman cult.[10] In some studies more categories are added, such as a Berbero-Roman cult.[11] I propose a division of the cult into one with Graeco-Roman elements and one with provincial/local elements. By defining the second category as a cult of Asclepius with provincial/local elements, I pay attention to the two centuries between the Roman conquest of the first African province and the first appearance of evidence of Asclepius in Roman times in North Africa. Moreover, there is a lack of evidence for a clear connection of Asclepius with Eshmun in the 2nd

century AD. This division will be demonstrated in the following two sections.

Elements of the Graeco-Roman cult

Several elements in temple architecture and epigraphy that are typical of the cult of Asclepius in the eastern part of the Roman Empire can be found in the North African provinces. The cult of Asclepius in the eastern provinces, including Asia Minor, has a long tradition dating back to classical times, yet new elements developed in the Roman era, such as the inclusion of baths in sanctuaries or the introduction of *Leges Sacrae*.[12] These elements can also be found in North Africa. In Thuburbo Maius (Henchir Kasbat) a *Lex Sacra* dating to the second half of the 2nd century was found. It follows the tradition of the *Leges Sacrae* dated to the early 2nd century AD found in the Asclepieion in Pergamon and describes a purification ritual before the entrance of the podium of Asclepius:[13]

Iussu domini / Aesculapi / L.Numisius L.f. / Vitalis / podium de / suo fecit / quisq(ue) intra(t) / podium ad/scendere vo/ let a muli/ere a suilla / a faba a ton/sore a bali/neo commu/ ne custodi/at triduo / cancellos / calciatus / intrare no/lito.

The content of the inscription is similar to the one from Pergamon, because it mentions that abstinence from certain activities and foods has to occur for three days. This 3-day purification ritual is comparable to an inscription from Balagrae (El Beida), a city which was very much influenced by the Greeks.[14] The evidence provided by the inscription for the existence of a purification ritual is supported by two mosaics found in the Asclepieion in Lambaesis (Tazzoult). The mosaics were found in two annex buildings of the Asclepieion and bear the inscriptions *bonus intra melior exi* and *B(onis) b(ene)*.[15] The *epitheton dominus* refers to the eastern part of the empire where the Greek equivalent κύριος was used in inscriptions dedicated to Asclepius.[16] The use of the *epitheton dominus* for Asclepius is only known in North Africa, Rome (two inscriptions), and Dacia (one inscription). The latter was probably dedicated by a North African soldier.[17]

Two mosaics found in Thuburbo Maius and Althiburos depict agonistic crowns, while an inscription from Ostia dating to the reign of Gallienus refers to the *Asclepia Karthagini*, games performed in honour of the god.[18] The tradition of the *Asclepia* originated in the eastern part of the Roman Empire, where they were amongst the major pan-Hellenic games in the Hellenistic period.[19]

Africa Proconsularis: Bordj Ab del Malek-Hr Chett, Gammarth, Hr Bir el Afu, Karthago, Maxula, Musti, Thignica, Thisiduo, Thugga, Thysdrus, Vazi Sarra; Numidia: Castellum Dimmidi; Mauretania Caesarensis: Auzia (nur für Valetudo), Caesarea,

[3] Hangartner 2018, 33: Althiburos, Bulla Regia and Lambaesis.
[4] Hangartner 2018, 27: Hr Bir el Afu, Gammarth, Thignica, Thysdrus, Castellum Dimmidi.
[5] Hangartner 2018, 83. Ammaedara, Castellum Tidditanorum, Djebel Oust, Gigthis, Rapidum, Tebessa Khalia, Timgad.
[6] Benseddik 2001, 2692.
[7] Benseddik 2001, 2691; Benseddik 2005, 272.
[8] Benseddik 2005, 277; Van der Ploeg 2018, 258 on this topic as well.
[9] Benseddik 2010a, Benseddik 2010b, Musso 2009, Cadotte 2007, Bénabou 1976a and 1976b, Charles-Picard 1954.
[10] Van der Ploeg 2018, Benseddik 2010a.
[11] Benseddik 2001, 2696.

[12] Riethmüller 2005, 379.
[13] Thuburbo Maius: IlAfr 225, for the ones in Pergamon: Habicht 1969, 169 Nr. 161 and IvPII 264, LSAM 14.
[14] SEG 20.759.
[15] Groslambert 2009, 86, CIL VIII 2584. Benseddik 2010a, II, 126 Nr. 14.
[16] Robert 1989, 252 n. 5.; Habicht 1969, 106.
[17] Carthage: AE 1949, 00056; Thisiduo: CIL VIII, 1267; Dacia: CIL III, 1079; Rome: CIL VI, 17 and 18.
[18] CIL XIV, 474 = Dessau, ILS, 5233.
[19] Robert 1982, 228.

The discovery of many statues of Asclepius in the Roman baths of North Africa may indicate another Graeco-Roman attribute in the cult of Asclepius, as their number (21) surpasses other provinces.[20] A strong connection of the cult to water, especially in the eastern part of the empire, has been demonstrated by several inscriptions that mention bathing as beneficial in connection to a visit of the Asclepieion and the inclusion of baths in association with his temples.[21]

The architecture and the syncretic arrangement of the worshipped gods of the Asclepieion in Lambaesis yields excellent proof of the transfer and adaptation of the cult's traditions from the east. This tripartite temple, built in the Doric order, was dedicated to Asclepius, Salus, Jupiter Valens, and Silvanus by the emperors through the *III Augusta* legion.[22] The arrangement of several baths around the complex and the inclusion of a porticus in the sanctuary are typical elements of Greek *asclepieia*, especially in the 2nd century AD. The grandiose architecture forming a religious complex on its own deepens this argument. The eight chapels (also interpreted as *scholae* or *sacella*) that lead up to the temple and many inscriptions which substantiate that they were used for the worship of other gods such as Apollo, Aquae Sinuessae, Medaurus, or Mercury demonstrate the influence of the legionary fortress and the diverse composition of the legion on the cult. As in other parts of the Roman Empire, Asclepius was a much-worshipped god by the military in North Africa.[23]

The existence of several versions of the god Asclepius worshipped under the same name is illustrated by an inscription found in Gammarth, dedicated to the *Aesculapio ab Epidauro*.[24] Mention of the Asclepius from Epidauros implies that there were also other forms of Asclepius. This was not a new phenomenon in North African religion. Inscriptions addressing Saturn also have the epitheton *achaiae*.[25] The phenomena of the *interpretatio romana* and *africana* made it necessary to specify to whom the inscription was dedicated.

The presence of so many elements of the cult, which seem to have originated in the eastern area of the Roman Empire, shows the importance a Graeco-Roman Asclepius achieved. It coexisted amongst the Punic pantheon in cities such as Thuburbo Maius, or was combined with other gods into a syncretic arrangement such as in Lambaesis.

Elements of provincial/local character

The cult of Asclepius in North Africa also shows traits that are unique compared to other regions of the Roman Empire, but only appeared from the moment of Roman rule. I, therefore, propose to call them elements of local/provincial character, as it is not possible to clearly associate them with a single, local Punic or Numidian deity. These elements consist of the combined worship of many deities that are usually not worshipped together. This phenomenon may have been the result of a syncretism between different belief systems or an *interpretatio romana*.[26] It is manifested in the cult of Asclepius by the dedication of altars or temples to Asclepius together with other deities he is usually not worshipped together with in the rest of the Roman Empire. For example, in Althiburos, Asclepius is worshipped with Mars and Jupiter and has a Punic inscription dedicated to him,[27] whilst in Bulla Regia he is associated with Apollo and Ceres.[28] These unusual combinations of deities also relate to the priests. The *sacerdotes* of Asclepius in North Africa are often also *sacerdotes* of Caelestis.[29] This suggests there is a strong probability that the combination of Asclepius and Caelestis was likely to have its origin in the Punic world and was maintained in Roman times. This connection to Punic religion is apparent because of the accumulation of priests of Asclepius in Carthage and the cities around it, which used to be the centre of the Punic health god Eshmun.[30] There is evidence of him being worshipped in Carthage as early as the 4th century BC.[31] Ancient sources mention a temple of Asclepius on the Byrsa hill in the 2nd century BC.[32] Because Eshmun is known to have been called Asclepius in the Graeco-Roman world, it is assumed that this temple was dedicated to Eshmun whose name was translated by the ancient authors.[33] After the third Punic war and the transformation of the region into a Roman province, there is no more evidence of the Eshmun cult in North Africa. It appears that he was worshipped under the name of Asclepius in Roman times.[34] Unfortunately, so far, it is not possible to prove a seamless passage from Eshmun to Asclepius since the earliest testimony of the cult of Asclepius is an inscription only in Claudian times.[35]

Another connection that is not manifested in the rest of the Empire is the role Asclepius played in the imperial cult.

---

[20] Manderscheid 1981, 31.
[21] Baths were added to the Asclepieia in Epidauros, Kos, Argos and Lebena, Riethmüller 2005, I, 379. Furthermore, several written sources attest to bathing activities in connection to a visit in the Asclepieia in Pergamon (Ael. Arist., Or., XXXIX, 1 – 17; Pausanias, Graeciae Descriptio 5.13.3) and Epidauros (Pausanias, Graeciae descriptio, II, 27, 6; IG IV²,1 126).
[22] CIL VIII, 2579 a, b, c= 18089 = I.L.S., 3841. *Iovi Valenti Aesculapio et Saluti Silvano / Imp(erator) Caes(ar) M(arcus) Aurelius Antoninus Aug(ustus) Pont(ifex) Max(imus) et / Imp(erator) Caes(ar) L(ucius) Aurelius Verus Augustus / has aedes per [[leg(ionem) III]] Aug(ustam) fecerunt.* For the Doric order as reference to Asclepius: Janon 1985, 84-86.
[23] For other regions: Van der Ploeg 2018, 169-214.
[24] Benseddik 2005, 284: AÉ 1968, 0553.
[25] CIL VIII, 12331.

[26] Cadotte 2007
[27] AÉ 1908, 0168 = CIL VIII, 27776. Merlin 1913, 15.
[28] Merlin 1908, 16.
[29] Musso 2009, 127f.
[30] Musso 2009, 124.
[31] Benseddik 2001, 2693. Lipinski 1994, 22.
[32] E. g. Livius, Ab urbe condita libri CXLII: XLI, 22,2; XLII, 24,3. Strabon, Geographia, XVII, 3, 14. Appian, Punica, 130.
[33] E.g., on the trilingue from Sardinia dating to the 2nd century BC: CIS I, 143; Lipinski 1994, 24.
[34] Toutain 1907, 468, Charles-Picard 1954, 125, LeGlay 1975, 129, Bénabou 1976a, 359, Benseddik 2010a, I, 124, Cadotte 2007, 171.
[35] AÉ 1914, 0166. Benseddik 2010a, II, 93.

At ten sites temples are dedicated to *Aesculapio Augusto, pro salute Imperatore/is* or the *Dii Augusti*.[36] Many other inscriptions to Asclepius contain the formula *pro salute Imperatoris* as well.[37] The great number of dedications for the emperors, in contrast to dedications *pro salute* of the person dedicating the inscription or a relative of theirs, is unusual. By comparison, most dedications throughout the empire ask for personal health instead of the emperor's health.

The Cult of Asclepius in Dacia

Dacia only became part of the Roman Empire at the beginning of the 2nd century AD. *Religionspolitik* was introduced into the newly composed province by the imperial government, and immigrants, mostly from the high social and economic spheres of the empire, brought their traditions and religious practices to the economic centres of the province.[38] A cohabitation of the new gods with the local gods, which were not easy to understand in Roman Dacia, most likely began.[39] The response of the local inhabitants of Dacia remains a highly discussed topic. Were certain Graeco-Roman gods worshipped by local inhabitants as their old gods with new names, therefore performing an *interpretatio romana*? Did they give up their gods? Or, did they keep worshipping their gods in local sanctuaries, which have not left archaeological remains?[40] Unlike the situation in other provinces, there is no evidence that any Graeco-Roman god was an *interpretatio romana*, e.g., due to special *epitheta* or by attributes of the statues.[41] This can also be observed in the cult of Asclepius which stands in the pure Graeco-Roman tradition.

So far only four temples in Dacia are known to have been dedicated to Asclepius: in Apulum (Alba Iulia), Micia (Veczel), Ulpia Traiana Sarmizegetusa (Várhely), and Ampelum (Zlatna). Nevertheless, the cult has been recognized at many other sites thanks to inscriptions on votive altars: e.g., in Arcobadara (Uriu), Alburnus Maior (Roşia Montană), Băile Herculane, Germisara (Geoagiu), Potaissa (Turda), Fort Săcelu, and Ungra.[42] In fact, more than 80 inscriptions dedicated to Asclepius yield insights into who dedicated the inscriptions, the motivation for their dedication, and the gods Asclepius was worshipped with. Additional evidence is in the form of statues,[43] votive reliefs,[44] coins, and gems. There is a concentration of

finds in the urban centres of Apulum and Ulpia Traiana Sarmizegetusa, as well as at the bathing resorts, such as Germisara and Băile Herculane, at military camps such as Micia, and at the mines, such as Ampelum.[45]

In Ulpia Traiana Sarmizegetusa, a sanctuary dedicated to Asclepius and Hygieia, probably together with other gods, has been excavated, whilst at Apulum, a *locus sacer* dedicated to these healing gods has probably been identified based upon inscriptions and a program of geophysical research to the north of the city. The other two sites with temples of Asclepius are at Ampelum, where architectural remains and an inscription have been found,[46] and in Micia, which is only known through an unpublished inscription.[47] The sanctuaries in Apulum and Ulpia Traiana Sarmizegetusa, which yielded the greatest number of dedications to Asclepius are presented in more detail in the following sections in order to analyse the cult in terms of similarities and differences with the one from North Africa.

Apulum

In Apulum, where the *XIII Gemina* legion was stationed, a considerable amount of material, mainly inscriptions, shows that Asclepius was among the most important god worshipped here. 26 inscriptions concerning Asclepius were found in Apulum.[48] In the 1970s two inscriptions mentioning a *locus salutaribus* were found outside the ancient city. They were dedicated to Asclepius and Hygieia, Apollo, Diana and Leto by C. Iul. Frontonianus and are dated to the late 2nd /early 3rd century AD.[49] Mention of a *locus salutaribus* implies that there was a sanctuary dedicated to the healing gods on public ground.[50] Since three other inscriptions mention a *huiusque (huiusce) loci*, A. Szabó thinks a cult district standing under public law existed outside the colonia which accommodated several sanctuaries for divinities, such as Nemesis, Venus and the healing gods.[51] Already in the 1970s I. Crişan highlighted the fact that the *Asclepieion* was outside the city, based upon the location of the inscriptions by Frontonianus.[52] This area is located approximately 200m to the north of the city and is called *locus apulensis* or *locus sacer*

---

[36] Aradi: CIL 08, 27356; Maxula: AE 1937, 72; Musti: AÉ 1968, 586; Thibicaa: CIL 08, 12228; Thugga: CIL 08, 26456a; Uchi Maius: CIL 08, 15446; Bulla Regia: CIL 08, 25513 Thisiduo: CIL 08, 1267; Vazi Sarra: CIL 08, 12006, Lambaesis: CIL 08, 18089.

[37] Aquae Flavianae: CIL 08, 17726. Carthage: CILPCart 00001. Lambaesis: CIL 08, 18091. Mactaris: AÉ 2002, 1667.

[38] Bologa 1966, 224; Nemeti 2005, 402.

[39] Nemeti 2005, 415.

[40] Bodor 1989, 1138.

[41] Bodor 1989, 1155.

[42] Riethmüller 2005, II, 457-460. For Arcobadara: CIL 03, 00786; Ungra: CIL 03, 07720.

[43] Apulum: Bodor 1989, 1123; Romula: ebd. Sarmizegetusa: ebd. Anm. 324.

[44] Apulum: CIL 03, 979; Potaissa: CIL 03, 12545; Sarmizegetusa: IDR 3, 2, 156, 160, 166, 170, 174.

[45] Bodor 1989, 1122.

[46] Szabó 2018, 161. AÉ 1959, 0306. (B) = AÉ 2007, 1188.
[Numi]ni Aesculapi / [et Hyg(iae)?] templum / [a solo c]onstituit / [---]es Aug(usti) lib(ertus) / [adiutor] tabul(arii) / [------

[47] Bodor 1989, 1122. Riethmüller 2005, II, 458 Kat. 725.

[48] Beu-Dachin 2010, 187.

[49] IDR 3, 5, 021; Aesculapio / et Hygiae ce/terisq(ue) diis dea/busq(ue) huiusq(ue) /loci salutarib(us) / C(aius) Iul(ius) Fronto/nianus vet(eranus) ex / b(ene)f(iciario) co(n)s(ularis) leg(ionis) V M(acedonicae) p(iae) / redditis sibi lumi/nibus grat(ias) age(ns) ex / viso pro se et Carteia / Maxima coniug(e) et Iul(ia) / Frontina filia / v(otum) s(olvit) l(ibens) m(erito). AÉ 1980, 0735 = IDR 3, 5, 36 Apol[l]ini Dianae / et Leto(!) ceterisque / dis deab[us]q(ue) huiusq(ue) / loci salutar[ib]us ex / imperio numi[n]is C(aius) Iul(ius) / Frontonia[nu]s vet(eranus) / leg(ionis) V M(acedonicae) p(iae) e[x b(ene)f(iciario) co(n)s(ularis)] / dec(urio) col(oniae) Apul(ensis) pr[o se et] / suis p(ecunia) s(ua) pontem / exstruxit

[50] Szabó 2004, 787, 790.

[51] Szabó 2004, 791. Inscriptions: IDR 3, 5, 297; IDR 3, 5, 356; IDR 3, 5, 364. Nemesis: IDR 3, 5, 293, Szabó 2015, 139f.

[52] Crişan 1971, 316; Szabó 2004, 788; Szabó 2018, 69.

by archaeologists.[53] It has been investigated through geophysical prospection, but the results were never fully published. A theatre seems to be located next to some monumental buildings.[54] Through other inscriptions, also dedicated to Asclepius and very likely also belonging to this sanctuary, it is probable that this complex consisted of at least three *porticoes* (perhaps following each other consecutively), a fountain, and a bridge.[55] The architecture with the *porticoes*, the presence of water, and the worship of several healing gods evoke a picture of a monumental sanctuary in the tradition of Greek *Asclepieia*, such as the complexes in Pergamon or Epidauros. Some inscriptions are dedicated to Asclepius and other gods not necessarily linked to healing which could be a syncretic element, e.g., when he is mentioned together with Jupiter Dolichenus[56] or with Jupiter Optimus Maximus and Juno and Minerva.[57]

An inscription associated to the *locus* notes the birth of the dedicator in the sanctuary of Jupiter Optimus Maximus.[58] A. Szabó compares this to the *Asclepieion* in Epidauros where a place was erected on the grounds of the sanctuary dedicated to visitors who gave birth at the site.[59] Other finds strengthen the hypothesis of this sanctuary being an *Asclepieion* in the tradition of the sanctuaries in the eastern part of the Roman Empire. The use of the formula *ex viso* in combination with the healing report in the inscription of Frontonianus could be an indicator for the practice of incubation.[60] The presence of doctors in the *locus* is indicated by inscriptions that mention a *haruspex* as the *antistes*, the caretaker of the *locus*, another similarity to *Asclepieia* in the eastern part of the empire.[61] An inscription with a relief of two hands could be a body part votive as they are also found in other sanctuaries of Asclepius in the eastern part of the empire.[62]

In contrast to the *Asclepieia* in the eastern part of the empire and in Rome, most dedications at Apulum were from high-ranking military officials and the local elite, such as *sacerdotes, augustales*, and *decuriones*, whereas in the eastern part of the empire, slaves and women represent the largest group of dedicators.[63]

E. Beu-Dachin analysed the usage of the name *Asclepius*, as being the transliterated Greek version versus *Aesculapius*, the Latin version, to determine whether the cult in Dacia was more influenced by the Greek or the Roman traditions. She concluded that it was important to most dedicators in Dacia to show how latinized they were

by using *Aesculapius*.[64] This is true for Apulum where only one inscription uses the transliterated Greek version, whilst another one is in Greek.[65] Therefore, the cult was strongly influenced by the eastern part of the empire in terms of its location, architectural elements, and possible ritual of incubation. The people who practiced the rituals emphasize Roman culture by using the latinized name.

Ulpia Traiana Sarmizegetusa

Ulpia Traiana Sarmizegetusa was a veterans' colony and, after Apulum, the most important city of the province. During excavations that took place in 1973 and 1974 to the north of the northern city gate, a concentration of inscriptions addressed to Asclepius and Hygieia were discovered at a sanctuary.[66] The unearthing of doctor's equipment, in addition to the inscriptions, led scholars to designate this zone as an area sacred to Asclepius and Hygieia.[67] 28 inscriptions mentioning Asclepius have been found at Ulpia Traiana Sarmizegetusa, most of which were not *in situ*.

The area referred to as the sanctuary of Asclepius and Hygieia consists of five temple-like buildings surrounded by a wall. At least three construction phases can be documented.[68] Buildings I, II, and III can be identified as temples due to their architectural features.[69] Temple I follows the typology of a *gallo-römischer Umgangstempel*.[70] Its dedication remains unclear and A. Schäfer proposes a local/provincial deity such as Apollo Grannus because of its architecture.[71] Temple II consists of two building units, one in front and one in the back, which are preceded by an altar. Temple III may have had a tetrastyle prostyle plan. Building IV is not identified and the remains of Building V consist of a square platform in the south-east.[72] Many lamps were found in front of Temple II, which A. Schäfer sees as evidence of the practice of incubation at the sanctuary.[73] G. Renberg showed, however, that for a secure identification of the practice of incubation more than one kind of evidence should be considered, unless the source is an inscription that unmistakably mentions the ritual of incubation.[74]

Inside a well to the north of the buildings, a marble statue of Asclepius and a relief of Asclepius and Hygieia were found.[75] The marble was most likely from Asia Minor. A. Schäfer interprets this as an intentional deposition in pagan times and not a disposal during the Christian period.[76]

[53] Szabó 2015, 133.
[54] Szabó 2018, 65.
[55] Portikus: CIL 03, 975; CIL 03, 976; IDR 3, 5, 013 = AÉ 1993, 1337. Fountain: IDR, 3, 5, 31. Bridge: AÉ 1980, 0735
[56] CIL 03, 01614.
[57] CIL 03, 01079.
[58] CIL 03, 1084.
[59] Szabó 2004, 796. Pausanias II.27.1.
[60] Renberg 2006, 139. IDR 3, 5, 021.
[61] Szabó 2018, 64f. Szabó 2004, 794f. Caius Iulius Valens, haruspex of the locus: AÉ 1930, 0006. IDR 3, 5, 356.
[62] CIL 03, 12558. *(A)escula/peo / et (H)y/gi(a)e / Resti/tuta / [------;* Hughes 2017, 166.
[63]   For Rome: Musial 1990, 236. For Apulum: Szabó 2004, 787.

[64] Beu-Dachin 2010, 187.
[65] CIL 03, 07740. IDR 3, 5, 15.
[66] Daicovicu-Alicu-Nemes-Piso-Pop-Rusu 1981, 231.
[67] Schäfer 2007, 147, 153. Inscription numbers: AÉ 1977, 0675 - 0677.
[68] Schäfer 2007, 65.
[69] Schäfer 2007, 64.
[70] Schäfer 2007, 65.
[71] Schäfer 2007, 69.
[72] Schäfer 2007, 145f.
[73] Schäfer 2007, 67.
[74] Renberg 2006, 106; Renberg 2017, 34f.
[75] Schäfer 2007, 66.
[76] Schäfer 2007, 66.

He compares this deposition to those in springs or wells in other parts of empire, such as the spring-sanctuary of Germisara where golden plates dedicated to the nymphs, Diana, and Hygieia have been found.[77]

The inscriptions dedicated to Asclepius are mainly from the urban upper classes such as *procuratores*, *duumviri* and *flamines*, while some inscriptions were dedicated by people who emphasise their Greek background.[78] Two altars were dedicated by women.[79] One inscription depict upside down ears, signifying that Asclepius and Hygieia were gods that listened.[80] In comparison to Apulum, there are fewer inscriptions from dedicators with a military background, even though Ulpia Traiana Sarmizegetusa was a veterans' colony.[81] There are also more inscriptions in Ulpia Traiana Sarmizegetusa that do not mention the name of the dedicators at all.[82]

The area of Asclepius and Hygieia is surrounded by other sanctuaries, including a temple of Liber Pater, a sanctuary of Nemesis, and a sanctuary dedicated to Domnus and Domna.[83] It is also close to the amphitheatre. Inside the sanctuary are dedications for other gods, such as Hercules and Jupiter Optimus Maximus.[84]

Since we do not know much about the architecture of the sanctuary in Apulum it is difficult to compare the two sanctuaries with each other. The extra-urban location of the two sanctuaries is similar, and they are both located close to a sanctuary of Nemesis and the amphitheatre. Considering the inscriptions in Apulum that mention a porticus it seems that the one in Ulpia Traiana Sarmizegetusa has a character that is more typical of sanctuaries in the north-western provinces and does not follow a classical Graeco-Roman canon.[85] The sanctuary at Apulum, on the other hand, could stand in the architectural tradition of the sanctuaries in Epidauros or Pergamon. This cannot be proven until further research is conducted.

Comparison of the cult in North Africa and Dacia

The character of the cult of Asclepius in North Africa and the one in Dacia is both similar and different. The archaeological evidence of the cult is quite similar in both regions. Inscriptions represent the most frequent type of evidence, followed by statues and architectural remains. Well documented and excavated temples do not exist in either North Africa or Dacia.[86] The cult seems to have been more wide-spread in Africa Proconsularis than in Dacia, suggested by the number of inscriptions that mention a temple and architectural remains that clearly pertain to the cult.[87] This might be due to the fact that there were more urban settlements in Africa Proconsularis in the pre-Roman period into whose religious pantheon Asclepius could have been added. The presence of the cult in the context of thermal baths is accounted for in Dacia (Băile Herculane, Germisara, and Toplița) as well as in North Africa (Aquae Aptuccensium, Aquae Persianae, Hammam Djedid, Hammam Mellègue, and Hammam Zriba). This presence may have been an attribute of the cult throughout the Roman empire.

When analysing the inscriptions in terms of their dedicators some differences can be discerned. In most sanctuaries of Asclepius in the eastern part of the empire dedications were primarily from women, slaves, and freedmen. This is different in North Africa and Dacia.

The dedications in Sarmizegetusa are almost exclusively civilian and were dedicated mostly by the male political elite, such as *flamines*, *duumviri*, *procuratores, and decuriones*. Only one inscription from Sarmizegetusa is dedicated by a soldier of the legion *V Macedonica*.[88] This is also true for Apulum where most dedications were made by the male political elite, such as *sacerdotes, augustales*, and *decuriones*. An exception to this is a dedication of a temple by a freedman in Ampelum.[89] In the North African provinces the dedications come from the political elite as well as from high-ranking members of the military, especially in Lambaesis where the dedications are almost exclusively of military origin.[90] Such a centre of military dedications is lacking in Dacia, even though Apulum and Ulpia Traiana Sarmizegetusa are strongly connected to the military, the former having had a legionary fortress and the latter having been a veterans' colony. In contrast to Dacia, the civilian dedications to Asclepius in North Africa seem to be more connected to a latinized elite, which is of local origin. They generally carry two names or served functions that belonged to this local elite, such as *sufet* or *magistros*, whereas in Dacia there is no evidence of a continuous local elite and the names of the dedicators follow the *tria nomina*. The priest of Asclepius is also connected to the one of Caelestis which is an argument for the partial *interpretatio romana* of the cult. The presence of several healing gods at the sanctuaries in North Africa and Dacia, among them Asclepius, Hygieia, Jupiter, and Silvanus can be explained by the syncretism that often occurred in the Roman provinces, especially at military sites, where many cultures met.

When analysing the way the dedicators wrote the god's name, there seems to be a larger immigrant community

---

[77] Schäfer 2007, 67.

[78] Inscription with Greek background: IDR 3, 2, 157; CIL 03, 07899.

[79] IDR 3, 2, 154; AÉ 1977, 0678.

[80] Bodor 1989, 1121; AÉ 1977, 0675.

[81] Only CIL 03, 01427.

[82] IDR 3, 2, 172-177. IDR 3, 2, 179. IDR 3, 2, 183.

[83] Schäfer 2007, 30.

[84] Hercules: IDR 3, 2, 221; IOM: AÉ 1977, 0674.

[85] Schäfer 2007, 148 compares the architecture with sanctuaries in Heckenmünster. Kempten, Margerides, Trier, auf Metzenberg bei Tawern.

[86] North Africa: Althiburos, Bulla Regia, Lambaesis. Dacia: Sarmizegetusa.

[87] Hangartner 2018, 83-85. Asclepius temples in Africa Proconsularis: Althiburos, Carthage, Maxula, Musti, Thibicaae, Thugga, Thisiduo. Vazi Sarra.

[88] CIL 03, 01427.

[89] AÉ 2007, 1188.

[90] Benseddik 2010a, I, 132f.

from the eastern part of the empire in Dacia than in North Africa. In North Africa the term *Asclepius* instead of *Aesculapius* is never used. Another significant difference in inscriptions is the use of the term *pro salute*. In Dacia as well as in other Roman provinces it is common to dedicate an inscription to Asclepius while asking for one's own health and/or the health of family members.[91] Only one inscription, from Potaissa, is dedicated to the health of the emperors.[92] In North Africa the inscriptions to Asclepius with the formula *pro salute* are all dedicated to the emperors.[93] This coincides with the lack of healing inscriptions in North Africa, whereas in Dacia several healing inscriptions have been found.[94] This could imply that the cult of Asclepius in North Africa may not have been dedicated to the health of individuals but was more closely associated to the *Religionspolitik*.

The cult in Dacia shows many Greek elements, present in the epigraphically noted architecture in Apulum (*Porticus*, Fountain) and in the votive inscriptions that probably mention the practice of incubation with accounts of individuals healing. In Ulpia Traiana Sarmizegetusa the architecture seems to be more influenced by the north-western provinces than the one in Apulum. Inscriptions are comparable to the one at Apulum. An inscription dedicated to *Aesculapio Pergameno* implies that there were different kinds of Asclepius worshipped, which made it necessary to specify.[95] This is similar to North Africa where an inscription from Gammarth is dedicated to *Aesculapio ab Epidauro*.[96] But unlike the case of North Africa there is no evidence for an *interpretatio romana* of the cult of Asclepius in Dacia, which would have made it necessary to specify. It is possible that the specification occurred according to the *Asclepieia* in the Greek east and, therefore, with regard to whether they were referring to the god in Pergamon or Epidauros. In North Africa there is a considerable amount of evidence of the cult having been influenced by the eastern part of the Roman Empire. This was demonstrated in the architecture of the *Asclepieion* in Lambaesis (*porticus*, Doric order) as well as the inscription on two mosaics which remind the visitor to enter with a good mind.[97] These examples stand in the tradition of the inscription that according to Porphyrios was written on the temple of Asclepius at the sanctuary in Epidauros.[98] Other influences of the Greek cult of Asclepius in North Africa are the *Asclepia* mosaics in Althiburos and Thuburbo Maius as well as the *Lex Sacra* from Thuburbo Maius.

A phenomenon that has not been widely discussed until now, but seems to be a ritual that took place in several locations of the Roman cult of Asclepius are deposits of inscriptions and/or statues in wells. In North Africa and in Dacia, evidence of ritual discard in wells has been identified. In the former, such rituals may have taken place in at least four sites (Castellum Dimmidi, Hammam Djedid, Naraggara, and Lambaesis). In Castellum Dimmidi a votive inscription to Asclepius, Hygieia, and Apollo was found in a pit.[99] In Hammam Djedid two statues of Asclepius and one of Hygieia were found in a cistern, and in Naraggara statues of Silvanus, Asclepius, and Hercules were found in a well.[100] Unfortunately, no information about the stratigraphy was recorded by the early 20th century excavators. In Naraggara, however, three pieces of gold were found together with the statues, making it probable that the deposit was an intentional and careful act of discard in pagan times, rather than a destructive campaign by Christians. At Ulpia Traiana Sarmizegetusa a marble statue of Asclepius and votive relief for Asclepius and Hygieia were found in a well at the sanctuary. The finds in Dacia and North Africa could be exemplary for a practice that took place throughout the empire. There is a similar find from Lauriacum (Enns) located in the Roman province of Noricum where the torso of an Asclepius statue was discovered in a Roman fountain.[101] Another similar situation with a very late chronology appears in Milet at the Asclepieium, underneath the theatre.[102]

In terms of the architecture of the sanctuaries nothing final can be said at the moment as there are almost no excavated sanctuaries. The sanctuaries at Apulum and Lambaesis are very similar to each other, which makes sense as there were legions in both cities. Furthermore, both were large sanctuary complexes (a *locus* implies that it is bigger) located outside the city and dedicated to several healing gods, including Asclepius, Hygieia, Jupiter, Silvanus, and other gods.

Conclusion

By comparing the cult of Asclepius in North Africa and Dacia, especially the two most important Dacian sites, Apulum and Ulpia Traiana Sarmizegetusa, it is possible to elucidate the degree to which the cult was influenced by local/provincial religious beliefs and by the large cult centres in the eastern part of the empire.

In both regions dedications by the political elite and members of the military prevail over inscriptions by slaves, freedmen, and women. But unlike in North Africa, there is no site in Dacia where the cult was almost exclusively documented through members of the military, even though the urban centres of the province were very much

---

[91] Apulum: CIL 03, 975; IDR 3, 5, 013 = AÉ 1993, 1337, CIL 03, 987, CIL 03, 14468, Sarmizegetusa: AÉ 1914, 0111 = AÉ 1933, 0019, AÉ 1977, 0676. Baile Herculane: CIL 03, 01561.

[92] Potaissa: AÉ 2012, 1215

[93] Aquae Flavianae: CIL 08, 17726. Carthago: CIL PCart 00001. Lambaesis: AÉ 1967, 0571, Mactaris: AÉ 2002, 1667. Mustis: AÉ 1968, 0586. Thibicaaes: CIL 08, 12228. Thisiduo: CIL 08, 01267. Vazi Sarra: CIL 08, 12006.

[94] e. g. Apulum: CIL 03, 987, Baile Herculane: CIL 03, 01561.

[95] CIL 03, 01417a.

[96] AÉ 1968, 0553.

[97] CIL VIII 2584, Benseddik 2010a, II, 126 Nr. 14.

[98] Porph., abst. II, 19. ἁγνὸν χρὴ ναοῖο θυώδεος ἐντὸς ἰόντα ἔμμεναι· ἁγνεία ἐστὶ φρονεῖν ὅσια.

[99] Benseddik 2010a, I, 143. AE 1948, 213.

[100] Hammam Djedid: Merlin 1913, A. Merlin, Rapport, BCTH 1913, CCXV-CCXVIII. Naraggara: Benseddik 2010a, II, 73.

[101] Varga 2015, 242. CSIR – Österreich III/2, 14,

[102] Niewöhner 2016, 86.

influenced by it. This shows how unique the *Asclepieion* in Lambaesis is. Moreover, Asclepius was worshipped in both provinces together with other (healing) gods. This leads me to the conclusion that it was typical for Asclepius to be worshipped together with other healing gods. This does not necessarily have to be a sign of *interpretatio romana*, except when the association with the other gods was unique in the Roman Empire, e.g., in North Africa with Ceres and Caelestis.

The Roman cult of Asclepius in North Africa and Dacia was dominated by elements that originated in the eastern part of the empire. But the characteristics that prove this connection are quite different in the two regions. In Dacia we have evidence of the healing cult through healing inscriptions which is similar at Pergamon and other Greek sites. There are also many inscriptions that ask for the health of oneself or family members. In North Africa the evidence lies in the architecture of the temple in Lambaesis, the *Asclepia* mosaics in Althiburos and Thuburbo Maius, and the games with the same name held in Carthage as well as the *Lex Sacra* for which we can find parallels in Epidauros and Pergamon. This difference in the archaeological material can either be explained by the fragmentary transmission or the different attribution of values to certain elements in the two regions. Perhaps, for the population in North Africa the ritual of purification and the games were more important, while the individual healing aspect was fulfilled by another deity (e.g., African Saturn). In Dacia we do not have evidence of a deity ascribed to this role, which might explain the focus on the individual healing aspect. The differences might also be explained by the fact that Dacia's pre-Roman political structures were destroyed and the province was colonized with people from Asia Minor and Italy whose belief systems dominated over the former local gods. This would have resulted in a lack of *interpretatio romana*.[103] This seems probable, as the situation is the same when we look at the archaeological sources for other gods in Roman Dacia. There is almost no evidence of local cults (through *epitheta*, onomastics, lack of clearly defined local iconographies), which could mean that the Dacians adopted the Roman gods.[104]

By contrast, in North Africa many local political structures remained intact even after the Roman conquest, and there is much evidence of Roman gods serving as *interpretatio romana*.[105] The amount of evidence connecting the cult to the imperial cult is surprising because Asclepius was not a typical god used for this purpose in other parts of the empire. In Dacia most inscriptions *pro salute imperatoris* are found in the context of the cult of Jupiter Optimus Maximus. J.B. Rives showed, however, that there was a comparable imperial cult already under the Numidian kings.[106] Since it was mostly the political elite who

dedicated to Asclepius with *epitheta*, such as *augustus* or for the health of the emperors, it demonstrates that in North Africa Asclepius was part of the state religion and not only an important local deity.

Bibliography

Bénabou 1976a: Bénabou, M., *La résistance africaine à la romanisation.* Paris (1976).

Bénabou 1976b: Bénabou, M., "Résistance et romanisation en afrique du nord sous le Haut-Empire". In *Assimilation et résistance à la culture gréco-romaine dans le monde ancien: travaux du Vième Congrès international d'études classiques*, D. M. Pippidi (ed.). Bucarest-Paris (1976): 367-375.

Benseddik 2010a, I: Benseddik, N., *Esculape et Hygie en Afrique. Recherches sur les cultes guérisseurs. Volume 1.* Paris (2010).

Benseddik 2010a, II: Benseddik, N., *Esculape et Hygie en Afrique. Textes et images. Volume 2.* Paris (2010).

Benseddik 2010b: Benseddik, N., "Asklépios, Eshmun mais encore...". *Bolletino di archaeologia on line*, volume speciale (2010): 11-21.

Benseddik 2005: Benseddik, N., "Esculape et Hygie Les cultes guérisseurs en Afrique". *Pallas 68* (2005): 271-288.

Benseddik 2001: *Encyclopédie Berbère* (2001): 2691-2698 s. v. "Esculape africain" (N. Benseddik).

Beu-Dachin 2010: Beu-Dachin, E., "Asclepius-Aesculapius în inscripții din Dacia". In *Studia Archaeologica et Historica in Honorem Magistri Dorin Alicu*, V. Rusu-Bolindeț, T. Sălăgean, R. Varga, (eds.). Cluj-Napoca (2010): 181–199.

Bodor 1989: Bodor, A., "Die griechisch-römischen Kulte in der Provinz Dacia und das Nachwirken einheimischer Traditionen". *ANRW* II 18.2 (1989): 1077-1164.

Bologa 1966: Bologa, V., "Äskulap und andere Heilgottheiten im römischen Dazien". In *Internationaler Kongress für Geschichte der Medizin/19e Congrès International d'Histoire de la Médecine : Basel, 7.-11. September 1964*, R. Blaser-H. Buess (ed.). Basel (1966): 223-228.

Cadotte 2007: Cadotte, A., "La romanisation des dieux. L'interpretatio romana en Afrique du Nord sous le Haut-Empire". *Religions in the Graeco-Roman World 158.* Leiden (2006).

Charles-Picard 1954: Charles-Picard, G., *Les religions de l'afrique antique.* Paris (1954).

Crişan 1971: Crişan, H., "Asclepeionul roman de la Apulum". *Apulum* 9 (1971): 341–346.

Daicovicu et al. 1981: Daicovicu, C., Alicu, D., Nemes, E., Piso, I., Pop, C., Rusu, A., "Principalele rezultate ale sapaturilor din 1973". *Sargetia* 15 (1981): 225-231.

---

[103] Florea-Pupeză 2008, 289; Nemeti 2005, 410.
[104] For this phenomenon in general: Nemeti 2005, 409.
[105] E. g. Saturn.
[106] Rives 2001.

Florea, Pupeză 2008: Florea, G., Pupeză, P., "Les Dieux Tués. La destruction du chef-lieu du royaume dace". In *Die römischen Provinzen. Begriff und Gründung. Kolloquium Cluj-Napoca 28. September – 1. Oktober*, I. Piso (ed.). Cluj-Napoca (2008): 281-295.

Groslambert 2009: Groslambert, A., *Lambèse sous le Haut-Empire (Ier-IIIe siècles) du camp à la cite*. Paris (2009).

Habicht 1969: Habicht, C., "Die Inschriften des Asklepieions". *Altertümer von Pergamon 8.3*. Berlin (1969).

Hangartner 2018: Hangartner, J., *Der Askelpiuskult im römischen Nordafrika*. University of Vienna (2018): manuscript.

Kleijwegt 1994: Kleijwegt, M., "Beans, Baths and the Barber…A Sacred Law from Thuburbo Maius". *Antiquites Africaines* 30 (1994): 209-220.

LeGlay 1975: LeGlay, M., "Le syncrétisme dans l'afrique ancienne". In *Les syncrétismes dans les religions de l'antiquité*, F. Dunand, P. Leveque (eds.). Leiden (1975): 123-151.

Lipinski 1994: Lipinski, E., "Apollon/Eshmun en afrique proconsulaire". In *L'Afrique, la Gaule, la Religion à l'époque romaine. Mélanges à la mémoire de Marcel LeGlay*, Y. LeBohec (ed.). Bruselas (1994): 19-26.

Manderscheid 1981: Manderscheid, H., *Die Skulpturenausstattung der kaiserzeitlichen Thermenanlagen*. Berlin (1981).

Merlin 1913: Merlin, A., "Forum et Maison d'Althiburos". *Notes et documents 6*. Paris (1913).

Merlin 1908: Merlin, A., "Le temple d'Apollon à Bulla Regia". *Notes et documents 1*. Paris (1908).

Musial 1990: Musial, D., "Sur le culte d'Esculape à Rome et en Italie". *Dialogue d'Histoire Ancienne 16/1* (1990): 231-238.

Musso 2009: Musso, L., "Esculapio in Africa romana: tradizione punica, ellenizzazione, integrazione imperiale". In *Il culto di asclepio nell area mediterranea. Atti del convegno internazionale, Agrigento il 20-22. novembre 2005*, E. DeMiro, G. Sfameni Gasparro, V. Calì (eds.). Roma (2009): 113-144.

Nemeti 2005: Nemeti, S., *Sincretismul religios în Dacia romană*. Cluj-Napoca (2005).

Niewöhner, Huy 2016: Niewöhner, P., Huy, S., "An Ancient Cave Sanctuary underneath the Theatre of Miletus. Beauty, Mutilation, and Burial of Ancient Sculpture in Late Antiquity, and the History of the Seaward Defences". *Archäologischer Anzeiger* (2016/1): 67-156.

Riethmüller 2005 I: Riethmüller, J. W., "Asklepios". *Heiligtümer und Kulte*. Band ½. Heidelberg (2005).

Riethmüller 2005 II: Riethmüller, J. W., "Asklepios". *Heiligtümer und Kulte*. Band 2/2. Heidelberg (2005).

Renberg 2006: Renberg, G., "Was Incubation Practised in the Latin West?". *Archiv für Religionsgeschichte* 8 (2006): 105-147.

Renberg 2017: Renberg, G., "Where Dreams May Come. Incubation Sanctuaries in the Greco-Roman World". *Religions in the Graeco-Roman World 184*. Leiden/Boston (2017).

Robert 1982: Robert, L., "Une vision de perpétue martyre à Carthage en 203". *Académie des inscriptions et belles-lettres. Comptes rendus des séances de l'Académie 126* (1982): 228-276.

Schäfer 2007: Schäfer, A., *Tempel und Kult in Sarmizegetusa. Eine Untersuchung zur Formierung religiöser Gemeinschaften in der Metropolis Dakiens*. Paderborn (2007).

Szabó 2004: Szabó, Á., "Der ‚Locus' von Apulum". In *Orbis Antiquus. Studia in Honorem Ioannis Pisonis*, R. Ardevan, C. Ciongradi, C. Găzdac, L. Ruscu (eds.). Cluj-Napoca (2004): 787–801.

Szabó 2015: Szabó, C., "Placing the Gods. Sanctuaries and Sacralized Spaces in the Settlements of Apulum". *Revista doctoranzilor în istorie veche şi arheologie 3* (2015): 123-160.

Toutain 1907: Toutain, J., *Les cultes païens dans l'Empire romain. Première partie, les provinces latines*. Paris (1907).

Varga 2015: Varga, T., "Hypnos and the incubatio ritual at Ulpia Traiana Sarmizegetusa". *Acta Musei Porolissensis 37* (2015): 241-251.

Van der Ploeg 2018: van der Ploeg, G., *The impact of the Roman Empire on the Cult of Asclepius*. Leiden/Boston (2018).

6

The Cults of Serapis and Isis in Roman Serdica

Vessela Atanassova

(Institute of Balkan Studies with Centre of Thracology "Professor Alexander Fol", Bulgarian Academy of Sciences)

Abstract: This contribution reassesses archaeological evidence from Sofia, Bulgaria in order to demonstrate that the cults of Serapis and Isis played an important role in Serdica between the late Antonine period and the 3rd century. Coins minted in Serdica as well as an inscription on an architectural fragment suggest that a temple of Serapis stood in or immediately outside the city. In addition to the imperial function of the Isiac cults in Serdica, artifacts, such as lamps and a bone pin, indicate that some residents of the city privately venerated Serapis and Isis.

Keywords: Isiac cults, Serdica, epigraphic and numismatic sources, iconography

Introduction

The cults of Serapis and Isis became popular amongst the Greeks and the Romans following the conquest of Egypt by Alexander the Great. While never exceptionally popular cults, there is evidence of worship in both major and minor centres of the Mediterranean and Europe. Given its close proximity to Macedonia, a growing number of people living in the region of Thrace venerated Serapis and Isis by the 3rd century BC,[1] first in the coastal areas and later in land-locked cities, such as Serdica.

According to Cumont,[2] the introduction of Isiac cults to Thrace was part of a program of propaganda implemented by the Ptolemaic dynasty aimed at consolidating their supremacy in the region. On the contrary, Fraser suggests that the propagation of these cults was based upon personal choice and had no political basis.[3] More recent research proposes that neither hypothesis is categorical and that the penetration of the Egyptian cults into Thrace had different nuances and was affected by local factors.[4]

Regardless of the reasons for their introduction, the earliest evidence of these cults is observed along the Thracian coast of the Aegean Sea and the Propontis at Maroneia, Rhedestos and Perinthos. A century after the expansion of the Ptolemaic dynasty, the cults spread to Mesambria, Tomis, and Dionyssopolis, all of which were important, multi-ethnic trade centres. Of these cities, Mesambria has yielded the most abundant evidence pertaining to Egyptian cults.[5] The first indisputable proof of the existence of a temple dedicated to Serapis in Thrace is also from this site.[6] Although the cult may not have been deliberately imposed for political reasons, the inhabitants clearly sought to expand trade relations by permitting Egyptian merchants and seafarers to establish a short- or long-term presence at this emporium. Thracian merchants who traded with cities in Greece and the island of Delos would have been familiar with the cults and may have been instrumental in the spread of worship within their homeland.[7]

The proliferation of the cult of Isis in Thrace occurred at a slower pace.[8] Votive inscriptions dedicated uniquely to the goddess are rare,[9] and she appears infrequently on coins.[10] However, there is information from Egypt that pertains to the spread of her cult in Thrace, namely a hymn honouring Isis inscribed by Isidorus on the pilasters of her temple in Medinet-Madi.[11] In this hymn, composed during the 22nd year of the reign of Ptolemy II Soter, Isidorus lists the assimilations of Isis by the numerous populations that worshipped her.[12] According to his words, "for Thracian men [she] was mother of the gods."[13] The Egyptian priest describes Isis as the founder of world order, who gives the gift of life created by her to people and to all living creatures, a benefactress of humans in their lifetime, and the guardian of the power and riches of rulers. These

---

[1]   Bricault 2004, 266.
[2]   Cumont 1929, 74-77.
[3]   Fraser 1960.
[4]   Bricault 2004, 245.
[5]   *RICIS*, 114/1401-1405.

[6]   *RICIS* 114/1403. This is a marble slab found in Nessebar in 1969, which refers to a decree that was to be engraved on a white marble slab and was to be placed in the "temple of Serapis."
[7]   Judging from the votive inscriptions from Delos, the island was visited by worshippers from the entire Greek world, as well as from Thrace (Тачева-Хитова 1982, 93).
[8]   Тачева-Хитова 1982, 96.
[9]   *RICIS* 114/0501.
[10] *SNRIS*, 27.
[11] Vogliano, 1936, 34-35, pl. 14.
[12] The reason for the assimilations of Isis, listed by Isidorus, was intended to present the greatest goddesses of the respective people as incarnations of Isis (Dunand 1973, 71, Тачева-Хитова, 1982, 69).
[13] Vogliano 1936, 34-35, pl. 14:1, 20.

are all qualities attributed in Thrace to Bendis, the Great Goddess/Mother,[14] with whom Isis was assimilated.

There are very few Hellenistic monuments in Thrace connected with Serapis, all of which are situated in the coastal cities (Maroneia, Rhedestos, Mesambria, Dionyssopolis and Tomis). Similar to Isis, Serapis rarely appears in autonomous votive inscriptions. This changed during the period of the Roman Empire. At first, the Romans did not intervene in the traditions and religious life of the newly-conquered lands, such as Thrace.[15] This policy was not entirely effective and, therefore, manifestations of the Egyptian cult were subdued in the early 2nd century AD. This repressive trend persisted until the reigns of Antoninus Pius and Marcus Aurelius, when Egyptian deities were not only accepted, but were directly related to imperial rule. This is demonstrated in both the epigraphic monuments and the coinage of Thracian cities. Serapis was now perceived as a deity who brought protection and victory to the emperors, and the release of coin issues with images of Serapis and Isis became a manifestation of the province's allegiance to the empire.[16]

Serdica is one of the major inland centres of Thrace in which the two Egyptian deities were worshipped during the Roman Empire.

Overview of Serdica

Serdica and its hinterland were inhabited by at least the Neolithic Age,[17] but it was only in the Bronze Age, in the late third or early second millennium BC, that we observe evidence of a proto-Thracian settlement near a mineral spring that exists to this day in the heart of Sofia. Elements of dwellings, roads, and fortifications have been identified.[18] During the Early Iron Age the settlement developed towards the south, still maintaining its proximity to the spring. By the early Hellenistic period, the city of Serdonpolis (city of the Serdi) flourished. Archaeological finds show that the city had strong connections with Seuthopolis and other cities further south.[19]

Serdonpolis became a Roman city in the late 1st century BC, and was renamed, Serdica. The city proved to be situated at a strategic location, and under Trajan, Ulpia Serdica acquired the status of a Roman municipium. Serdica became the administrative centre of Dacia Interior and served as the seat of one of the most important coin mints of the late Roman period. Several late 3rd and 4th century emperors, including Gallerius and Constantine, governed from an imperial palace in this city.[20]

Many archaeological objects unearthed in Sofia, including coin issues of Serdica, indicate that a wide variety of Greco-Roman and Eastern deities were worshipped here. This was certainly due to the city's location along the Via Diagonalis, the primary land route between Aquileia and Byzantium. The presence of Egyptian deities in the city is, therefore, not surprising, and according to recent reassessments of artifacts, it appears that the Egyptian cults carried more weight than was previously believed.[21]

Material evidence connected with Serapis

The evidence for the cult of Serapis in Serdica is abundant, yet until the 1980s the presence of the cult in Serdica was only known from a single inscription. In April 1940, architect S. Bobchev conducted excavations near Graf Ignatiev and Denkoglu streets, where he found the remains of a "large ancient cult building with peristyle and many architectural fragments, one of which bears an inscription with a dedication to Serapis".[22] The fragment in question pertains to a pediment with a chiselled votive inscription to the right of an image in relief of a round shield decorated with a head (Fig. 6.4). The inscription is dated to AD 161–163 and indicates that the temple, dedicated to Jupiter Capitolinus-Helios-Serapis, was constructed by the city's magistrates. Bobchev was convinced that this was also the site of a temple of Serapis, based, in part, upon the presence of a "shaft filled with a great quantity of bovine bones."[23]

According to T. Gerassimov, however, the components of the building and associated finds, including the torso of an aristocratic woman from Serdica, were not related to the pediment; hence, the inscription must have been brought from somewhere else.[24] According to another study, the inscription was added onto the pediment of an older building, probably a temple, which was located somewhere within the city's confines, not outside it.[25]

An examination of the coins minted and found in Serdica with representations of Serapis reveals that the cult of this deity was popular in the city for at least one century. Seven different coin types are observed, minted under at least seven Roman emperors between Marcus Aurelius (AD 161–180) and Gallienus (AD 255–268):

[14] Popov 1976, 292.
[15] Тачева-Хитова 1982, 96.
[16] Тачева-Хитова 1982, 96–97.
[17] Станчева 1989, 8.
[18] Станчева 1989, 9.
[19] Станчева 1989, 9–10.
[20] De Sena 2014.

[21] Prof. M. Tacheva-Hitova cites in her monograph only one monument connected with Serapis in Serdica: the pediment of the temple of Jupiter Capitolinus-Helios-Serapis (Тачева-Хитова 1982, 38–39, No 34). According to her, "there is no doubt that this inscription does not prove the dissemination of the cult in the city, but the act of the city's gratitude for imperial benevolence" (Тачева-Хитова 1982, 102).
[22] Бобчев 1989, 39.
[23] Бобчев 1942: 219. According to P. Wild's study, two things are frequently associated with cult buildings connected with Serapis: water and bovine bones (Wild 1981: 191–206). Moreover, Bricault indicates that Serapeums in the Graeco-Roman world were usually located outside fortification walls and close to markets and trade centres. The most frequent orientation of these temples was south-southeast (Bricault 2005: 252).
[24] Герасимов 1942, 260–261.
[25] Тачева-Хитова 1982, 39.

1. head of Serapis with *calathos* decorated with stylised olive leaves (under Marcus Aurelius, Lucius Verus and Septimius Severus) (Fig. 6.1.3);
2. head of Serapis with *calathos* (under Caracalla) (Fig. 6.1.4);
3. Serapis on Caracalla's shield (under Caracalla) (Fig. 6.1.5);
4. Serapis standing, with *calathos* on his head; his right hand is raised forward and in his left hand he is holding a sceptre. A burning sacrificial altar is depicted at his feet (under Julia Domna, Geta) (Fig. 6.1.6);
5. Serapis standing, with *calathos* on his head; his right hand is raised forward and in his left hand he is holding a sceptre (without a sacrificial altar) (under Caracalla, Gallienus) (Fig. 6.1.7);
6. Hades-Serapis seated on a throne, to the left, stretching his hand above the three-headed Cerberus seated on his hind legs at the deity's feet, his left hand resting on a sceptre (under Julia Domna, Caracalla) (Fig. 6.1.8);
7. Hades-Serapis seated *en face* in a temple with four columns, with a sceptre in his left hand. The three-headed Cerberus is seated at his feet (under Gallienus) (Fig. 1.9).

It is clear that the Roman emperors considered Serapis to be a deity who brought protection and victory. The image on Caracalla's shield is indisputable evidence of the deity's military characteristics. The coin minted under Gallienus, on which Serapis is depicted in a temple, has evoked a significant amount of interest (Fig. 6.1.9). According to M. Tacheva-Hitova, coins bearing images of temples should not always be considered as evidence that an actual temple existed.[26] This eminent scholar did not have the Gallienus coin at her disposal, because it was only unearthed in the 2000s.[27] In fact, the most recent studies of images on coins with depictions of Serapis in a temple indicate that they can be reliable sources of the existence of a temple[28] and may even be considered as evidence of the temple's actual architectural style.[29] Intriguingly, a comparison of the pediment of the temple of Serapis and the image on the coin from the reign of Gallienus, shows that they are similar in style, and, in particular, a round decorative element at the centre of the coin is similar to the round head at the centre of the pediment from Serdica. Another important piece of information gleaned from that coin concerns the time during which the temple of Serapis in Serdica existed. If the pediment, and hence the consecration of the temple, can be dated to the beginning of the reign of Marcus Aurelius, and the coin was minted under Gallienus, this means that the temple stood for at least one century.

The worship of Serapis in Serdica was not limited to imperial circles. This is proven not only by the possible location of the deity's temple, i.e., *extra muros*, but also by several artifacts demonstrating that residents of the city privately venerated the god. Such is the case of a ceramic lamp with an image of Serapis found during the excavations at Alexander Battenberg Square in 1958 (Fig. 6.5).[30] This is a round lamp with a single wick hole, which shows traces of having been used. Its handle is ring-shaped, flat on the sides, with two flutes on its upper part, where there is a concave disc on which the bust of a man is seen in relief. The figure is presented in profile, facing left. The head and the hand are clearly discernible, while the other elements of the image are less distinct. The man depicted is middle-aged and has a large, well-outlined nose. The upper part of his face is framed by abundant hair in large curls falling back on his neck and blending with his beard in front. A moustache is visible above his lips. The man is wearing a medium-sized *calathos* that becomes slightly wider in its upper part and ends with a prominent rim. There is no doubt that this is a depiction of Serapis with his typical *calathos* and beard.[31] Similar images of Serapis, in profile, with a *calathos* and beard, occur on lamps from Greece (Corinth and Armatova).[32] The lamp from Serdica was a funerary offering, suggesting that the deceased person was a follower of Serapis.[33]

Another fascinating artefact, recently found during excavations near the Central Department Store by Mario Ivanov, is also connected with Serapis. This is a small rectangular ceramic tile, measuring 6.2 x 5.4 cm, with an inscription in Greek (Fig. 6.6). The object was found in the southeastern sector of the site near the (residential?) building A3 in a 3rd century context. The inscription consists of four lines, presented in retrograde:

Εὐτυχῶ διά σέ Σάραπι

"I thrive through you, Serapis."

According to Ivanov, the text is a religious formula expressing satisfaction with life thanks to Serapis. It was probably not a votive tablet in view of the reversed inscription, but rather a kind of seal. The tile was probably used to make a votive impression on sacred bread consumed during festivals in honour of Serapis. Feasts including ritual breads are well attested in Roman religious practices.[34]

Material evidence connected with Isis

Two coin issues of the Serdica mint with images of Isis are known. The first is from the time of Marcus Aurelius, when coins were first minted in Serdica (Fig. 6.1.1). In this case, the goddess is depicted standing, with a *sistrum* in her left hand and a *situla* in her right hand; a *baselion* is on her head. According to some researchers,[35] this indicates that the cult of Isis was already honoured in the city. The

[26] Тачева-Хитова 1982, 84.
[27] Божкова 2009.
[28] Bricault 2008, 60; Божкова 2009, 82.
[29] Bricault 2008, 60–62.
[30] Станчева 1967, 8–9, No 2.
[31] Станчева 1967, 8.
[32] See Sbd.m(2) and Sbd.m(3) in Podvin 2011, 138, pl. 27.
[33] See Podvin 2011.
[34] Glinister 2014, 215–227.
[35] Мушмов 1926, 20.

1)

2)

3)

4)

5)

6)

7)

8)

9)

Fig. 6.1. Coins with the effigies of Isis and Sarapis.

Fig. 6.2. Marble torso of Isis. National Archeological Institute К 8536.

Fig. 6.3. Bone needle with Isis-Thermuthis (?). Regional History Museum-Sofia 1608.

Fig. 6.4. Fragment of pediment with dedication to Zeus-Capitolian-Helios-Sarapis. Regional History Museum-Sofia A 4929

second coin issue with Isis is from the time of Caracalla. These coins bear a bust of the goddess with a *baselion* on her head (Fig. 6.1.2).

Two objects connected with Isis were revealed through archaeological excavations in the last 25 years. The first is a marble torso from the excavations at the intersection of Lege and Saborna streets. The torso was found in the context of a Roman building outside the fortification wall and dates to late 2nd or early 3rd century AD.[36] The torso bears a so-called Isis knot, tied twice (Fig. 6.2). According to some researchers, when a double knot is depicted, the image refers to a priestess of Isis, and when it was tied on only one side, asymmetrically, this represented the goddess herself.[37] More recently, M. Malaise and R. Veymiers suggest that this rule was not mandatory and it is possible for the goddess to bear the double tied knot.[38] Therefore, in the absence of a head, it is difficult to decide who is depicted in the statue, the goddess or one of her priestesses.

Another object is a bone needle recovered during the 2016 excavation campaign at the Western Gate of Serdica (Fig. 6.3).[39] The object depicts a woman with curly hair drawn together at the back of her head. On her head there is an accessory that appears to be an article of adornment on account of its trapezoidal shape, rather than a hair bun. The woman's body is of greater interest to us. The arms and breasts are missing, while the end of the body is twisted. The twisted lower part of her body returns as a continuation of the body. This could be perceived as a cloak covering the woman's shoulders and entire torso, but the twist in its lower part evokes questions and tends to suggest another interpretation. In fact, images of Isis as a cobra are known in her form of Isis-Thermuthis, where a similarly stylised appearance of the body is found.[40] In this way, the unusual appearance of the body seems much more comprehensible and the object can undoubtedly be associated with the goddess. The lead researcher of the site, Dr Iliyana Borissova, hesitates to state whether this

---

[36] Динчев, Гатев 1999, 49, 53, Fig. 10.

[37] Tran tam Tinh 1984, 1726–1727; Eingartner 1991, 13; Walters 1988, 7.

[38] Malaise, Veymiers 2018, 480.

[39] Personal communication with Dr Iliyana Borissova. The photograph is from the archive of the Regional History Museum in Sofia, for which the author expresses gratitude to its Director Assoc. Prof. Dr Veneta Handjiyska.

[40] See, e.g., London BM 2001, 0329.1, Cairo CG 26925.

Fig. 6.5. Ceramic lamp with Sarapis. Regional History Museum-Sofia A 1454.

Fig. 6.6. Ceramic tile with dedication to Sarapis. Regional History Museum-Sofia A 6848.

represents Isis or some other deity (or simply a woman with hair knotted on her head).

Conclusion

An analysis of all known artefacts from Serdica with a connection to Serapis and Isis demonstrates that the two deities were worshipped in the city during the Roman period. From what we can surmise, Serapis, and possibly Isis, had an official temple that existed for at least a century. For the time being, however, it is not possible to know with certainty whether the temple was located at the place of the building excavated by S. Bobchev at Graf Ignatiev and Denkoglu streets. Nevertheless, based upon this summary, it appears that the cults of these deities were not exclusively imperial and restricted to the minting of coins as a part of a provincial policy. Based upon a fresh analysis of the objects presented here, it becomes clear that there were true followers of the Egyptian cults in Serdica, who believed in and worshipped the deities as their own.

Bibliography

Божкова 2009: Божкова, Б., *Култът на Сарапис в Сердика по нумизматични данни. Нумизматика,* сфрагистика и епиграфика 5 (2009): 77–84.

Бобчев 1942: Бобчев, С. Н., "Храмъ на Сераписа в София". *ИБАИ* 14. София (1942): 218–222.

Бобчев 1989: Бобчев, С. Н., "Списък на откритите останки от сгради на Сердика в границите на вътрешната стена и около нея". In *Сердика: археологически материали и проучвания,* том 2, М. Станчева (ed.). (1989): 30–40.

Герасимов 1942: Герасимов, Т., "Новооткрити паметници в София". *ИБАИ* 14 (1940-1942): 260–262.

Динчев, Гатев 1999: Динчев, В. and Гатев, Й., "Разкопките при археологическия музей в София". *Археология кн.* 3-4 (1999): 49–61.

Мушмов 1926: Мушмов, Н., *Монетите и монетарниците на Сердика.* София (1926).

Станчева 1967: Станчева, М., "Към изучаването на езическите култове в Сердика". *Музеи и паметници на културата* VII/2 (1967): 6–10.

Станчева 1989: Сердика, М., *Археологически материали и проучвания,* т. 2. София (1989).

Тачева-Хитова 1982: Тачева-Хитова, М., *История на източните култове в Долна Мизия и Тракия V в. пр. н. е. – IV в. от н. е.* София (1982).

Bricault 1998: Bricault, L., "Serapis dans l'empire kouchan". In *Bulletin de la société française de numismatique,* 53e année, n°10 (1998): 249–254.

Bricault 2004: Bricault, L., "La diffusion isiaque: une esquisse". In *Fremdheit-Eigenheit. Ägypten,* Griechenland und Rom. Austausch und Verständnis, P. C. Bol (ed). Stuttgart (2004): 548–556.

Bricault 2005: Bricault, L., "Iseum et Serapeum". In *Thesaurus Cultus et Rituum Antiquorum IV: Cult Places, Representations of Cult Places,* B. Jaeger (ed.). The J. Paul Getty Museum. Los Angeles (2005): 251–259.

Bricault 2007: Bricault, L., "Isis des eaux du Nil à celles de la Méditerranée". In *Actes du colloque La Méditarranée d'une rive à l'autre: Culture classique et cultures périphériques,* A. Laronde, J. Leclant (eds.). Paris (2007): 261–269.

Cumont 1929: Cumont, F. *Les religions orientales dans le paganisme romain.* Paris (1929).

De Sena 2014: De Sena, E.C., "Constantine in the Imperial Palace of Serdica," in Nenad Lemajić (ed.), *Constantine, Sirmium and Early Christianity* (2014): 7-24.

Doetsch-Amberger 1998: Doetsch-Amberger, E., "Osiris-Apis". In *Göttinger Miszellen* 165 (1998): 39–43.

Dunand 1973: Dunand, Fr., *Le culte d'Isis dans le basin oriental de la Méditerranée, Vol. II: Le culte d'Isis en Grèce.* Leiden (1973).

Eingartner 1991: Eingartnerm, J., "Isis und ihre Dienerinnen in der Kunst der römischen Kaiserzeit". *Mnemosyne Suppl.* 115. Leiden (1973).

Fraser 1960: Fraser, P. M., "Two studies on the cult of Serapis in the hellenistic world". *Opuscula Atheniensia* 3 (1960): 1–54.

Glinister 2014: Glinister, F., "Festus and Ritual Foodstuffs". *Erudito Antiqua* 6 (2014): 215–227.

Grandjean 1975: Grandjean, J., *Une nouvelle arétalogie d'Isis à Maronée.* EPRO 49. Leiden (1975).

Malaise 1976: Malaise, M., "Histoire et signification de la coiffure hathorique à plumes". *Studien zur Altägyptischen Kultur* 4 (1976): 125–236.

Malaise 2000: Malaise, M., "Le problème de l'hellénisation d'Isis". In *De Memphis à Rome, Actes du Ier Colloque international sur les etudes isiaques, Poitiers-Futuroscope, 8-10 avril 1999,* L. Bricault (ed.). RGRW 140. Leyde/Boston/Cologne (2000): 1–17.

Malaise 2009: Malaise, M., "Le basileion, une couronne d'Isis : origine et signification". In *Elkab and Beyond. Studies in Honour of Luc Limme,* W. Claes, H. de Meulenaere, St. Hendrickx (eds.). OLA 191. Leuven (2009): 439–455.

Malaise, Veymiers 2018: Malaise, M. and Veymiers, R., "Les dévotes isiaques et les atours de leur déesse". In *Individuals and Materials in the Greco-Roman Cults of Isis. Agents, Images, and Practices, Proceedings of the VIth International Conference of Isis Studies (Erfurt, May 6–8, 2013 – Liège, September 23–24, 2013),* V.

Gasparini, R. Veymiers (eds.). RGRW 187. Leiden/ Boston (2018): 470–508.

Pfeiffer 2008: Pfeiffer, St., "Ptolemy II, Serapis and the Beginnings of Ruler-Cult in Ptolemaic Egypt". In *Ptolemy II Philadelphus and His World*, P. McKechnie, Ph. Guillaume (eds.). Mnemosyne Supplements: History and Archaeology of Classical Antiquity. Leiden (2008): 387–408.

Podvin 2011: Podvin, J.-L., *Luminaire et cultes isiaques*. Monographies Instrumentum 38. Montagnac (2011).

Popov 1976: Popov, D., "Essence, origine et propagation du culte de la déesse thrace Bendis". *Dialogues d'histoire ancienne* 2 (1976): 289-303.

RICIS: Bricault, L., *Recueil des inscriptions concernant les cultes isiaques*, 3 vol. Paris (2005).

Sabottka 2008: Sabottka, M., *Das Serapeum in Alexandria: Untersuchungen zur Architektur und Baugeschichte des Heiligtums von der frühen ptolemäischen Zeit bis zur Zerstörung 391 n. Chr.* Études Alexandrines 15. Cairo (2008).

Schoske, Wildung 1992: Schoske, S. and Wildung, D., *Gott und Götter im alten Ägypten*. Mayence (1992).

SNRIS: Bricault, L., *Sylloge nummorum religionis isiacae et sarapiacae*. Mémoires de l'Académie des Inscriptions et Belles-Lettres 38. Paris (2008).

Stambauch 1973: Stambauch, J. E., *Serapis. EPRO* 32. Leiden (1973).

Swiderek 1975: Swiderek, A., "Serapis et les Hellénomemphites. *Mélanges Claire Préaux*. Bruxelles (1975): 670– 675.

Tran tam Tinh 1984: Tran tam Tinh, V., "État des études iconographiques relatives à Isis, Serapis et Sunnaoi Theoi". *ANRW* 11,17.3 (1984): 1710-1738.

Velkov, Fol 1977: Velkov, V. and Fol, A., *Les thraces en Égypte gréco-romaine*. Studia Thracica 4. Sofia (1977).

Veymiers 2014: Veymiers, R., "Le basileion, les reineset Actium, dans L. Bricault". In *Power, Politics and the Cults of Isis. Proceedings of the Vth International Conference of Isis Studies, Boulogne-sur-Mer, October 13-15 2011*, M. J. Versluys (ed.). RGRW 180. Leiden/ Boston (2014): 195–236.

Vogliano 1936: Vogliano, A., *Primo rapporto degli scavi condotti dalla missione archeologica d'Egitto della R. Università di Milano nella zona di Madinet Madi*. Milano (1936).

Walters 1988: Walters, E. J., *Attic Grave Reliefs that Represent Women in the Dress of Isis*. Hesperia Supplements 22. Princeton (1988).

Wild 1981: Wild, P., *Water in Cultic Worship of Serapis and Isis*. Leiden (1981).

7

Les Cultes isiaques à Sarmizegetusa*

Laurent Bricault
(Toulouse Jean Jaurès University/Institut Universitaire de France)

Dan Deac
*(Zalău County Museum of History and Art; Center for Studies on the Middle
East and the Mediterranean, Babeș-Bolyai University, Cluj-Napoca)*

Ioan Piso
(Center for Roman Studies, Babeș-Bolyai University Cluj-Napoca)

Abstract: Dacia, which became a Roman province in AD 106, offers an interesting glimpse
into the nature of public and private religion of the empire in the 2nd and 3rd centuries. Although
much work has been conducted on the Isiac cults in Dacia, new evidence and new ideas demand
a new approach. 17 pieces related to the Isiac cults originate from Sarmizegetusa and its initial
territory, which included Apulum and Micia. Special attention is given to the Serapeum built in
the *praetorium procuratoris* of Sarmizegetusa under Caracalla and to the important inscriptions
uncovered here. Inscription no. 7 is of special interest because it seems to contain exhortations for
the initiation into the cult of Isis, which provides a parallel to Book XI of Apuleius' Metamorphoses.
Our analysis demonstrates a strong link between the Isiac cults and the imperial cult, which does
not contradict the reality of the great popularity of these cults among all social groups.

Keywords: Roman Dacia, Sarmizegetusa, Isiac cults, *praetorium procuratoris*, *Serapeum*

La dimension sociale de la diffusion et de la réception des cultes isiaques dans l'Occident romain a véritablement commencé à être prise en compte par les historiens à la fin des années soixante et au début des années soixante-dix, notamment dans les synthèses pionnières de Ladislav Vidman[1] et Michel Malaise[2]. Pour l'Italie, l'analyse minutieuse de Valentino Gasparini montre que les particularismes locaux empêchent toute définition d'un cadre général, « chaque contexte local [développant] son micro-environnement social propre, ce qui déterminait les institutions et influençait l'habitus des élites, *ingenui* et affranchis. La spécificité de la préférence religieuse au sein du pouvoir est ainsi inextricablement liée à son contexte social immédiat »[3]. Ainsi, par exemple, si les *Augustales* et les décurions apparaissent très présents dans les *civitates* de la *regio X* et notamment à *Verona* et *Aquileia*, en Campanie, les individus les plus investis dans les cultes isiaques sont des *ingenui* et des magistrats. Les disparités observables entre la *regio I* et la *regio X* trouvent assurément leur explication dans la diversité des dynamiques de diffusion

et de réception de ces cultes. Celles-ci varient en fonction des lieux et de la chronologie, mais aussi suivant les facteurs et les vecteurs qui déterminent la mobilité des cultes. Dans ce double processus de diffusion/réception, les caractéristiques spécifiques des acteurs locaux, à un moment donné, l'emportent sur toute velléité de vouloir imposer le paradigme d'un développement universel du culte d'Isis, de Sérapis et des divinités qui leur sont associées.

Faute d'un modèle directement imposable d'en haut, il faut au préalable multiplier les études de cas pour tenter de mieux appréhender ces phénomènes. Le cas particulier de la Dacie, devenue pour partie province romaine en 106, est intéressant à plus d'un titre. Il offre un espace vierge de toute présence isiaque avant cette date, mais aussi une documentation relativement riche et, souvent, datable avec une relative précision.

Pour l'historiographie, le culte de Sérapis et d'Isis est entré en Dacie[4] avec les troupes romaines et les colons

---

* Le présent article a pu être réalisé grâce au projet de PN-III-P4-ID-PCE-2020-038, financé par le Ministère roumain de la Recherche et de l'Innovation.

[1] Toutes les dates, dans cette étude, s'entendent après J.-C. Vidman 1970.
[2] Malaise 1972, 67-95.
[3] Gasparini 2014, 299.

[4] Voir, pour le culte de Sérapis et d'Isis en Dacie, Drexler 1890, 52-58 ; Popescu 1927, 159-209 ; Jones 1929, 245-305 ; Floca 1935, 204-249 ; *SIRIS* 680-699 ; Petolescu 1971, 649-651, n° 3 ; Sanie 1975, 529-537 ; Berciu, Petolescu 1976, 5-7, 30-34; Popa 1979, 8-74; Popa 1983, 71-80; Malaise 1984, 1677-1680; Vidman 1989, 1000-1004; Takács 1995, 194-

venus de toutes les parties de l'Empire[5] dès la constitution de la nouvelle province. Les nombreux mouvements de troupes qui se sont succédés durant plus de deux siècles (guerres de Trajan en 114-117, de Lucius Verus en 161-165, de Septime Sévère en 195-198, de Caracalla en 214-217[6]) ont été l'occasion d'échanges, de rencontres, de transferts culturels et cultuels multiples. Il serait cependant probablement exagéré d'accorder une trop grande importance aux guerres livrées par Rome dans la propagation des cultes isiaques. La mobilité des soldats n'était qu'un aspect de l'extraordinaire mobilité humaine sous le Principat.

Dans sa synthèse sur les témoignages isiaques de Dacie, Marie-Christine Budischovsky considère que les premières inscriptions relatives à Isis et Sérapis n'apparaissent pas avant le règne conjoint de Marc Aurèle et Lucius Verus, et que le premier centre de diffusion de ces cultes aurait été Apulum[7]. Trois dédicaces y sont adressées à nos dieux sous le règne de Marc-Aurèle : l'une *Sarapi et Isidi* de L. Iunius Rufinus Proculianus, tribun laticlave de la *legio XIII Gemina*[8] au début du règne commun de Marc Aurèle et de Lucius Verus[9], la deuxième *Sarapi Aug(usto)* de Tib. Iulius Flaccinus, gouverneur de Dacie Supérieure[10] vers 164-168[11], et la troisième *Sarapidi Iovi Soli Isidi Lunae Dianae* de L. Aemilius Carus, gouverneur des trois Dacies[12], entre 173 et 175. Cependant, comme on le verra plus bas, la première inscription (n° **1**), que nous localisons à Sarmizegetusa, date déjà des années 156/7-158.

Rappelons toutefois qu'avant le règne de Marc Aurèle et Lucius Verus, il est difficile de faire une séparation nette entre Apulum et Sarmizegetusa. Au début, le territoire de la colonia Ulpia Traiana Augusta Dacica Sarmizegetusa s'étendait jusqu'au Danube et jusque dans la vallée moyenne du Mureş. À l'exception du camp légionnaire et de la zone *intra leugam*, Apulum était un *pagus* de Sarmizegetusa. C'est seulement sous le règne conjoint de Marc Aurèle et Lucius Verus que le *vicus* de Partoş et le territoire afférent reçurent le statut de *municipium (Aurelium)*. Significatif est le fait que beaucoup de citoyens d'Apulum conservèrent

la tribu *Papiria* de Sarmizegetusa[13]. N'oublions pas non plus que C. Iulius Metrobianus, qui dédia à Apulum, à la fin du IIe ou au début du IIIe siècle, un monument *Numini Serapis*[14], était non seulement *pontif(ex) q(uin)q(uennalis) IIvir col(oniae) Apuli*, mais aussi, semble-t-il, *IIvir* de la colonie de Sarmizegetusa.

Voyons maintenant ce que les sources nous apprennent sur la présence isiaque à Sarmizegetusa.

Les inscriptions isiaques en dehors du *praetorium procuratoris*

La première inscription datable attestant le culte d'Isis en Dacie est liée au nom de M. Statius Priscus, gouverneur de Dacie Supérieure en 156/7-158[15].

1. – Plaque de marbre, fragmentaire[16]. Dimensions: 21 x 21 x 5 cm. H. des lettres: 5 cm ligne 1; 4,5 cm ligne 2; 4 cm ligne 3. (**Fig. 7.1**)

Popa 1962, 149; *SIRIS* 687; Popa 1979, 24, n° 79; Russu 1975, 417; *IDR* III/2, 229; Piso 1993, 67, n° 8; Takács 1995, 198; *RICIS* 616/0302; Carbó García 2010, 999-1000, n° 290; Cristea, Tecar 2010, 265, n° 5: *[-?- I]sidi [- - -] | [-?-] M(arcus) Stati[us Priscus leg(atus) / Au]g(usti) pr[o pr(aetore) - - -].*

La pièce est conservée au Musée de la Civilisation Dace et Romaine de Deva (MCDRD) qui, pendant sa longue existence, a rassemblé des monuments non seulement de Sarmizegetusa, Micia et Germisara, mais aussi d'Apulum. Il était donc permis de faire des suppositions sur l'origine de la pièce. Selon A. Popa, son premier éditeur, elle proviendrait d'Apulum ou de Sarmizegetusa, selon L. Vidman (*SIRIS*), L. Bricault (*RICIS*) et J. R. Carbó García de Micia, selon I. I. Russu (*IDR*) et I. Piso avec certitude de Sarmizegetusa, selon M.-Ch. Budischovsky[17] sans aucun doute d'Apulum. En consultant l'ancien registre du musée de Deva, nous avons trouvé la notice suivante: « Fragment de inscripţie. Aflat la Germisara. Materialul: Marmoră. Dimensiuni: 13 x 21 cm. N° 8687 = 2042 » (= « Fragment d'inscription. Trouvé à Germisara, etc. »); la notice est accompagnée d'un dessin. Le toponyme initial de *Germisara* a été rayé d'un trait de crayon et remplacé par *Ulpia*, ce qui désigne *Sarmizegetusa*. En supposant que celui qui a opéré la modification savait bien ce qu'il faisait, on gagne en certitude sur l'origine de la pièce.

203; Piso 1998, 253-271; Sanie 2004, 61-82; Budischovsky 2004, 171-191; S. Nemeti 2005, 316-322; I. Nemeti 2005, 279-282; Budischovsky 2007, 267-288; Dunand 2000 2008, 260-269; Cristea, Tecar 2010, 255-282; Deac 2012, 159-174; Nicolae 2012, 127-133; Deac 2013; Deac, Varga 2014; Deac 2016, 59-70; Deac 2017, 241-256; Piso 2020b, 127-137.

[5]   Eutropius 8, 6, 2 : - - - *Traianus victa Dacia ex toto orbe Romano infinitas eo copias hominum transtulerat ad agros et urbes colendas*; Cassius Dio 68, 14, 3 : - - - καὶ οὕτως ἡ Δακία Ῥωμαίων ὑπήκοος ἐγένετο καὶ πόλεις ἐν αὐτῇ ὁ Τραϊανὸς κατῴκισεν ; pour la colonisation comme politique d'état, voir Piso 2008, 316-318.

[6]   Carbó García 2016.

[7]   Budischovsky 2007, 272; Deac, Varga 2014, 11-19.

[8]   *CIL* III 7770 = *ILS* 4398 = *SIRIS* 691 = *IDR* III/5, 318 = *RICIS* 616/0403; Deac, Varga 2014, 12-13.

[9]   L. Petersen, *PIR*[2], J 810.

[10]   *CIL* III 7768 = *SIRIS* 689 = *IDR* III/5, 317 = *RICIS* 616/0401; Deac, Varga 2014, 12-13.

[11]   Piso 1993, 77-79.

[12]   *CIL* III 7771 = *ILS* 4398 = *SIRIS* 690 = *IDR* III/5, 319 = *RICIS* 616/0402; Deac, Varga 2014, 12-13; datation erronée chez Mora 1990, 465.

[13]   Voir, pour ces développements, Piso 1995, 73-77 = Piso 2005, 284-287.

[14]   *CIL* III, 973 = *IDR* III/5, 316 = *RICIS* 616/0406; voir aussi Bricault 2013, 186, n° 57 b; Deac, Varga 2014, 14.

[15]   Voir, pour ce personnage, Piso 1993, 66-73; K. Wachtel, PIR[2], S 880.

[16]   Musée de la Civilisation Dace et Romaine de Deva (dorénavant MCDRD), inv. 8687 = 2042. Russu, *IDR*: *[Deae? I]sidi [et Serapidi | - - -] M(arcus) Stati[us Priscus | - - - leg(atus) Au]g(usti) pr(o) [pr(aetore) Dac- - - | - - - - - -].*

[17]   Budischovsky 2007, 272, 274, 277.

Fig. 7.1. L'inscription n° 1.

L'origine d'Apulum était soutenue par M.-C. Budischovsky[18] également en raison de la qualité de gouverneur de M. Statius Priscus, dont le centre de commandement se trouvait à Apulum. Il faut cependant tenir compte du fait qu'à Sarmizegetusa se trouvait un des plus importants tribunaux du gouverneur, que l'on connaît approximativement l'endroit où il rendait justice[19], que le *forum novum*, construit à peine quelques années avant la mission de M. Statius Priscus était rempli de statues de gouverneurs et qu'une bonne partie de ceux-ci étaient patrons de la colonie[20]. Les rapports des gouverneurs avec Sarmizegetusa étaient donc particulièrement étroits. N'oublions pas non plus que M. Statius Priscus était devenu, par ses victoires remportées à la frontière occidentale de la province, une célébrité et qu'il avait érigé des monuments votifs dans plusieurs localités[21].

À la ligne 1, les lettres SIDI sont suivies de la trace d'un pied de haste, mais on ne peut pas décider s'il s'agit d'une haste verticale ou oblique. Il n'y a donc pas lieu de penser que la ligne 1 soit brève et centrée sur le seul nom d'Isis. Si on envisage une lacune au début de la ligne 1, cela pourrait justifier l'hypothèse que le nom de Sérapis – s'il doit être restitué, ce qui ne s'impose pas – ait pu se trouver avant et non après le nom d'Isis, comme l'avait supposé I. I.

Russu. Ce nom pouvait éventuellement être accompagné d'une épithète, tout comme celui d'Isis. L'épithète d'Isis pouvait être *Aug(usta)*, qui n'est pas encore attestée pour cette déesse en Dacie, mais est très répandue en Pannonie Supérieure, où M. Statius Priscus avait justement commandé la *legio XIIII Gemina*[22]. Si on admet une lacune au début de la ligne 1, on peut en supposer également une à la ligne 2, avant le nom du gouverneur et, peut-être, aussi au début de la ligne 3. Dans ce cas, la plaque pourrait avoir eu une largeur d'au moins 80 cm, mais il est plus probable que la dédicace s'adressait à la seule Isis pourvue d'une épithète. Quoi qu'il en soit, il est peu recommandé d'essayer une reconstitution graphique.

Il peut s'agir d'une inscription de construction d'un temple ou bien d'une plaque d'une base de statue, toujours dans un temple. Pour un temple de Sérapis construit à l'initiative d'un gouverneur, on a l'exemple très proche de la plaque de Byala Slatina, qui provient plutôt d'Oescus que de Montana. Oescus était pour la Mésie Inférieure ce que Sarmizegetusa était pour la Dacie : de rang colonial, la plus ancienne et la plus vénérable ville romaine de la province, avec les institutions religieuses les plus représentatives et donc une relation spéciale avec le gouverneur. M. Iallius Bassus, gouverneur de Mésie Inférieure vers 163-165, y avait initié – *[in|ch]oavit* – la construction d'un *t[emplum*

---

[18] Budischovsky 2007, 274.

[19] C'est l'édifice T, qui limitait vers l'Est le *forum novum* ; voir Piso 2005, 442.

[20] Ardevan 1979, 185-190.

[21] Piso 1993, 66-73.

[22] *CIL* VI, 1523 = *ILS* 1092.

Laurent Bricault, Dan Deac, Ioan Piso

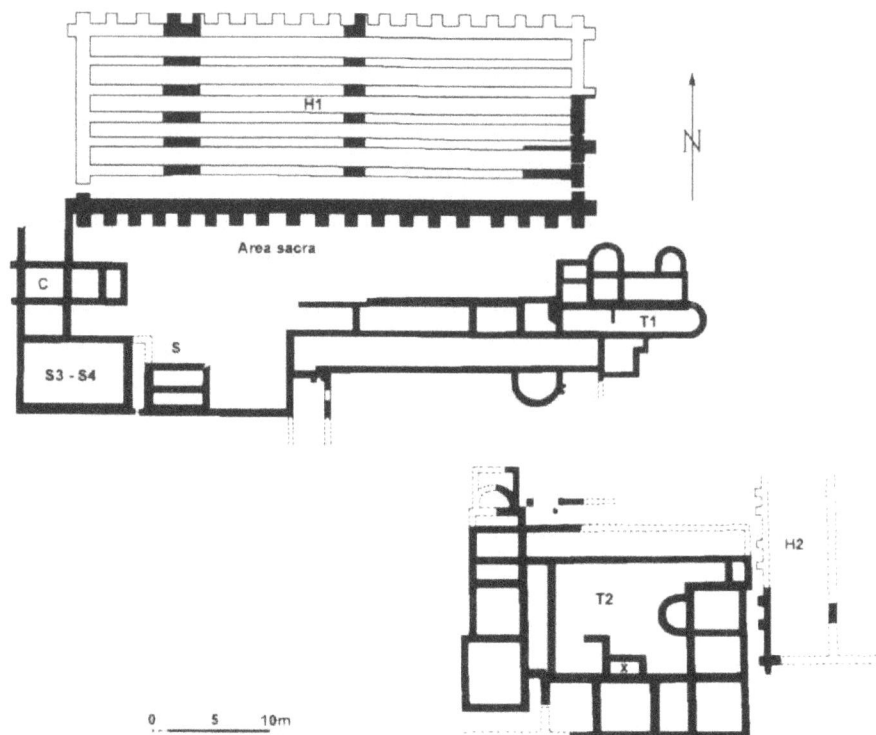

Fig. 7.2. Le *praetorium procuratoris* de Sarmizegetusa.

cum sig\ni]s pour Sérapis[23]. Il est peut-être significatif que M. Statius Priscus et M. Iallius Bassus ont exercé auparavant, tous les deux et presque pendant les mêmes années, des charges dans les Pannonies, où les cultes isiaques étaient bien présents depuis la fin du Ier siècle[24].

Un temple d'Isis [et Sérapis ?] existait donc à Sarmizegetusa avant 159. Il est pour le moment impossible de le localiser. On peut supposer qu'il se trouvait, comme à Savaria, en dehors du *pomerium*[25]. Une bonne possibilité serait l'énorme *area sacra* se trouvant au nord du mur septentrional de la colonie et qui est incomplètement fouillée[26].

2. – Autel ou base de statue votive, perdue.

Neigebaur 1851, 25, n° 27; *CIL* III 1428; Drexler 1890, 56; Popescu 1927, 199; Floca 1935, 220, 238; Tudor 1957, 251, n° 49; *SIRIS* 683; Russu 1975, 417; *IDR* III/2, 228; Popa 1979, 23-24, n° 28; Takács 1995, 196-197; Ardevan 1998, 379, n° 147; *RICIS* 616/0203; Carbó García 2010, 1008-1009, n° 299; Cristea, Tecar 2010, 266-267: *De[a]e Isidi | Priscianus Aug(ustalis) | col(oniae) Sarmiz(egetusae) metrop(olis) et Aurelia Fortunata |5 liberta eius.*

En tant qu'Augustale, (Aurelius) Priscianus était un affranchi, qui eut à son tour une esclave, Fortunata[27]. Celle-ci, libérée, est peut-être devenue sa *coniux*. L'inscription est datable à partir du règne de Sévère Alexandre, lorsque Sarmizegetusa fut honoré par l'épithète de *metropolis*[28].

Le *Serapeum* du *praetorium procuratoris*

Le *praetorium* du procurateur financier se trouve à Sarmizegetusa *intra muros*, près de la porte nord de la colonie (**Fig. 7.2**)[29]. Il s'étend sur environ un hectare, dont un tiers à peu près a été fouillé dans les années 1979-1989. Il est délimité au nord par le mur de la ville, au sud par un *decumanus* et à l'ouest par le *cardo maximus*. Ses parties

[23] *CIL* III 12387 = *SIRIS* 702 = *RICIS* 618/0102; pour M. Iallius Bassus voir L. Petersen, *PIR²*, J 4; Thomasson 1984, 136, n° 94; Fitz 1993, I, 489-493, n° 290; pour le parallèle avec M. Statius Priscus, voir Budischovsky 2004, 173-174; pour l'inscription de Byala Slatina, voir encore Christodoulou 2015, 170.
[24] Budischovsky 2004, 171. Remarquable est en Pannonie la popularité des cultes isiaques dans le milieu du *portorium publicum Illyrici* (*CIL* III 4015 = *SIRIS* 654 = *RICIS* 613/0301 et *CIL* III 4017 = *SIRIS* 656 = *RICIS* 613/0303 – Poetovio) et de l'office du procurateur financier (*CIL* III 4044 = *SIRIS* 657 = *RICIS* 613/0304).
[25] Il est à noter que les règles qui s'appliquaient au *pomerium* de Rome s'appliquaient aussi aux *pomeria* des colonies: à l'intérieur de ceux-ci, on n'avait pas le droit de construire des temples pour les dieux étrangers; voir Blumenthal 1952, 1871; pour Savaria voir Mráv 2016, 105-106. Ces règles n'existaient plus sous les Sévères. C'est sous les Sévères que fut construit à Sarmizegetusa un temple palmyrénien *intra muros*, près du *forum vetus*; voir Piso, Țentea 2011, 111-121.
[26] Voir, pour cette *area sacra*, Piso 2005, 440-445, 450.

[27] Cf. Mora 1990, 467, n° 19, p. 477, n° 80.
[28] C. Daicoviciu 1966, 161 = C. Daicoviciu 1970, 393-394.
[29] Voir H. Daicoviciu et alii 1981, 246-277; H. Daicoviciu et alii 1982, 121-134; H. Daicoviciu, Alicu 1984, 132-145; voir le plan chez Piso 1998, 253-255, fig. 1; Piso 2005, 443, 454, fig. 7 et pour les aspects religieux voir Schäfer 2007; Boda 2015, 291-292; Szabó 2018, passim; Szabó 2020, 299-300, I.34; récemment Piso 2020b, 127-130.

nord et est sont constituées par des *horrea*. Les parties que nous connaissons le mieux sont du côté ouest avec un temple du culte impérial (C), devant lequel s'étend une vaste *area sacra*, limitée au nord par un des *horrea* (H 1), à l'est par les petits thermes (T 1) et à l'ouest par les édifices S, S3 et S4. Dans cette *area sacra*, on a trouvé environ 50 monuments votifs dédiés par des procurateurs à des divinités très diverses, en vertu de leurs obligations de service, sans donc user de formules comme *v(otum) s(olvit) l(ibens) m(erito)*[30]. Du point de vue épigraphique, on constate qu'aucune inscription n'est antérieure à celles érigées par C. Sempronius Urbanus, procurateur de Dacie Apulensis vers 184-186[31]. On peut, pour le moment, invoquer des arguments logiques, mais nulle preuve épigraphique pour affirmer la présence, dans cet espace, des procurateurs financiers de Dacie Supérieure entre 118 et 168. Du point de vue archéologique, on constate une phase en bois, qui préfigure les édifices en pierre, et deux phases en pierre. La succession des phases en pierre est très claire dans le secteur sud, celui qui nous intéresse. Il y avait au IIe siècle une salle au plan basilical de 18,50 x 8 m, divisée en deux nefs et délimitée par les murs Z1, Z2, Z3 et Z4[32]. Dans une seconde phase, le mur Z1 a été démantelé et la basilique a été transformée en une cour. Dans la partie ouest de la cour a été construit un édifice de 3,80 m (nord-sud) x 6,80 m (est-ouest), délimité par les murs Z5 (adossé au Z3), Z6, Z7 et Z8 **(Fig. 7.3)**. C'est cet édifice qu'il faut identifier avec le *Serapeum*. Tout comme la basilique antérieure, cet édifice est divisé par un mur (Z9) en deux nefs. Les compartiments nord et sud communiquaient soit par une porte soit à travers une colonnade. L'entrée se trouvait sur le mur nord (Z7)[33]. Le grand trou d'environ 1 m de diamètre se trouvant devant l'entrée supposée semble avoir été fait par des chercheurs de trésors, qui auront sorti la fondation d'un autel, d'un vase d'ablution ou, plus probablement, d'un nymphée. Le corridor large d'environ 1 m entre les murs Z8 et Z4 peut être interprété comme une *crypta*. Le *Serapeum* n'appartient donc pas au plan initial du *praetorium* en pierre. On l'a implanté là à la suite d'une pressante nécessité politique.

La stratigraphie et la position initiale des monuments ont été totalement dérangées à l'aube de l'époque moderne, lors de l'aménagement de canaux de drainage, pour lesquels ont été utilisés des monuments épigraphiques. D'autres inscriptions ont été cassées et déplacées afin d'être transformées en chaux. C'est pourquoi les inscriptions isiaques s'étendent à travers tout l'espace entre le mur Z7 du *Serapeum* et l'*horreum* H1.

3. – Cinq fragments d'une plaque votive de construction, en marbre, dont trois ont été trouvés près du trou devant l'entrée dans le *Serapeum*[34]. Dimensions totales: 28 x 96 x

11 cm. H. des lettres: 5 cm ligne 1; 2,5 cm; lignes 2-3; 3,5 cm ligne 4; 2,2-2,4 cm ligne 5. **(Fig. 7.4a-b)**

Piso 1998, 255-257, n° 1 (photo, dessin) (= *CIL* III 7920 ; *SIRIS* 684 + *CIL* III 7958; Drexler 1890, 56; Popescu 1927, 200; Floca 1935, 220, 239; Popa 1979, 30, n° 41; *IDR* III/2, 227); *AE* 1998, 1088; *ILD* I 265; *RICIS* 616/0204; Schäfer 2007, 251-252, H 12, 9; Carbó García 2010, 1017-1019, n° 309; Cristea, Tecar 2010, 275-276, n° 21; Opreanu 2016, 83-86[35]: *[Invicto deo Sera]pidi | et Is[idi frugi]ferae pro salute | atque incolumitate Imp(eratoris) Caes(aris) | M(arci) [A]urel(ii) Antonini [p]ii felicis |⁵ [Aug(usti)] Part(hici) max(imi) p[ontif(icis) max(imi)? B]ritt(anici) max(imi) | [et Iuliae Domnae A]ug(ustae) m[atri]s | [Aug(usti) et castrorum --- | ---].*

Le texte ressemble beaucoup à celui de deux inscriptions de Carnuntum[36] et Ad Statuas[37], datables de 213, ce qui suggère des circonstances et une datation semblables. Il semble maintenant prouvé qu'au début de l'automne 213 Caracalla, venant de Pannonie, visita la Dacie[38], ce qui détermina la dédicace, partout dans la province, de nombreuses statues et de monuments votifs pour le salut de l'empereur. Ce serait peut-être un argument supplémentaire pour la construction du *Serapeum* dans le *praetorium procuratoris* en 213. On a donc toutes les raisons de croire que l'inscription n° 3 est l'inscription de construction d'un nymphée plutôt que du *Serapeum* lui-même, ou bien, comme on va le voir plus bas, une des inscriptions de construction du temple. Pour la mise en

---

[30] Piso 1983, 234-235; Piso 1998, 255-271.
[31] Voir Piso 2013, 197-200.
[32] H. Daicoviciu et alii 1984, 2-3.
[33] H. Daicoviciu et alii 1984, 3-5.
[34] Les fragments se trouvent aux musées de Lugoj, de Sighişoara et de Sarmizegetusa.

[35] Dans la lecture et l'interprétation d'Opreanu, seule est correcte l'observation qu'à la ligne 5, entre *Part(hico) max(imo)* et *Britt(anico) max(imo)*, pouvait se trouver *p[ontif(ici) max(imo)]*, car la même erreur apparaît aussi dans trois inscriptions impériales de construction, de Porolissum, datées de 213 (*AÉ* 1944, 51; *AÉ* 1979, 491 = *ILD* I, 658 ; *AÉ* 1958, 230 = 1979, 491). C'est un argument de plus pour dater l'inscription de Sarmizegetusa de 213 également. Le même auteur a toutefois tort de compléter à la ligne 6 la titulature de l'empereur, car dans cette ligne on distingue clairement les lettres VG M....S, qui ne peuvent appartenir qu'à *[A]ug(ustae) m[atri]s*. Pour parachever sa déconstruction de l'ancienne lecture de Piso, l'auteur (Opreanu 2016, 84-85) plaide contre la restitution *[Invicto Deo Sera]pidi* à la ligne 1, lui préférant *[Deo Invicto Sera]pidi*, en oubliant qu'au même endroit et à la même divinité a été érigé un monument *Invicto deo Serapidi* (n° **5** de notre liste).
[36] *AÉ* 1992, 1412 = *AÉ* 2000, 1209 = *RICIS* 613/0703 (Carnuntum): *[Deo invicto] Sarapidi et [Isidi reginae | pro salute victoria et in]columitate Imp(eratoris) C[aes(aris) M(arci) Aureli(i) Antonini Pii Felicis | August(i) Parth(ici) Max(imi) Brit(annici) Max(imi)] pont(ificis) max(imi) | (tr)ibunicia pot(estate) XVI imp(eratoris) III co(n)s(ulis) IIII p(atris) p(atriae) et |⁵ Iuliae Piae Aug(ustae) matris cas]trorum ac patri[ae templum vetustate conlapsum | restitut P(ublius) Cornelius Anu]llinus leg(atus) leg(ionis) X[IIII G(eminae) M(artiae) V(ictricis) | Antoninianae d(evotus) n(umini) m(aiestati)q(ue) eorum].*
[37] *AÉ* 1947, 36 = *RIU* III, 645 = *AE* 2000, 1202 = *RICIS* 614/0501 (Ad Statuas): *[Deo invicto Sarapidi et Isidi reginae pro s]alute et victoria | [Imp(eratoris) M(arci) Aur(elii) Antonini Aug(usti) et Iuliae Aug(ustae) matris Augus]ti et senat(us) et | [castrorum patriaeque et populi senatusque] Romani et genio | [---]nus b(ene) f(iciarius) sac[erdos et --- tem]plum a so[lo cum --- a fundamen]tis a novo | [impendiis suis ---] renova(verunt).* Il apparaît clairement que le formulaire de l'inscription de Ad Statuas est très proche de celui de Sarmizegetusa.
[38] SHA, Caracalla 5, 4: *--- dein ad orientem profectionem parans omisso itinere in Dacia resedit*, information soutenue par un grand nombre d'inscriptions. C'est à un défaut de méthode qu'il faut imputer l'acharnement d'Opreanu 2016, 89-93 à nier la réalité de cette visite impériale en Dacie; sur cette question, voir récemment Piso, Deac 2018, 756-762.

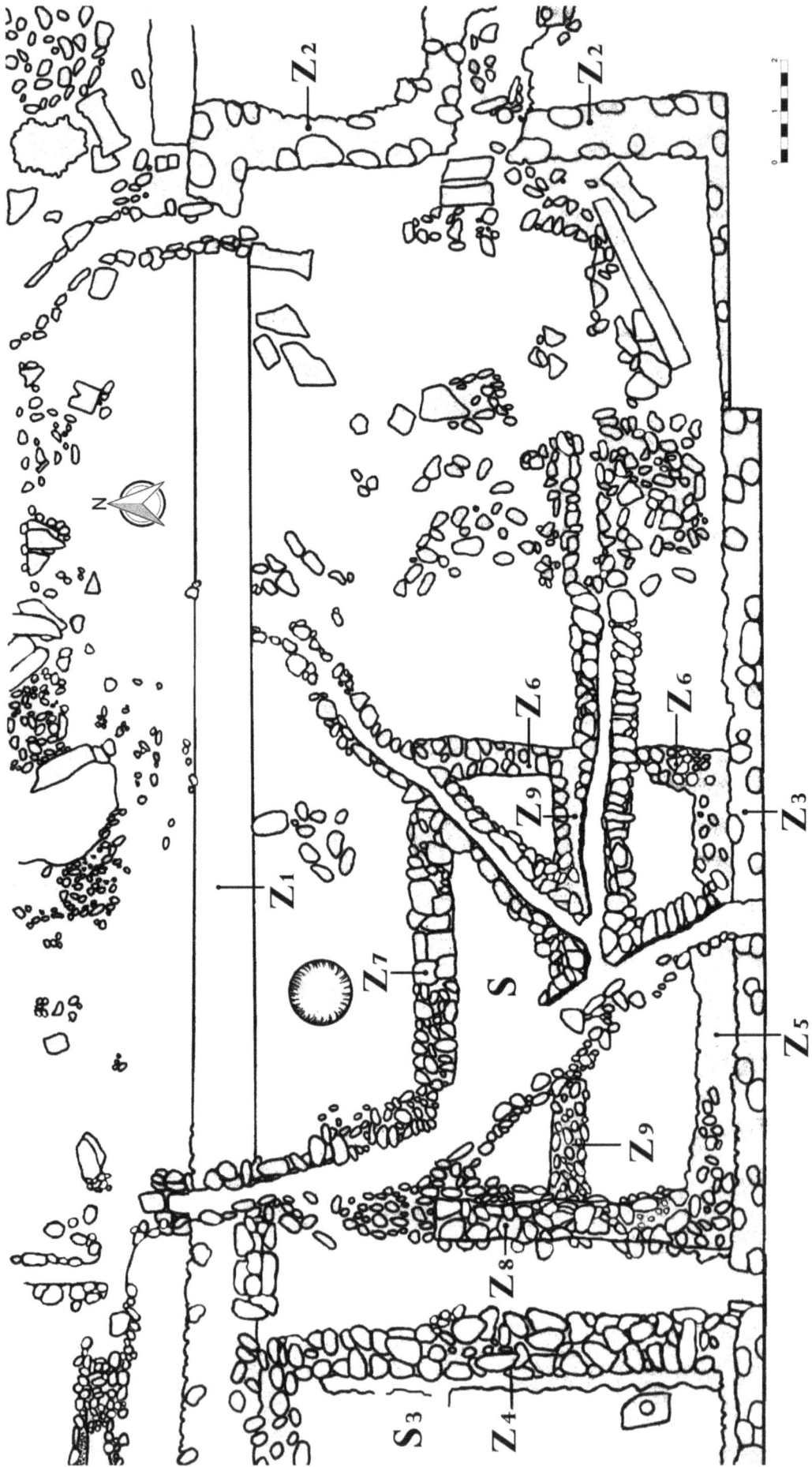

Fig. 7.3. Le *Serapeum* du *praetorium procuratoris*.

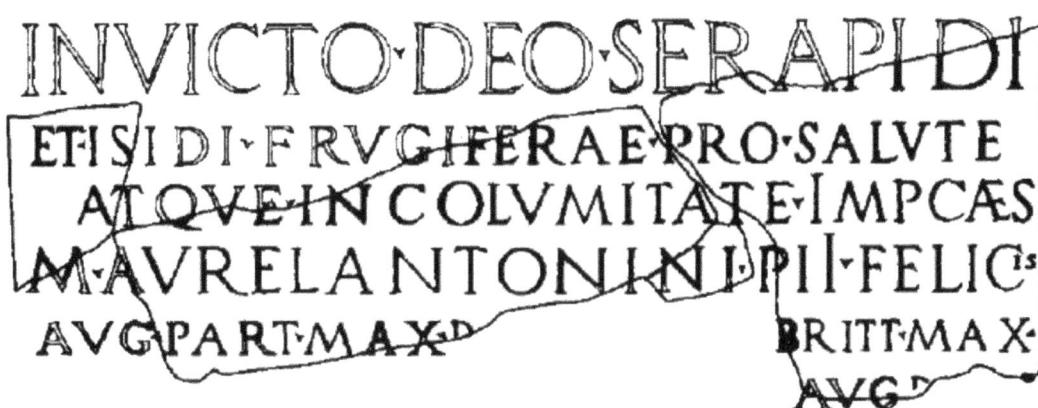

Fig. 7.4 a-b. L'inscription nᵒ 3.

circuit d'un pareil temple, il faut pourvoir non seulement aux murs et au toit, mais aussi aux statues, au bassin d'eau, à la crypte, à l'appareil et à la peinture. Chacun de ses éléments peut avoir eu son propre initiateur. *Isis frugifera*[39] désigne la déesse en tant que puissance nourricière et correspond au grec Ἶσις καρποφόρος[40], Ἶσις καρποτόκος[41] ou ἡ καρπὸν ἀνθρώποις εὑροῦσα[42]. Elle est rarement attribuée à la déesse en latin et on ignore la raison pour laquelle c'est le cas ici, même si on peut faire l'hypothèse d'une intervention divine lors d'un problème de ravitaillement. Rappelons qu'avec Sarapis, Isis est celle qui veille au bon acheminement de l'annone[43]. Le nom du procurateur de Dacie Apulensis qui initia cet ouvrage reste inconnu.

4. – Sept fragments d'une plaque votive de construction, en marbre[44], dont trois ont été trouvés devant le *Serapeum*. Le champ de l'inscription était bordé de *tabulae ansatae*,

qui, avec la partie inférieure, au-dessous du champ épigraphique, suggèrent une pièce d'architecture fixée au-dessus de l'entrée. Dimensions totales: ca 56 x 140 x 3,5 cm. H. des lettres: 5,5-6 cm. (**Fig. 7.5a-b**)

Piso 1998, 257-258, nᵒ 2 (photo, dessin) (= Téglás, König 1884, 54, nᵒ 9; *CIL* III 7995; *IDR* III/2, 68); *AE* 1998, 1089; *SEG* 48, 1998, 985; *ILD* I 266; *CIGD* 110; *RICIS* 616/0206; Schäfer 2007, 259, H 12, 23; Carbó García 2010, 1020-1021, nᵒ 311; Cristea, Tecar 2010, 270, nᵒ 14; Piso 2013, 205-206, nᵒ 1: Ζηνὶ θ[εῶ?]ν π[άντων κρατοῦ?]ντι Σαράπι[δι?] / Κάσ[σ]ιος Αλ?[..... κατασκευ]ασθέν[τα ἐπὶ?] / ΑΙ[..]Λ?ΑΣ[--- κατ'] ἐπιτ[αγήν] sive [---] ἐπιτ[ρόπου].

À la ligne 1, on peut hésiter entre les participes présents κρατοῦντι[45], βοηθοῦντι[46], βροντῶντι[47] et κοσμοῦντι[48]. À la fin de la ligne 3, on peut lire tout aussi bien ἐπιταγῇ, κατ'ἐπιταγήν ou κατ'ἐπίταγμα. Le premier personnage nommé à la ligne 2, un Κάσσιος Αλ[- - -], ne peut être que le procurateur financier[49]. Dans ce cas, au début de la ligne

---

[39] Bricault, Dionysopoulou 2016, 73; voir *CIL* VI 351 = *ILS* 4354 = *SIRIS* 379 = *RICIS* 501/0111 (Rome).

[40] Bricault, Dionysopoulou 2016, 33; voir *SIRIS* 317 = *RICIS* 301/0601 (Hamamlu/Mysie).

[41] Bricault, Dionysopoulou 2016, 73; voir Bernand 1969, n° 166 et *RICIS* 101/0233.

[42] *IG* XII Suppl., 98-99 = *I. Kyme* nᵒ 41 = *RICIS* 302/0204 (Kyme).

[43] Bricault 2000; Bricault 2006, 75-80.

[44] Musées de Sarmizegetusa et Deva.

[45] *SIG*³ 1138 = *IG* XI/4, 1234 = *RICIS* 202/0173 (Délos).

[46] Bernand 1969, n° 227.

[47] *IGUR* I 138.

[48] Plut., *De Iside et Osiride* 29.

[49] Voir, pour ce procurateur, Piso 2013, 205-207.

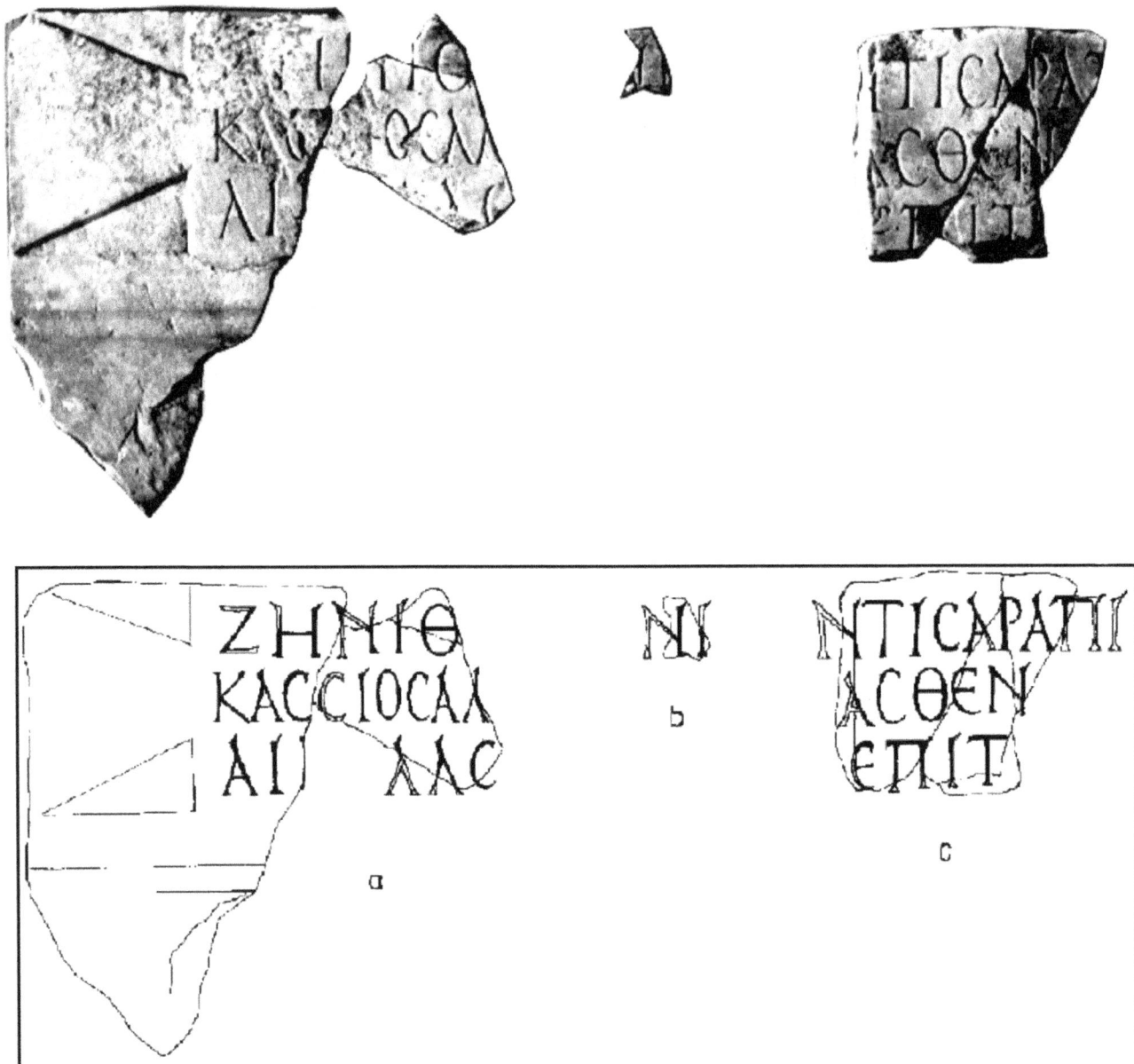

Fig. 7.5 a-b. L'inscription nᵒ 4.

3, pourrait être mentionné un personnage subordonné. Il est toutefois possible que nous ayons affaire à la ligne 1 au procurateur qui a initié l'ouvrage et à la ligne 3 au procurateur qui l'a accompli[50]. Il n'est pas nécessaire de supposer que l'inscription nᵒ 4 exprime la réfection de l'édifice[51]. Il nous semble probable que ce soit l'inscription de construction du temple, certes rédigée en grec, peut-être parce qu'il ne s'agit pas de *dei consentes*, mais bien d'un

culte très populaire dans un monde devenu cosmopolite. À notre avis, l'inscription est datable du règne de Caracalla[52].

5. – Autel ou base de statue, en marbre, trouvée dans l'*area sacra* en position secondaire près de l'*horreum* H1. Dimensions: 80 x 41 x 34 cm. H. des lettres: 5 cm ligne 1; 4,5 cm lignes 2-7. **(Fig. 7.6)**

Piso 1998, 263, nᵒ 9; *AE* 1998, 1096; *ILD* 273; *RICIS* 616/0207; Schäfer 2007, 257-258, H 12, 20 (photo); Carbó García 2010, 1022-1023, nᵒ 313; Cristea, Tecar 2010, 271, nᵒ 16; Piso 2013, 222-223, nᵒ 9: *Invicto | deo | Serapidi | M(arcus) Lucceius |⁵ Felix | proc(urator) Aug(usti) | n(ostri)*.

---

[50] Piso 1998, 258. Le nom au début de la ligne 2, Κάσσιος Αλ[.....] - peut-être Ἀλ[έξανδρος] -, appartient au procurateur; voir, pour ce procurateur inconnu, Piso 2013, 205-206. On remarque le *nomen* complet, non abrégé. Il est difficile de trouver une solution pour le début de la ligne 3. Si l'on proposait le *nomen* Αἴλιος, *exempli gratia* Αἴλιος Κλάσσικος ou Αἰ[λ(ίου)] Κ]λασ[σικοῦ], il serait difficile d'expliquer pourquoi le *nomen* du second procurateur est abrégé mais pas celui du premier. On ne procédait pas ainsi dans les inscriptions officielles. La prudence est donc requise.

[51] Ce que propose Budischovsky 2007, 281.

[52] Piso 1998, 258.

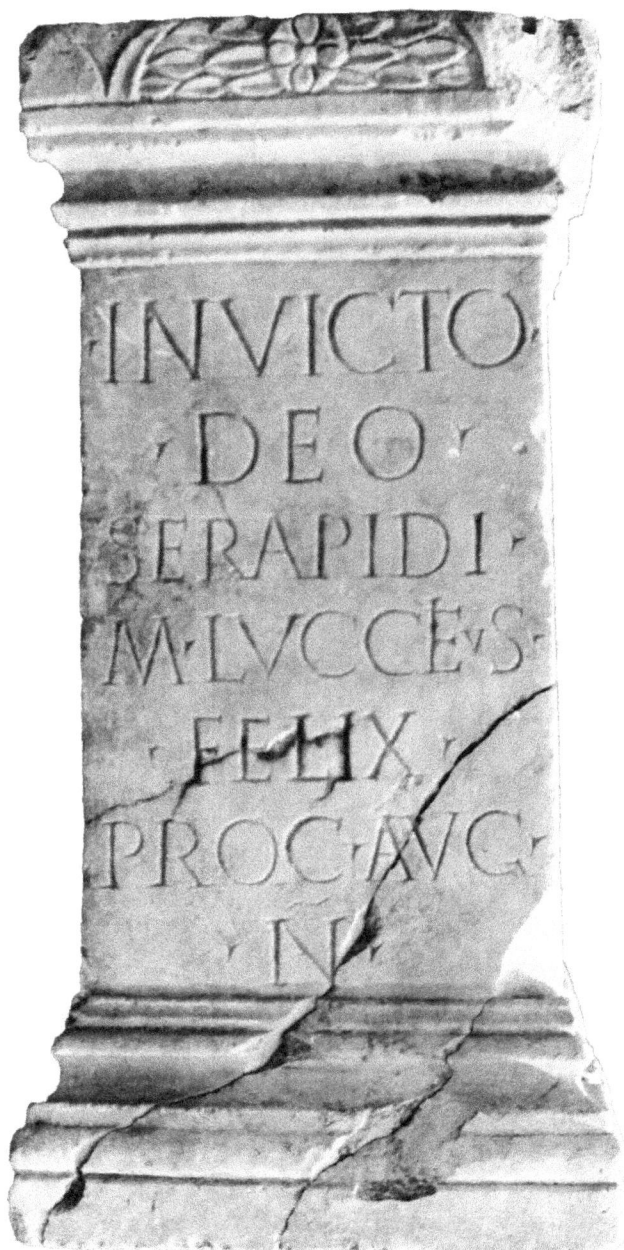

Fig. 7.6. L'inscription n° 5.

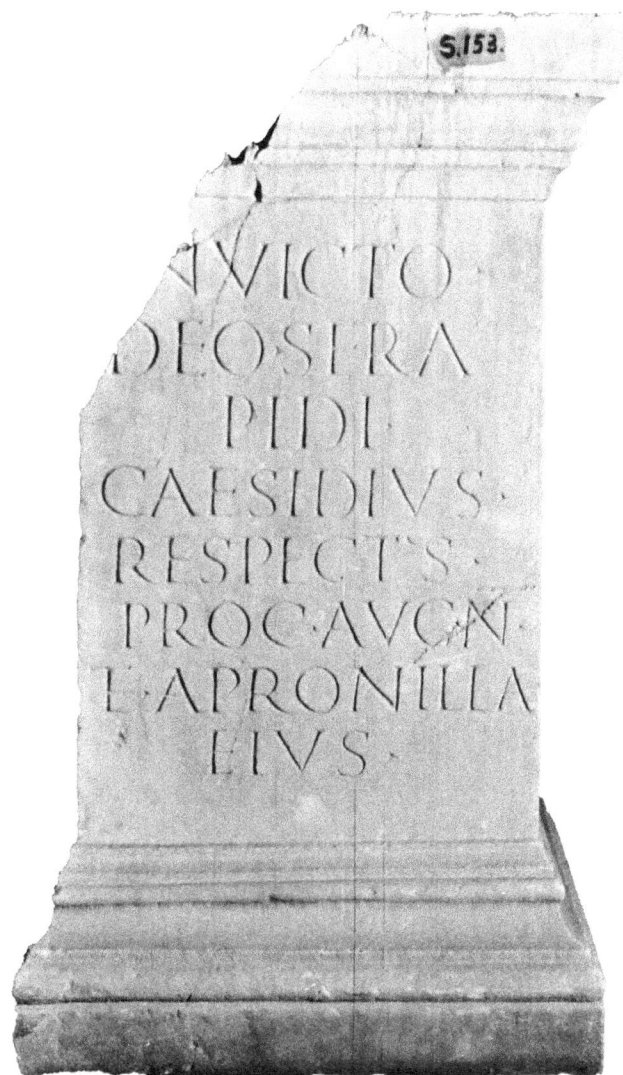

Fig. 7.7. L'inscription n° 6.

Les épithètes *invictus deus*[53] peuvent avoir été inspirées du culte de Mithra, auquel M. Lucceius Felix avait dédié un relief[54]. Datation: ca 230-235.

6. – Autel ou base de statue, en marbre trouvée par C. Daicoviciu vers 1928 dans l'*area sacra* du *praetorium procuratoris*. Dimensions: 90 x 42 x 28 cm. H. des lettres: 4,5-5 cm. **(Fig. 7.7)**

Daicoviciu 1928-1932, 82-84, n° 1 (= Daicoviciu 1970, 202, n° 1); *AE* 1930, 134; 1933, 12; Stein 1944, 82; *SIRIS* 685; *IDR* III/2, 331; *RICIS* 616/0205; Schäfer 2007, 259-260, H 12, 24; Carbó García 2010, 1019-1029, n° 310; Cristea, Tecar 2010, 270, n° 13; Piso 2013, 226-227, n° 1: *[I]nvicto | deo Sera|pidi | Caesidius |⁵ Respectus | proc(urator) Aug(usti) n(ostri) | et Apronilla | eius.*

Les mêmes épithètes sont déjà attribuées à Sérapis dans l'inscription précédente. Elles pourraient être relativement contemporaines, ca 230-235[55].

7. – Deux ou trois plaques en marbre, dont sont conservés 19 morceaux, groupés en 11 fragments (**a-j**)[56]. Le fragment **f** a été trouvé devant l'entrée du *Serapeum*, les autres ont été dispersés dans l'*area sacra*. Les plaques avaient été encastrées dans le mur de part et d'autre de l'entrée du *Serapeum*. Les lettres sont d'environ 2,5 cm. Les dimensions initiales des plaques et un texte continu n'ont pas pu être établis.

---

[53] Bricault, Dionysopoulou 2016, 118-119.
[54] *CIL* III 1437; Cumont 1896, II, 107, n° 189 bis; *CIMRM* II 323, n° 2149-2150; *IDR* III/2, 286; Carbó García 2014, 796-797, n° 90; voir les justes remarques de Carbó García 2014, 1022.

[55] Pour Caesidius Respectus, voir Piso 2013, 227.
[56] Les fragments se trouvent au Musée de Sarmizegetusa et au MCDRD, à l'exception du fragment **d**, perdu.

Laurent Bricault, Dan Deac, Ioan Piso

Piso 2020b, 130-137 (**Fig. 7.8 a-j**): a) *Ṣi defit aurum I[--
-] | numen quod omnẹ Isiḍ[---] | sacṛis ramis fonte ỵ[--- |
.... fi?]nito ḟinis est ce[rimoniarum --- |⁵ .... r]ẹcuṛ[r]ẹns
muḷ[t---].*

b+c) *[- - -]m salu[tem(?) - - - | - - -] q[uis?]qu[e - - -| - - -]
dignam(?) - - -|- - -]CA[- - -].*

d) - *[- - -]RETEMPIA[- - -|- - -]S secun[d- - -|- - -]TE[- -
-].*

e) - *[- - -]am recurr[- - - | - - -]a et iubente le[- - -].*

f) - *[- - - reme?]ạbis ad [- - - | - - -]s et vers[us? - - -].*

g) - *[- - - exaudi?]enti precem | [- - -] centri locus | [- - -]
is aequo vocat | [- - - i]usto cum | [- - -].*

h) - *[- - - i]mmoṛ[tal - - -].*

i) - *[- - - iu?]nxit [- - -].*

j) - *[- - - n]ostram [- - - | - - -]ur coles taụ[ru]ṃ doniquae
mundum [hunc relinques?].*

Pour I. Piso, malgré l'état très fragmentaire des plaques,
on trouve assez d'arguments pour soutenir qu'elles
contiennent des exhortations pour les initiés dans le culte
isiaque et pour leur vie future. En somme, il s'agirait de
rituels décrits un demi-siècle auparavant dans le livre XI
des *Métamorphoses* d'Apulée. Nous nous trouvons en tout
cas devant un monument épigraphique unique. Comme
l'analyse détaillée du texte a été faite ailleurs[57], nous nous
limiterons, dans ce qui suit, aux idées générales.

Fragment **a**. La ligne 1 fait allusion à la faim d'or des
temples isiaques et aux dépenses qui incombaient par
conséquent aux fidèles qui voulaient accomplir les rites
de l'initiation. Ligne 2 est exprimé le caractère universel
d'Isis, dans une forme qui ressemble à la formule utilisée
dans une célèbre inscription de Capua: *te tibi una quae
es omnia*[58]. Ligne 3, il s'agit de rameaux, abondamment
utilisés dans des actions sacrées. On passe ensuite au
rôle exceptionnel joué dans le rituel isiaque par l'eau,
notamment par l'eau du Nil, provenant de la source ou
bien déclarée comme telle. Ligne 4, on aura probablement
précisé les actions qui allaient être accomplies à la suite
de la cérémonie d'initiation. Ligne 5, *recurrens* fait
allusion au retour de l'initié du voyage symbolique qu'il
avait fait dans l'au-delà; la même idée est présente dans
le fragment **e**, où l'on rencontre deux éléments indiquant
le voyage: *remeare* et *versus*. Dans les fragments **b+c** et
d, on trouve l'idée du salut du monde et de l'individu
par la grâce divine. Le fragment **g** évoque la divinité, qui
écoute les prières des mortels – *[exaudi?]enti precem* – et
fait mention d'un *centri locus*, synonyme du *meditullium*
d'Apulée: on y désigne le milieu du sanctuaire, d'où

l'initié exprime des remerciements à la déesse[59]. Dans
le fragment **h**, le terme *immortalis* peut s'appliquer à la
divinité, mais plutôt au suprême but de l'initiation, qui
est celui d'obtenir la promesse de l'immortalité. Enfin,
dans le fragment **j**, on communique à l'initié l'obligation
de vénérer jusqu'à la fin de sa vie terrestre le bœuf Apis
(*taurum*), qui était en fait le porteur de l'âme d'Osiris. On
peut aussi y comprendre un hommage à Sérapis.

L'aménagement d'un *Serapeum* dans le *praetorium
procuratoris* exprime une préoccupation politique forte,
en lien direct avec le culte impérial dans sa forme de *pro
salute Imperatoris*. On n'a pas la certitude que tous les
monuments pour les divinités isiaques aient été érigés
dans le *Serapeum* ou dans son voisinage immédiat.
Des autels ou des bases de statues comme les n°s **5** et **6**
ont pu être placés dans la grande *area sacra*, auprès
de monuments dédiés à d'autres divinités. C'était une
obligation générale qui incombait aux procurateurs.
Le *Serapeum* de Sarmizegetusa n'était assurément pas
réservé au seul procurateur et à son *officium*, les cultes
isiaques étant ouverts à toutes les couches sociales et à
tous les individus[60].

8(?). – Deux fragments appartenant à la partie moyenne
supérieure d'une plaque votive de construction en marbre,
trouvés dans l'*area sacra*, près de l'*horreum* H1[61].
Dimensions: 30 x 18,5 x 2 cm. H. des lettres: 3,3 cm. (**Fig.
7.9**)

Piso 1983, 240-241, n° 7 (photo, dessin); *AE* 1983, 832;
Haensch 1997, 692; *ILD* I, 256; Schäfer 2007, 265, H 12,
33; Piso 2013, 252, n° 2: *[Te]mplum [--- | de]dicatum [a
Temonio? | Se]cundo v(iro) [e(gregio) proc(uratore) | per]
Messiu[--- | cu]m s[uis?].*

On n'a aucune certitude qu'il s'agisse du *Serapeum*, car,
comme nous l'avons montré plus haut, l'*area sacra* était
dominée par le temple du culte impérial (C). La datation
assez tardive de l'épithète *v(ir) e(gregius)* et l'acte de la
dédicace, qui habituellement se rapporte à une nouvelle
construction, parleraient toutefois en faveur du *Serapeum*.
Le procurateur Tem[---] Secundus est connu par une autre
inscription fragmentaire de la même *area sacra*[62]. Quant
au second personnage, Messius [---], ce pourrait être un
successeur de Tem[---] Secundus.

9(?). – Quatre fragments d'une plaque de construction en
marbre, trouvés dans l'*area sacra*. Dimensions: 47,5 x 31
x 3 cm. H. des lettres: 4 cm ligne 1; 3,5 cm lignes 2-5.

---

[57] Piso 2020b, 130-137.
[58] *CIL* X 3800 = *ILS* 4362 = *SIRIS* 502 = *RICIS* 504/0601.

[59] Apul., *Met.* XI, 24, 2.
[60] Benoît 1973, 78: « La nouveauté des cultes orientaux est de s'adresser
non plus au citoyen, au père de famille, mais à la personne considérée
comme telle; on abolit des distinctions de classes, de races, voire de
sexes »; voir aussi Bricault 2012, 100-101.
[61] Les pièces n°s 8-10 se trouvent au Musée de Sarmizegetusa.
[62] *IDR* III/2, 338 = *AÉ* 1982, 829 = Piso 2013, 252, n° 1 = Schäfer
2007, 265, H 12, 34 : *[------| II?[---] | Ter[rae matri ?] | Tem[onius ?]
| Secund[us pr]o|⁵curator Clodius* ; pour le procurateur, voir Piso 2013,
252-253.

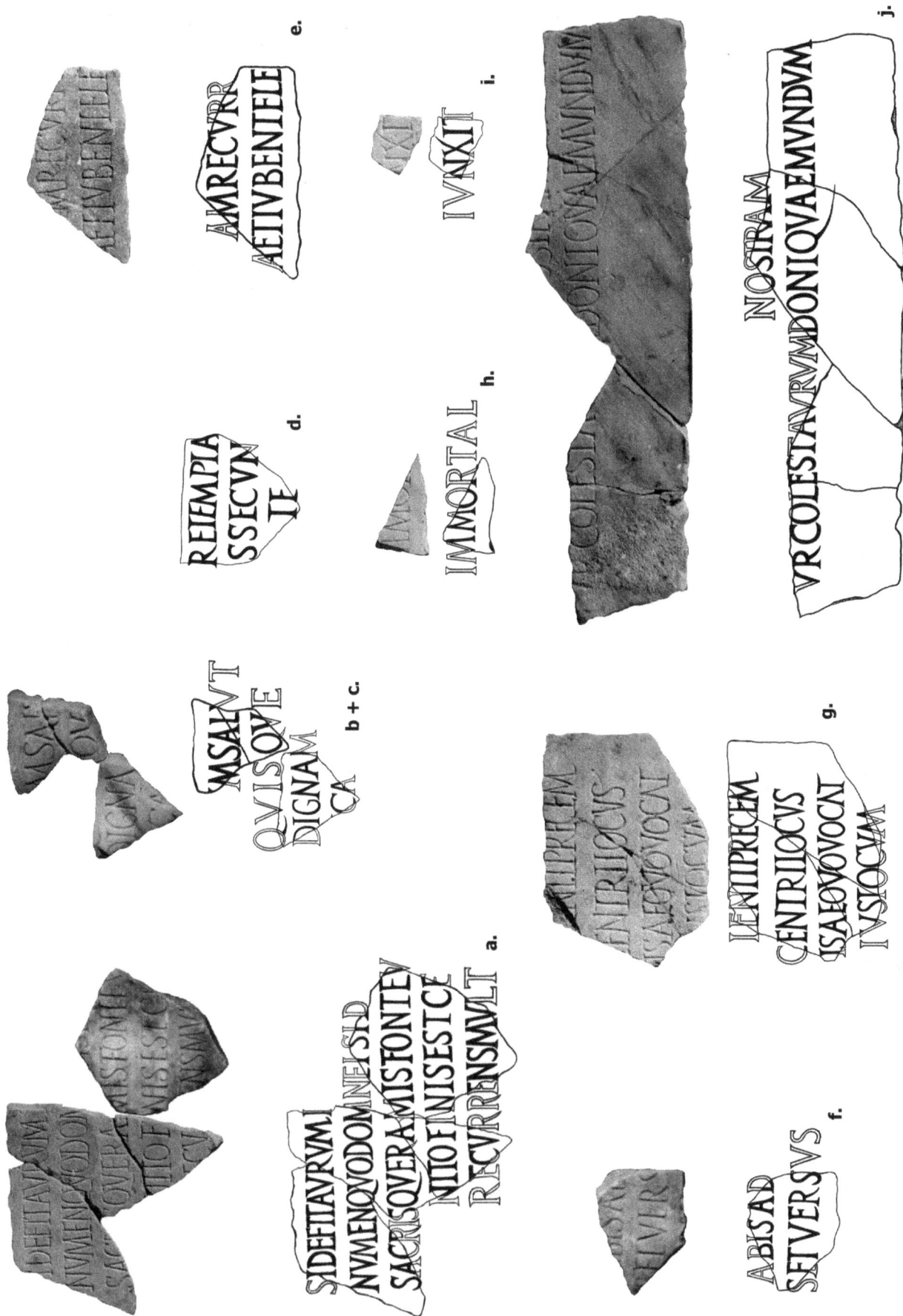

e.

AMRECVRR
AEITVBENIELE

i.

IXI

IVNXIT

d.

REIEMPIA
SSECVM
IE

h.

IMMORTAL

SONTONAEMVNDVM

COELSIB

j.

NOSTRAM
VRCOELESTAVRVMDONIQVAEMVNDVM

b + c.

MSANVT
OVISOVE
DIGNAM
CA

g.

AHPRECEM
ENRITOCVS
ISAEOVOVOCAT

LEMTIPRECEM
CENTRIIOCVS
ISAEOVOVOCAT
IVSTOCVM

a.

SIDEFITAVRVM
NVMENOVODOMNEISD
SACRISOVERAMISFONTEN
NTIOFINISESTCE
RECVRRENSMVLT

f.

ABISAD
SETVERSVS

Fig. 7.8. a-j. L'inscription n° 7.

55

Fig. 7.9. L'inscription nᵒ 8(?).

Piso 1998, 261-262, nᵒ 6; *AE* 1998, 1093; Schäfer 2007, 256-257, H 12, 18; Carbó García 2010, 1021-1022, nᵒ 312; Cristea, Tecar 2010, 271, 275-276, nᵒˢ 15, 22: *Pro salute ae[terna]* | *Ịṃp(eratoris) Caes(aris) M(arci) Aurelli(i) Se[veri Alexandri Aug(usti) et]* | *[[Iuliae Mameae]] s[anctissimae Augustae]* | *[[ma[tris]] Aug(usti) n(ostri) et castrorum]* |⁵ *templi sị[--- | ------].*

Il ne s'agit pas d'une inscription de construction du *Serapeum*, car le nom de la divinité manque. À la ligne 5, on a plutôt affaire à *si[gnis]* ou *si[gillis]* qu'à *Se[rapis].* Le temple pourrait être aussi bien celui du culte impérial (C). Le procurateur, dont le nom se trouvait dans la lacune, pourrait être M. Lucceius Felix, extrêmement actif dans l'*area sacra*⁶³. Datation: 230-235 ?

10(?). – Six fragments d'une plaque votive ou de construction, dont un a été trouvé dans la zone du *Serapeum*. Dimensions totales: ca 150 x ? x 2,5 cm. H. des lettres: 4,5 cm ligne 1; 3,5-4 cm les autres lignes.

Piso 1998, 259-260, nᵒ 4 (= *IDR* III/2, 145); *AE* 1998, 1091; *ILD* I, 268; *RICIS* 616/0208; Schäfer 2007, 255-256, H 12, 16; Piso 2013, 221, nᵒ 2: *[Invicto deo Serapidi(?)* | *pro salute(?) Imp(eratoris) Caes(aris) M(arci) Aurelli(i)* | *Severi [[Alexandri]] Pii Fel(icis) Aug(usti) et* | *[[Iul] iae M[ameae]] sanctissi]mae Aug(ustae)* |⁵ *[[m]atr[is]] Aug(usti) n(ostri) et cas[tro]rum* | *M(arcus) Luccei[us] Fe[li]x [pro]c(urator) Aug(usti) n(ostri)* | *[---]imu?[---* | *---* | *---]mus [------].*

À la ligne 1, le nom de Sérapis, complété dans le *RICIS*, est possible grâce au lieu de découverte du fragment **a**, mais il faut tenir compte aussi de l'existence du temple du culte impérial (C). Datation: ca 230-235.

11(?). – Cinq fragments d'une plaque en marbre, trouvés au cours du temps dans le *praetorium procuratoris*, mais pas nécessairement dans l'*area sacra*⁶⁴. Une division du texte en lignes a été impossible. Dimensions: 13 x 15 x 3 cm; 7 x 20 x 5 cm; 11 x 12 x 3 cm. H des lettres: 3,5 cm.

Piso 1998, 262-263, nᵒ 7 (= *CIL* III 7970; *IDR* III/2, 64); *AE* 1998, 1094; *ILD* I, 271; Schäfer 2007, 257, H 12, 19; Piso 2013, 222, nᵒ 4 : *[Pro salute?] aet[erna* | *Imp(eratoris) Caes(aris) M(arci) Aurelli(i)] Sever[i Alexandri Pii Felicis Aug(usti) et Iuliae Mameae matris Aug(usti) n(ostri) ca]str(orum) [--- et universi huma] ni gener[is] nymph[aeum --- M(arcus) Lucceius] Felix p[rocurator) Aug(usti) n(ostri)*⁶⁵.

Bien que la présence de l'eau soit vitale dans un *Serapeum*⁶⁶, il est impossible de décider si ce *nymphaeum* avait un rapport quelconque avec celui-ci⁶⁷. Datation: ca 230-235.

Les monuments anépigraphes

12(?). – Buste d'Isis(?) en marbre du Proconnèse/Marmara ou d'Usak⁶⁸. H.: 11,6 cm. **(Fig. 7.10).**

Andrițoiu-Mărghitan 1972, 35, fig. 62 (photo); Berciu-Petolescu 1976, 6 ; Alicu et alii 1979, 116, nᵒ 254, pl. XLI/254 (photo); Popa 1979, 24-25, nᵒ 30; Bricault 2001, 35; Carbó García 2010, 392; Müller et alii 2012, 90, SA 18 (photo); Deac 2013, 183, nᵒ 192.

La déesse est vêtue d'un chiton et d'un himation. Elle ne présente pas de nœud entre les seins. Une longue chevelure ondulée, séparée par une raie médiane, s'étend sur les épaules. Au sommet du crâne, restes d'une couronne

---

⁶³ Voir pour celui-ci Piso 2013, 221-227.

⁶⁴ Les fragments se trouvent au MCDRD.
⁶⁵ L'expression *matri --- universi generis humani* apparaît dans *CIL* II 3413 (Carthago Nova).
⁶⁶ Wild 1981, 49-53 et 126-148; Malaise 2005, 62-65; Kleibl 2007, 207-223.
⁶⁷ On se trouve dans la même incertitude concernant une autre plaque en marbre trouvée dans l'*area sacra* et sur laquelle sont mentionnés les noms des procurateurs M. Lucceius Felix et P. Aelius Hammonius: Piso 1998, 260-261, nᵒ 5 (=*AÉ* 1983, 834); *AÉ* 1998, 1092; *ILD* 269; Piso 2013, 222, nᵒ 3.
⁶⁸ MCDRD, inv. 392.

Fig. 7.10. Buste d'Isis, n⁰ 12 (photo Marius Barbu).

brisée (polos, calathos, croissant ?). La pièce présente une iconographie proche de celle d'un buste d'Isis ou de l'une de ses dévotes, retrouvé à Tomis et daté, en raison du contexte archéologique, du IIIe siècle[69], ainsi que d'un autre buste, également de Tomis, daté par G. Bordenache de l'époque flavienne[70]. Comme pour la pièce de Sarmizegetusa, le contexte archéologique fait défaut. Les deux *comparanda* étant datés d'une manière très variable[71], on est contraint de proposer une datation assez large, entre le milieu du IIe siècle et la première moitié du IIIe siècle[72].

Fig. 7.11. Buste de Sérapis, n⁰ 13 (photo Musée National d'Histoire de Roumanie).

13. – Buste en marbre de Sarapis. H.: 30 cm[73]. **(Fig. 7.11).**

Bordenache 1969, 86, n° 169, pl. LXXIII/169 (photo); Kater-Sibbes 1973, 176, n° 888; Alicu et alii 1979, 116, n° 256, pl. XLI/256 (photo); Popa 1979, 16, n° 13, pl. I/3 (photo); Carbó García 2010, 393; Deac 2013, 183, n° 191; Bâltâc et alii 2015, 115, n° 107 (photo).

Le dieu, barbu et à l'épaisse chevelure bouclée, est vêtu d'un chiton. Un orifice au sommet du crâne devait permettre la fixation d'un calathos aujourd'hui disparu. Le buste lui-même est pourvu d'un tenon d'encastrement. La pièce est dite provenir de Haţeg, c'est-à-dire probablement de Sarmizegetusa ou d'une *villa* de son territoire. On la date approximativement du milieu du IIe siècle[74].

---

[69] Musée National d'Histoire et Archéologie de Constanţa, inv. 2002 (h. 78 cm). Canarache et alii 1963, 46-51, n° 7, fig. 21-24 (photos); Bordenache 1964, 75-176, fig. 20-21 (photos), pour qui il s'agit d'une prêtresse d'Isis; Dunand 1973, II, 203, pl. XXII (photo); Tacheva-Hitova 1983, 14-15, n° 20, pl. VI/I.20 (photo); Tran tam Tinh, *LIMC* V/1, 1990, 770, n° 117, pl. 507, n° 117 (photo), s. v. *Isis*; Eingartner 1991, 136-137, pl. LI/78 (photo); Bricault 2001, 31; Covacef 2002, 162, pl. XXIII, fig. 2 (photo); Deac 2013, 218, n° 274. On doit à Budischovsky 2007, 276, fig. 2 (photo), 283, le rapprochement entre les deux bustes. Sur les cultes isiaques à Tomis, Bricault 2007.

[70] Musée National d'Histoire de Roumanie, Bucarest, inv. 18720 (= MNA L655) (h.: 23 cm). Tocilesco 1900, 235, n° 6, fig. 117 (photo); Bordenache 1969, 86-87, n° 170, pl. LXXIV/170 (photo); Tacheva-Hitova 1983, 14, n° 19; Eingartner 1991, 137, n° 79, pl. LII/79 (photo); Bricault 2001, 31; Covacef 2002, 162, pl. XXIII/ fig. 1 (photo); Deac 2013, 217-218, n° 273; Bâltâc et alii 2015, 118, n° 110 (photo).

[71] D'autres *comparanda* chez Tran tam Tinh, *LIMC* V/1, 1990, 761-796, pl. 501-526, s. v. *Isis*; Eingartner 1991, 135-138, n° 74-83, pl. XLIX-LIV, où sont incluses les pièces de Tomis mentionnées plus haut et un buste d'Isis découvert à Rome, qui, comme à Sarmizegetusa, ne porte pas le nœud isiaque (138, n° 83, pl. LIV/83, photo).

[72] Alicu et alii 1979 ont daté le buste du IIe siècle; cf. Deac 2013: IIe-IIIe siècles.

---

[73] Musée National d'Histoire de Roumanie, Bucarest, inv. 18780 (= MNA L293).

[74] Sur l'iconographie de Sarapis, Hornbostel 1973; Clerc, Leclant, *LIMC* VII, 1994, 666-692, pl. 504-518, s. v. *Sarapis*.

Fig. 7.12 a-b. Amulette en bronze provenant de Sarmizegetusa, nº 14 (photo Á. Alföldy-Găzdac).

14. – Amulette en bronze coulé représentant la triade Isis, Harpocrate et Sarapis[75]. Dimensions: H.: 3,7 cm. **(Fig. 7.12a-b)**

Paulovics 1927, 90, fig. 27 (photo); Kater-Sibbes 1973, 181, nº 916; Tran tam Tinh 1983, 106-107, IB 1, pl. XIV, fig. 29 (photo); Clerc, Leclant, *LIMC* VII/1, 682, nº 160, s. v. *Sarapis* = Alföldy Găzdac 2003, 175-176, nº 9, pl. 4/4-5 (photo); Alföldy Găzdac 2005, 43-44, nº 9, pl. 4, nº 4-5 (photo); Deac 2013, 183-184, nº 193, pl. 33/3 (photo); Mráv 2013, 106, cat. 8.33 (photo); Mráv, Szabó 2016, 144, nº 19, pl. 38a (photo).

Ce petit bronze a été vendu en 1926 par l'anticaire László Mauthner à la « Société des Amis du Musée National Hongrois » comme provenant de Sarmizegetusa. Les trois divinités, debout, sont fixées sur une base. À gauche, Isis, légèrement tournée vers la droite, est coiffée d'un *basileion* posé sur une chevelure composée de boucles torsadées qui tombent sur les épaules. Elle devait brandir un sistre dans la main droite et tient une situle de la main gauche. Au centre, le dieu Harpocrate, de face, nu, coiffé du *pschent* et portant la mèche de l'enfance tient une *cornucopia* de la main gauche et porte son index droit aux lèvres. À droite, Sérapis, légèrement tournée vers la gauche, est coiffé du *calathos*. Il devait tenir un sceptre de la main gauche et une patère de la droite[76].

Comme l'a précisé R. Veymiers, il s'agit d'une amulette portée sur la poitrine dans un collier[77], telle qu'on la reconnaît sur le cartonage d'une momie de femme découverte à Hawara en Égypte[78].

Pour les pièces nᵒˢ 12-14 manquent les conditions de découverte, ce qui restreint la portée des conclusions historiques. En tout cas, elles témoignent de manifestations religieuses individuelles.

Aliena

Les deux pièces suivantes n'ont, à notre avis, aucun rapport avec les cultes isiaques.

a) – Plaque de construction en marbre (74 x 90 x 5 cm), trouvée à Sarmizegetusa dans un endroit et dans des circonstances inconnues[79]. Normalement, elle était fixée au-dessus de l'entrée du temple.

Studniczka 1884, 44-45, nº 1; *CIL* III 7907; Popescu 1927, 199; *IDR* III/2, 19 (photo); *SIRIS* 681; Ardevan 1993, 228, nº 2; *AE* 1993, 1344; Rusu Pescaru, Alicu 2000, 177, nº 42; *RICIS* 616/0201; Carbó García 2010, 1006-1007, nº 297: *Deae [re]ginae | M(arcus) Com(inius) Q[u]intus eq(uo) p(ublico) | pon(tifex) et q(uin)q(uennalis) col(oniae) et Anto|nia Valentina eius | pro salute Claudi|⁵ae Valentinae | templ(um) a solo fecerunt.*

b) – Autel ou base de statue votive en marbre (64 x 32 x 25 cm), trouvé en 1889 à Sarmizegetusa dans des conditions inconnues[80].

---

[75] Musée National Hongrois, Budapest, inv. 1/1926.

[76] Une amulette tout à fait semblable, de provenance inconnue, est conservée à l'Ägyptisches Museum de Berlin, inv. 8871; voir Tran tam Tinh 1983, 115-116, cat. IB 30. Nous remercions N. Amoroso pour avoir attiré notre attention sur ce document.

[77] Veymiers 2020, 320, nº V.BCB.15.

[78] Pour cet artefact, Teasley Trope et alii 2005, 100, nº 76 (photo). Un autre cartonage de momie, réalisé dans une technique semblable, provenant toujours de Hawara et daté de la même époque, a sur la poitrine, à la place de l'amulette, le nœud isiaque. Il s'agit peut-être d'une prêtresse d'Isis ; Eingartner 1991, 168-169, nº 143, pl. LXXXVIII/143 (photo et bibliographie ancienne). Pour tels masques de momies, Grimm 1974.

[79] MCDRD sans nº inv.

[80] MCDRD sans nº inv.

Téglás 1890, 193, n° 6; *CIL* III 7908; Popescu 1927, 199; Tudor 1957, 250, n° 41; *IDR* III/2, 309 (photo); *RICIS* *616/0202; Carbó Garcia 2010, 1007-1008, n° 298: *Deae regi(nae) | Ael(ia) Primi|tiva ex vot(o) | pro Ael(io) Me|⁵trodoro | patrono suo | v(otum) s(olvit) l(ibens) m(erito)*.

La discussion sur l'identité de la *dea regina* a été longue. Pour commencer, il faut remarquer que, à l'exception des inscriptions citées, on ne trouve dans le *RICIS* aucun autre cas dans lequel *dea regina* serait susceptible d'être identifiée avec Isis. C'est une première raison de douter d'une pareille identification à Sarmizegetusa. Pourtant, cette identification a été acceptée par D. Popescu[81], O. Floca[82], S. Sanie[83], L. Vidman (*SIRIS*) et P. Christodoulou[84]. Une position ambiguë a été exprimée par I. I. Russu, qui considéra comme possible l'identification de la *dea regina* de l'inscription **a** « avec Iuno, mais surtout avec Isis ou Nemesis », tandis qu'il l'identifiait sans sourciller avec Nemesis dans l'inscription **b**[85]. Dans le *RICIS*, L. Bricault hésitait de même pour l'inscription **b**, mais proposait de retrouver Isis dans l'inscription **a** en considérant les liens familiaux qui unissent les dédicants de cette inscription et ceux de la dédicace d'un temple pour Isis à Micia[86]. O. Seeck se prononça pour une divinité autochtone[87], A. Popa l'élimina de son catalogue et M.-C. Budischovsky nia tout rapport avec Isis, la rapprochant soit de Iuno soit, plus probablement, de Nemesis[88]. À notre avis, Iuno devrait être exclue de la discussion. La déesse qui dominait ouvertement le panthéon romain n'avait aucune raison de se cacher sous des épiclèses. Tout au contraire, Nemesis symbolisait la mauvaise fortune et la vengeance et on avait parfois du mal à prononcer son nom. Il est donc probable que ce soit elle la *dea regina* des inscriptions **a** et **b**.

c) – Une statuette en bronze, qui avait été interprétée comme une figure d'Isis alors qu'elle est dépourvue de tout attribut iconographique isiaque représente en réalité Fortuna[89].

Conclusion

Le corpus épigraphique de Sarmizegetusa nous a fait connaître trois dédicaces à Isis datées des règnes d'Antonin, Caracalla et Alexandre Sévère (n°ˢ **1-3**) ainsi que quatre voire cinq dédicaces à Sarapis datées des règnes de

Caracalla et Alexandre Sévère (n°ˢ **3**, **4**, **5**, **6** et **10(?)**). Au moins deux (n°ˢ **5** et **6**, restitution probable au n° **3**) de ces dédicaces s'adressent à Sarapis *invictus deus*. Les fouilles récentes de l'*area sacra* du *praetorium procuratoris* de Sarmizegetusa ont permis d'identifier deux sanctuaires, pratiquement dans le même espace sacré: un temple du culte impérial et un *Serapeum*[90]. Le même rapprochement peut être opéré pour Eburacum, en Bretagne[91] et Apulum, où trois dédicaces aux divinités isiaques ont été retrouvées en 1878 dans l'*area* du *praetorium* du légat gouverneur de la Dacie Supérieure et des trois Dacies[92].

Une dédicace à Isis de la part d'un gouverneur de Dacie Supérieure (n° **1**), datable ca 156/7-158, indique le fait remarquable que la déesse (seule ou, moins probablement, accompagnée de Sarapis), était vénérée à Sarmizegetusa par un gouverneur dès le règne d'Antonin, sans que l'on puisse déterminer avec certitude où se trouvait ce lieu de culte dans la colonie. Enfin, une dédicace d'Apulum au *numen* de Sérapis faite par un prêtre du dieu Esculape, pontife, quinquennal, mais aussi ancien *duumvir* de la colonie de *Sarmizegetusa*, doit dater de l'époque sévérienne[93]. Dans ce contexte, il ne faut pas oublier Micia qui, à l'exception du camp et du *vicus* militaire, constituait un *pagus* de Sarmizegetusa[94]. Bien qu'aujourd'hui nous traitions ces localités séparément, le principe de l'unité du chef-lieu et du territoire d'une ville romaine nous obligerait peut-être à voir toujours Sarmizegetusa dans ce *pagus*. Ceci est d'autant plus intéressant qu'un temple semble y avoir été construit pour Isis par une Domitia, épouse de Varenius Pudens, un membre important de l'aristocratie de Sarmizegetusa[95].

Si l'on considère les quelque 17 inscriptions concernant les cultes isiaques attribuées à Sarmizegetusa, Micia et Apulum, 15 émanent de militaires, de gouverneurs, de magistrats municipaux et de prêtres du culte impérial. Il est clair que le lien, tout au moins en Dacie[96], entre les représentants du pouvoir central et les cultes isiaques est très fort dès le milieu du IIᵉ s. Sur la foi des inscriptions,

---

[81] Popescu 1927, 199.
[82] Floca 1935, 223.
[83] Sanie 2004, 62-64, qui s'est appuyé sur des sources littéraires, notamment Apulée, au lieu de prendre en considération exclusivement les inscriptions.
[84] Christodoulou 2015, 183-184.
[85] Russu, ad *IDR* III/2, 19 et 319.
[86] *CIL* III 1341 = *IDR* III/3, 48 = *RICIS* 616/0301.
[87] Seeck 1914, 472.
[88] Budischovsky 2007, 281, 283.
[89] Selon S. Nemeti 2005, 320-321, 391, fig. 36, il s'agit d'Isis-Fortuna. L'incertitude plane sur une autre statuette en bronze, censée représenter Anubis (Țeposu-Marinescu, Pop 2000, 161, n° 287), mais connue par un unique dessin peu probant. Enfin, une gemme de Sarmizegetusa qui présenterait, selon Popa 1979, 25-26, n° 32-33, des motifs isiaques, est perdue, sans qu'en soit connue la moindre image.

[90] Voir le plan supra fig. 2.
[91] *CIL* VII 240 = *ILS* 4394 = *SIRIS* 750 = *RIB* 658 = *RICIS* 604/0101: *Deo sancto | Serapi | templum a so|lo fecit |⁵ Cl(audius) Hierony|mianus leg(atus) | leg(ionis) VI Vic(tricis)*.
[92] Voir les notes 8, 10, 12. Le *praetorium* d'Apulum a été identifié comme tel par Piso 1993/1994, 205-207 = Piso 2005, 267-270.
[93] *CIL* III 973 = *SIRIS* 694 = *IDR* III/5, 316 = *RICIS* 616/0405; Deac, Varga 2014, 12-14.
[94] Voir Piso 1995, 72-74 = Piso 2005, 282-284.
[95] *CIL* III 1341 = *SIRIS* 686 = Angyal 1971, 20-21, n° 3 = *AE* 1975, 727 = *IDR* III/3, 48 = *RICIS* 616/0301. Il est toutefois curieux que l'inscription se trouve sur un autel et non une base de statue et non sur une plaque de construction. Liée au camp de Micia est la dédicace *CIL* III 1342 = *SIRIS* 688 = Russu 1969, 183 = *IDR* III/3, 75 = *RICIS* *616/0303 faite par un préfet d'aile, d'une lecture trop incertaine pour être attribuée avec certitude à Isis. On connaît, en revanche, de Micia, une gemme représentant Harpocrate assis sur une fleur de lotus; voir Țeposu-David 1964, 257-264, fig. 1/1; Michel 2004, 269, 19.A.1.a, n° 6. Pour les cultes isiaques à Micia voir aussi Mărghitan, Petolescu 1976, 723-724.
[96] Le même lien doit pouvoir être établi dans d'autres provinces danubiennes, même si la documentation fait pour le moment défaut. Voir cependant déjà le riche dossier relatif à l'*Iseum* de *Savaria*, en Pannonie, où le culte d'Isis fut étroitement associé au culte impérial; Sosztarits et alii 2013; Mráv 2016a, 29-34; récemment Piso 2020a, 139-142.

les cultes semblent toucher d'abord, sous les Antonins, les élites municipales, puis à la fin du IIe s. certains militaires[97] et enfin, à partir du règne de Caracalla - peut-être bien dès sa campagne de 213-214[98], les représentants directs de l'Empereur. Cependant, toute statistique faite sur la seule base des sources épigraphiques peut biaiser la réalité et entraîner de fausses conclusions. N'oublions pas que les cultes isiaques, aux IIe-IIIe s., avaient depuis longtemps conquis toutes les couches sociales de l'Empire, que les fêtes d'Isis étaient de grands spectacles goûtés par un nombreux public et que l'expression religieuse des catégories sociales les plus basses différait fortement de celle des élites[99].

Bibliographie

Ackner 1856: Ackner, M. J., *Decennal-Aufzeichnung der archäologischen Funde in Siebenbürgen von Jahre 1845 bis 1855, Mittheilungen der K.K. Central-Commission zur Erforschung und Erhaltung der Baudenkmale* 6 (1856): 93-103.

Alföldy-Găzdac 2003: Alföldy-Găzdac, Á., "Bronzuri romane din Dacia în Colecția Muzeului Național Maghiar din Budapesta". *Ephemeris Napocensis* 13 (2003): 149-185.

Alföldy-Găzdac 2005: Alföldy-Găzdac, Á., "Roman Bronzes from Dacia in the Hungarian National History Museum in Budapest". Dans *Corona laurea. Studii în onoarea Luciei Țeposu-Marinescu*, C. Mușețeanu, M. Bărbulescu, D. Benea (éd.). București (2005): 31-66.

Alicu et alii 1979: Alicu, D., Pop, C., Wollmann, V., *Figured Monuments from Sarmizegetusa*. BAR Int. Series 55. Oxford (1979).

Andrițoiu, Mărghitan 1972: Andrițoiu, I., Mărghitan, L., *Muzeul Arheologic din Deva*. București (1972).

Angyal 1972: Angyal, K. B., "Epigraphica: Contribution à l'étude historique des religions orientales de Dacie". *Studium* 2 (1971): 17–21.

Ardevan 1979: Ardevan, R., "Patronii coloniei Ulpia Traiana Sarmizegetusa". *Sargetia* 14 (1979): 185-190.

Ardevan 1993: Ardevan, R., "Die Cominii von Sarmizegetusa – ein prosopographisches und chronologisches Problem". Dans *Prosopographica*, L. Mrozewicz, K. Ilski (éd.). Poznań (1993): 227-236.

Ardevan 1998: Ardevan, R., *Viața municipală în Dacia romană*. Timișoara (1998).

Bâltâc et alii 2015: Bâltâc, A., Știrbulescu, C., Ștefan, A., *Catalogul Colecției Lapidarium I. Piese greco-romane*. București (2015).

Benoît 1973 : Benoît, A., "Les mystères païens et le christianisme". Dans *Mystères et syncrétismes*, F. Dunand, M. Philonenko, A. Benoît, J. E. Ménard, J. J. Hatt (éd.). Paris (1975): 73-78.

Berciu, Petolescu 1976: Berciu, I., Petolescu, C. C., *Les cultes orientaux dans la Dacie méridionale*. ÉPRO 46. Leiden (1976).

Bernand 1969: Bernand, É., *Les inscriptions grecques et latines de Philae II. Haut et Bas Empire*. Paris (1969).

Blumenthal 1952: Blumenthal, A. v., *Realenzyklopädie* XXI/2 (1952): 1867-1876, s. v. *pomerium*.

Boda 2015: Boda, I., "The Sacred Topography of Colonia Sarmizegetusa". *ArchHung* 66 (2015): 281-304.

Bordenache 1964: Bordenache, G., "Contributi per una storia dei culti e dell'arte nella Tomi di età romana". *Studii Clasice* VI (1964): 155-178.

Bordenache 1969: Bordenache, G., *Sculture greche e romane del Museo Nazionale di Antichità di Bucarest I. Statue e rilievi di culto, elementi architettonici e decorativi*. Bucarest (1969).

Bricault 2000: Bricault, L., "Un phare, une flotte, Isis, Faustine et l'annone". *Chronique d'Égypte* LXXV / 150 (2000): 136-149.

Bricault 2001: Bricault, L., *Atlas de la diffusion des cultes isiaques (IVe s. av. J.-C.- IVe s. apr. J.-C.)*. Mémoires de l'Académie des Inscriptions et Belles-Lettres XXIII. Paris (2001).

Bricault 2006: Bricault, L., Isis, *Dame des flots*. Aegyptiaca Leodiensia 7. Liège (2006).

Bricault 2007: Bricault, L., "La diffusion isiaque en Mésie Inférieure et en Thrace : politique, commerce et religion". Dans *Nile into Tiber. Egypt in the Roman World. Proceedings of the IIIrd International Conference of Isis Studies, Faculty of Arcaheology, Leiden University, May 11-14 2005*, L. Bricault, M. J. Versluys, P. G. P. Meyboom (éd.). RGRW 159. Leiden/ Boston (2007): 245-266.

Bricault 2012: Bricault, L., "Associations isiaques d'Occident". Dans *Demeter, Isis, Vesta and Cybele. Studies in Greek and Roman Religions in Honour of Giulia Sfameni Gasparro*, A. Mastrocinque, C. Giuffrè Scibona (éd.). Stuttgart (2012): 91-104.

Bricault 2013: Bricault, L., *Les cultes isiaques dans le monde gréco-romain*. La roue à livres/Documents 66. Paris (2013).

Bricault, Dionysopoulou 2016: Bricault, L., Dionysopoulou, E., *Myrionymi 2016. Épithètes et épiclèses grecques et latines de la tétrade isiaque*. Toulouse (2016).

---

[97] Comparer la dédicace à Jupiter-Sérapis pour le salut des empereurs Septime Sévère et Caracalla (avec noms complets) émanant de *Flavius Quirinalis Maximus*, tribun de la *legio X Gemina* stationnée à *Vindobona* (CIL III 4560 = *SIRIS* 667 = *RICIS* 613/0801, 198-209).

[98] Comparer les dédicaces *AÉ* 1992, 1412 = *RICIS* 613/0703 de Carnuntum (213), *AÉ* 1962, 40 = *SIRIS* 669 = *RIU* III 753 = *AÉ* 2000, 1209 = *RICIS* 614/0101 de *Crumerum* et CIL III 3637 = *SIRIS* 670 = *RIU* III 800 = *RICIS* 614/0201, de Piliscsév, en Pannonie Inférieure (toutes deux de 214, à l'occasion de la campagne de Caracalla contre les Parthes).

[99] Voir par exemple les très intéressants médaillons isiaques de Dacie étudiés en dernier lieu par Deac 2020, 121-125.

Budischovsky 2004 : Budischovsky, M.-C., "Témoignages de dévotion isiaque et traces culturelles le long du limes danubien". Dans *Isis en Occident, Actes du IIème Colloque international sur les études isiaques, Lyon III 16-17 mai 2002*, L. Bricault (éd.). RGRW 151. Leiden/Boston (2004): 171-191.

Budischovsky 2007: Budischovsky, M.-C., "Témoignages isiaques en Dacie (106-271 apr. J.-C.)". Dans *Nile into Tiber. Proceedings of the IIIrd International Conference of Isis studies, Faculty of Archaeology, Leiden University, May 11-14 2005*. L. Bricault, M. J. Versluys, P. G. P. Meyboom (éd.). RGRW 159. Leiden/Boston (2007): 267-288.

Canarache et alii 1963: Canarache, V., Aricescu, A., Barbu, V., Rădulescu, A., *Tezaurul de sculpturi de la Tomis*. București (1963).

Carbó García 2010: Carbó García, J. R., *Los cultos orientales en la Dacia romana. Formas de difusión, integración y control social e ideológico*. Salamanca (2010).

Carbó García 2016: Carbó García, J. R., "Studia Dacica et Parthica (III) : Las campañas Parthicas de Trajano a Galieno y la difusión de cultos de origen oriental en la Dacia Romana". *Acta Musei Napocensis* 53 (2016): 121-136.

Christodoulou 2015: Christodoulou, P., "Sarapis, Isis and the Emperor". Dans *Romanising Oriental Gods? Proceedings oft the International Symposium Skopje (18-21 September 2013)*, A. Nikoloska, S. Müskens (éd.). Skopje (2015): 167-211.

Covacef 2002: Covacef, Z., *Arta sculpturală în Dobrogea romană. Secolele I-III*. Cluj-Napoca (2002).

Cristea, Tecar 2010: Cristea, Ș., Tecar, T., "Isis și Serapis în epigrafia Daciei romane". Dans *Studia Archaeologica et Historica in honorem magistri Dorin Alicu*, V. Rusu-Bolindeț, T. Sălăgean, R. Varga (éd.). Cluj-Napoca (2010): 255-282.

Cumont 1896/1899: Cumont, F., *Textes et monuments figurés relatifs aux mystères de Mithra*. Bruxelles I (1899), II (1896).

C. Daicoviciu 1928-1932: Daicoviciu, C., "Contribuții la sincretismul religios în Sarmizegetusa". *AISC* I/1 (1928-1932): 81-88.

C. Daicoviciu 1966: Daicoviciu, C., "Severus Alexander și provincia Dacia". *Acta Musei Napocensis* 3 (1966): 153-171.

C. Daicoviciu 1970: Daicoviciu, C., *Dacica. Studii și articole privind istoria veche a pămîntului românesc*. Cluj (1970).

H. Daicoviciu et alii 1981: Daicoviciu, H., Alicu, D., Piso, I., Pop, C., Soroceanu, A., "Săpăturile din 1980 de la Ulpia Traiana Sarmizegetusa". *Materiale și Cercetări Arheologice. A XV-a sesiune anuală de rapoarte Brașov 1981*. București (1983): 246-277.

H. Daicoviciu et alii 1982: Daicoviciu, H., Alicu, D., Piso, I., Pop, C., Ilieș, C., Cociș, S., "Săpăturile arheologice din 1981 de la Ulpia Traiana Sarmizegetusa". *Materiale și Cercetări Arheologice. A XVI-a sesiune anuală de rapoarte Vaslui 1982*. București (1986): 121-134.

H. Daicoviciu et alii 1984: Daicoviciu, H., Piso, I., Alicu, D., Diaconescu, A., Opreanu, C., *Săpăturile arheologice de la Ulpia Traiana Sarmizegetusa din vara anului 1984*. ms. (1984).

H. Daicoviciu, Alicu 1984: Daicoviciu, H., Alicu, D., *Colonia Ulpia Traiana Augusta Dacica Sarmizegetusa*. Bucarest (1984).

Deac 2012: Deac, D., "Romanized Egyptian Gods from Porolissum". *Sargetia* (SN) 3 (2012): 159-174.

Deac 2013: Deac, D., *Prezența și influențele egiptene la Dunărea de Mijloc și de Jos : Provinciile pannonice, moesice și dacice (sec. I- IV e.n.)* (The Egyptian Influences and Presence at the Middle and Lower Danube : The Pannonian, Moesian and Dacian Provinces (1st-4th c. A.D.)). Diss. Cluj-Napoca (2013) ms.

Deac 2016: Deac, D., "Graffiti on Ceramic Medallions Depicting Isis and Sarapis from Roman Dacia". Dans *Mensa Rotunda Epigraphica Napocensis. Papers of the 4th Romanian-Hungarian epigraphic round table. Mensa rotunda epigraphiae Dacicae Pannonicaeque, Cluj-Napoca, 16-17 October 2015*, R. Ardevan, E. Beu-Dachin (éd.). Cluj-Napoca (2016): 59-70.

Deac 2017: Deac, D., "Shabtis and Pseudo-Shabtis from the Roman Provinces of Pannonia, Dacia and Moesia. An Overview". Dans *Egypt 2015. Perspectives of Research. Proceedings of the 7th European Conference of Egyptologists, 2nd-7th June, 2015, Zagreb, Croatia*, (Archaeopress Egyptology 18), M. Tomorad, J. Popielska-Grzybowska (éd.). Oxford (2017): 241-256.

Deac 2020: Deac, D., "A Terracotta Mold Depicting Sarapis from Micăsasa (Roman Dacia)". Dans *Bibliotheca Isiaca* IV, L. Bricault, R. Veymiers (éd.). Bordeaux (2020): 121-125.

Deac, Varga 2014: Deac, D., Varga, R., "Isiac Cults in the Settlements of Apulum (Dacia Apulensis)". Dans *Bibliotheca Isiaca* III, L. Bricault, R. Veymiers (éd.). Bordeaux (2014): 11-19.

Drexler 1890: Drexler, W., *Der Cultus der ägyptichen Gottheiten in der Donauländer*. Mythologische Beiträge I. Leipzig (1890).

Dunand 1973: Dunand, F., *Le culte d'Isis dans le bassin oriental de la Méditerranée. II. Le culte d'Isis en Grèce*. ÉPRO 26. Leiden (1973).

Dunand 2008 : Dunand, F., *Isis, mère des Dieux*. Paris (2008).

Eingartner 1991: Eingartner, J., *Isis und ihre Dienerinnen in der Kunst der römischen Kaiserzeit*. Leiden/New York/København/Köln (1991).

Floca 1935: Floca, O., "I culti orientali nella Dacia". *Ephemeris Dacoromana* 6 (1935): 204-249.

Gasparini 2014: Gasparini, V., "Les cultes isiaques et les pouvoirs locaux en Italie". Dans *Power, politics and the cults of Isis, Proceedings of the Vth International Conference of Isis Studies, Boulogne-sur-Mer, October 13-15 2011*, L. Bricault, M. J. Versluys (éd.). RGRW 180. Leiden (2014): 260-299.

Grimm 1974: Grimm, G., *Die römischen Mumienmasken aus Ägypten*. Wiesbaden (1974).

Haensch 1997: Haensch, R., *Capita provinciarum. Statthaltersitze und Provinzialverwaltung in der römischen Kaiserzeit*. Mainz (1997).

Hornbostel 1973: Hornbostel, W., *Sarapis. Studien zur Überlieferungsgeschichte, den Ercheinungsformen und Wandlungen der Gestalt eines Gottes*. ÉPRO 32. Leiden (1973).

Jones 1929: Jones, L. W., "The Cults of Dacia". *Classical Philology* 9/8. (1929): 245-305.

Kater-Sibbes 1973: Kater-Sibbes, G. J. F., *Preliminary Catalogue of Sarapis Monuments*. ÉPRO 36. Leiden (1973).

Kleibl 2007: Kleibl, K., "Water-crypts in Sanctuaries of Graeco-Egyptian Deities of the Graeco-Roman Period in the Mediterranean Region". Dans *Proceedings of the Fourth Central European Conference of Young Egyptologists, 31 August - 2 September 2006 Budapest*, K. Endreffy, A. Gulyás (éd.). Studia Aegyptiaca 18. Budapest (2007): 207-223.

Malaise 1972: Malaise, M., *Les conditions de pénétration et de diffusion des cultes égyptiens en Italie*. ÉPRO 22. Leiden (1972).

Malaise 1984: Malaise, M., "La diffusion des cultes égyptiens dans les provinces européennes de l'Empire romain". *ANRW* II.17/3 (1984): 1615-1691.

Malaise 2005: Malaise, M., *Pour une terminologie et une analyse des cultes isiaques*. Bruxelles (2005).

Mărghitan, Petolescu 1978: Mărghitan, L., Petolescu, C. C., "Les cultes orientaux à Micia". Dans *Hommages à Maarten J. Vermaseren*, M. B. de Boer, T. A. Edridge (éd.). ÉPRO 68-II. Leiden (1978): 718-731.

Michel 2004: Michel, S., *Die magischen Gemmen. Zu Bildern und Zauberformeln auf geschnittenen Steinen der Antike und Neuzeit*. Studien aus dem Warburg-Haus 7. Berlin (2004).

Mora 1990: Mora, F., *Prosopographia Isiaca I-II*. ÉPRO 113. Leiden / New York / København / Köln (1990).

Mráv 2013: Mráv, Z., "Catalogue items". Dans *A savariai Isis szentély. Sistrum Ser. A. No. 1*, O. Sosztarits, P. Balázs, A. Csapláros (éd.). Szombathely (2013).

Mráv 2016: Mráv, Z., "Considerations on the archaeological and natural contexts of cult places and sanctuaries in the Pannonian provinces". *Carnuntum Jahrbuch* (2016): 101-108.

Mráv 2016a: Mráv, Z., "The Gods of Alexandria". Dans *Saint Martin and Pannonia. Christianity on the Frontiers of the Roman World*, E. Tóth, T. Vida, I. Tákacs (éd.). Győr (2016): 29-34.

Mráv, Szabó 2016: Mráv, Z., Szabó, Á., "Aegyptiaca in the Hungarian National Museum. Exhibition in chamber gallery for the honour of the Vth Aegyptus et Pannonia symposium Lapidarium, 15th October – 31. December, 2008". Dans *Aegyptus et Pannonia 5. Acta Symposii anno 2008*, H. Győry, Á. Szabó (éd.). Budapest (2016): 117-148.

Müller et alii 2012: Müller, H., Piso, I., Schwaighofer, B., Benea, M., *Der Marmor im römischen Dakien*. Cluj-Napoca (2012).

Neigebaur 1851: Neigebaur, K. F., *Dacien. Aus den Ueberresten des klassischen Alterthums, mit besonderer Rücksicht auf Siebenbürgen*. Kronstadt (1851).

I. Nemeti 2005: Nemeti, I., "Osiris în Dacia". Dans *Antiquitas Istro-Pontica. Mélanges d'archéologie et d'histoire ancienne offerts à Alexandru Suceveanu*, M. V. Angelescu, I. Achim, A. Bâltâc, V. Rusu-Bolindeţ, V. Bottez (éd.). Cluj-Napoca (2005): 279-282.

S. Nemeti 2005: Nemeti, S., *Sincretismul religios în Dacia romană*. Cluj-Napoca (2005).

Nicolae 2012: Nicolae, M.-C., "Isiac Reliefs in Roman Dacia". *Marisia* 32 (2012): 127-133.

Opreanu 2016: Opreanu, C. H., "Relationship of temples of Deus Invictus Serapis at Sarmizegetusa and of Apollo at Tibiscum with Emperor Caracalla". *Studia Universitatis Babeş-Bolyai Journal. Historia* 61/1 (2016): 82-101.

Paulovics 1927: Paulovics, I., "Újabb synkretistikus bronzszobrocskák a Nemzeti Múzeumban". *ArchÉrt.* 41 (1927): 89-94.

Petolescu 1971: Petolescu, C. C., "Les cultes orientaux dans la Dacie inférieure", *Apulum* 9 (1971): 643-658.

Piso 1983: Piso, I., "Inschriften von Prokuratoren aus Sarmizegetusa (I)". *ZPE* 50 (1983): 233-251.

Piso 1993: Piso, I., *Fasti provinciae Daciae I. Die senatorischen Amtsträger*. Bonn (1993).

Piso 1993/1994: Piso, I., "Eine Parallele zwischen den praetoria der Statthalter in Carnutum und in Apulum". *Carnuntum Jahrbuch* (1993/1994): 203-209.

Piso 1995: Piso, I., "Le territoire de la colonia Sarmizegetusa". *EphNap* 5 (1995) : 63-82.

Piso 1998: Piso, I., "Inschriften von Prokuratoren aus Sarmizegetusa (II)". *ZPE* 120 (1998): 253-271.

Piso 2005: Piso, I., *An der Nordgrenze des Römischen Reiches. Ausgewählte Studien* (1972-2003). Stuttgart (2005).

Piso 2008: Piso, I., "Les débuts de la province de Dacie". Dans *Die römischen Provinzen. Begriff und Gründung, Colloquium Cluj-Napoca, 28. September – 1. Oktober 2006*, I. Piso (éd.). Cluj-Napoca (2008): 297-331.

Piso 2020a: Piso, I., "La grande inscription de l'Iseum de Savaria". Dans *Bibliotheca Isiaca* IV, L. Bricault, R. Veymiers (éd.). Bordeaux (2020): 139-142.

Piso 2020b: Piso, I., "Si defit aurum : l'initiation dans un Serapeum de Sarmizegetusa". Dans *Bibliotheca Isiaca* IV, L. Bricault, R. Veymiers (éd.). Bordeaux (2020): 127-137.

Piso, Deac 2018: Piso, I., Deac, D., "Eine neue kaiserliche Statuenbasis aus Buciumi und Caracallas Reise nach Dakien". Dans *Limes XXIII. Akten des 23. Internationalen Limeskongresses in Ingolstadt 2015*, C. S. Sommer, S. Matešić (éd.). Mainz (2018): 756-762.

Piso, Țentea 2011: Piso, I., Țentea, O., "Un nouveau temple palmyrénien à Sarmizegetusa". *Dacia* 55 (2011): 111-121.

Popa 1962: Popa, A., "O nouă inscripție închinată zeiței Isis la Apulum". *SCIV* 13/1 (1962): 147-152.

Popa 1979: Popa, A., *Cultele egiptene și microasiatice în Dacia romană*. Diss. Cluj-Napoca (1979): ms.

Popa 1983: Popa, A., "Câteva considerațiuni referitoare la divinitățile egiptene și microasiatice în epigrafia Daciei romane". *Apulum* 21 (1983): 71-80.

Popescu 1927: Popescu, D. O., *Le culte d'Isis et de Sérapis en Dacie*. Mélanges de l'École Roumaine en France. Paris (1927): 159-209.

Russu 1969: Russu, I. I., "Elementele syriene în Dacia Carpatică și rolul lor în "colonozarea" și romanizarea provinciei". *AMN* 6 (1969): 167-186.

Russu 1975: Russu, I. I., "Compte rendu de SIRIS". *AIIA* 18 (1975): 415-420.

Rusu Pescaru, Alicu 2000: Rusu Pecaru, A., Alicu, D., *Templele romane din Dacia (I)*. Deva (2000).

Sanie 1975: Sanie, S., "Quelques considérations sur les cultes gréco-égyptiens en Dacie romaine". Dans *Actes de la XIIᵉ Conférence Internationale d'Études Classiques Eirene, Cluj-Napoca 2-7 octobre 1972*. București/Amsterdam (1975): 529-537.

Sanie 2004: Sanie, S., "Cultele egiptene în Dacia romană". *Arheologia Moldovei* 27 (2004): 61-82.

Schäfer 2007: Schäfer, A., *Tempel und Kult in Sarmizegetusa. Eine Untersuchung zur Formierung religiöser Gemeinschaften in der Metropolis Dakiens*. Paderborn (2007).

Seeck 1914: Seeck, O., *RE* A1 (1914): 472-473. s. v. *Regina*.

Sosztarits et alii 2013: Sosztarits, O., Balázs, P., Csapláros, A., *A savariai Isis szentély*. Szombathely (2013).

Stein 1944: Stein, A., *Die Reichsbeamten von Dazien*. Budapest (1944).

Studnicka 1884: Studniczka, F., "Mithraeen und andere Denkmäler aus Dacien". *AEM* 8 (1884): 34-51.

Szabó 2018: Szabó, Cs., *Sanctuaries in Roman Dacia. Materiality and Religious Experience*. Archaeopress Roman Archaeology 49. Oxford (2018).

Szabó 2020: Szabó, Cs., "Sanctuaries of Roman Dacia. A Catalogue of Sacralised Places in Shared and Secondary Spaces". *JRGZ* 62 (2020): 255-340.

Tacheva-Hitova 1983: Tacheva-Hitova, M., *Eastern Cults in Moesia Inferior and Thrace (5ᵗʰ Century BC-4ᵗʰ Century AD)*. ÉPRO 95. Leiden (1983).

Takács 1995: Takács, S. A., *Isis and Sarapis in the Roman World*. RGRW 124. Leiden/New York/Köln (1995).

Teasley Trope et alii 2005: Teasley Trope, B., Quirke, S., Lacovara, P., *Excavating Egypt. Great Discoveries from the Petrie Museum of Egyptian Archaeology*. Atlanta (2005).

Téglás, Király 1890: Téglás, G., Király, P., "Neue Inschriften aus Dacien". *AEM* 13 (1890): 192-199.

Thomasson 1984: Thomasson, B. E., *Laterculi praesidum I*. Göteborg (1984).

Tocilesco 1900: Tocilesco, G., *Fouilles et recherches archéologiques en Roumanie. Communications faites à l'Académie des Inscriptions et Belles-Lettres de Paris, 1892-1899*. Bucarest (1900).

Tran tam Tinh 1983: Tran tam Tinh, V., *Sérapis debout. Corpus des monuments de Sérapis debout et étude iconographique*. ÉPRO 94. Leiden (1983).

Tudor 1957: Tudor, D., *Istoria sclavajului în Dacia romană*. București (1957).

Țeposu-David 1964: Țeposu-David, L., "O gemă de la Micia cu reprezentarea lui Harpocrate". *SCIVA* 15/2 (1964): 257-264.

Țeposu-Marinescu, Pop 2000: Țeposu-Marinescu, L., Pop, C., *Statuete de bronz din Dacia romană*. București (2000).

Veymiers 2020: Veymiers, R., "Ἴλεως τῷ φοροῦντι. Sérapis sur les gemmes et les bijoux antiques. Supplément III". Dans *Bibliotheca Isiaca* IV. L. Bricault, R. Veymiers (éd.). Bordeaux (2020): 307-342.

Vidman 1970: Vidman, L., *Isis und Sarapis bei den Griechen und Römern. Epigraphische Studien zur Verbreitung und zu den Trägern des ägyptischen Kultes*. Religionsgeschichtliche Versuche und Vorarbeiten XXIX. Berlin (1970).

Vidman 1989: Vidman, L., „Der ägyptische Kult in den Donauprovinzen". *ANRW* II.18/2 (1989): 976-1013.

Wild 1981: Wild, R. A., *Water in the Cultic Worship of Isis and Sarapis*. ÉPRO 87. Leiden (1981).

8

Egypt on the Danube. Egyptianizing the Material Agency of Roman Religious Communication in Western Illyricum

Csaba Szabó

(Research fellow, Department of Religious Studies, University of Szeged)

Abstract: Currently, Romanisation is interpreted as an interaction of material and human agency in an intra-connected world, where materiality played a key role in creating, maintaining and re-creating sacred spaces, but also local and global identities in the Roman Empire. One of the identities shaped by material agency was the Egyptianism(s), represented by the Isiac groups. This paper focuses upon the notion of Egyptianism(s), the mobility of Egyptianized objects, and the religious communication of the small group religions in the western part of the *Publicum Portorium Illyrici*, a major economic and cultural unit of the empire. The paper discusses Egyptianism(s) in the broader context of exoticism within the Roman Empire, used as cultural identity-marker for African cults and groups.

Keywords: Egyptianism(s), material agency, *Publicum Portorii Illyrici*, cultural identity

In the last decade, the number of studies focusing upon the Egyptian cults during the Principate and the cultural, economic, social, and religious relationship between Roman Egypt and the rest of the empire has increased significantly.[100] Since the dogmatic work of Franz Cumont on Oriental cults and religions, studies have introduced a variety of terminologies and approaches aimed at better understanding the cults associated with Egypt, as a geographic, mythological, and politico-administrative area.[101] Descriptive and paradigmatic concepts, as well as modern empty signifiers, such as the "mystery cults", Isiac cults ("isacology", etudes isiaque), "Alexandrian cults", "Romanising Oriental cults" or, more recently, "Orientalising Roman cults", emphasize aspects of the new gods and religious transformations, related to the historical territory and the memory of Egypt, which appeared between the 1st century BC and the 2nd century AD.[102] The abundance of literature on this phenomenon, can be compared only to studies of the cult of Mithras.[103] These modern notions have a common feature: they try to emphasize a single particularity or specificity of numerous gods, cults, agents of religious communication, most commonly their geographic origins, or the central divine agent. They emphasize the geographic and cultural "otherness" of these cults. Therefore, modern notions are little more than sophisticated intellectualisms in contemporary historiographic narratives, which often attempt to translate ancient religious communication into a modern one.[104]

More recently, the focus of scholarship on the Eastern divinities and their materiality has shifted from the divine agents to a quest for new questions and answers pertaining to the human and material agency of Roman religious communication, local appropriations, sense-scapes, space sacralisation, and embodiment.[105] New studies, which still focus on the "otherness" of these cults, use the notion of "Egyptianized materiality" as agents in Roman religious communication in the 1st century BC. Eva Mol, analysing the role of agency and this type of taxonomy of objects, argued that "in order to evaluate object agency – i.e., how objects shape our minds and influence Roman history – it is useful to analyse the emergence of mental classification and categorizations. Classifications or taxonomies are cultural constructs made to describe the external world, and are at the same time influenced by the world itself, in a process also called 'ecological hermeneutics. Although classifications are perceived as static bounded entities (otherwise they would not function), in effect they are a continuously changing network of links. As classifications are used to understand the world, exploring their dynamics and the influence of form and matter on this process is able to inform both about existing and changing worldviews."[106]

Similar to Persianism as a cultural agent that made the Roman cult of Mithras more attractive, exotic, and unusual

---

[100] The most detailed bibliography is Bibliotheca Isiaca I-IV. On the issues and paradigms of scholarship, see: Leclant 2000; Bricault 2000; Bricault, Bonnet 2013; Bricault 2015.

[101] Versluys 2010.

[102] Alvar 2008; Versluys 2013. For a detailed chronology of the diffusion and typology of Egyptianisms, see: Tomorad 2016; Gasparini, Gordon 2018.

[103] Gordon 2007; Belayche, Mastrocinque 2013; Mastrocinque 2017. See also: Szabó 2018a.

[104] Versluys 2018, 230-232. For a detailed discussion on archaeological imaginaries of ancient religions, see: Meier, Tillesen 2014.

[105] On the Isiac cults from the perspective of the Lived Ancient Religion approach, see: Gasparini 2016; Rüpke 2018, 264-272; Veymiers 2018. See also: Albrecht et al. 2018.

[106] Mol 2017, 171.

during the process of religious grouping,[107] Egyptianism represents a cultural agent and religious bricolage, that was used consciously by the first religious providers of new cults beginning in the Hellenistic period and, especially, the Principate to establish those small group religions which we label today as "Isiac cults", "Egyptian cults", etc.[108]

Egyptianism, in this sense, can be integrated within the Lived Ancient Religion approach as an important facet of religious competence, termed by J. Rüpke as religious agency.[109] Egyptianism, as agency in establishing and maintaining the success of sacred places in primary, secondary, and public spaces,[110] was used in numerous strategies by religious providers (priests): avoidance of magical practices,[111] Egyptian behaviour (the spectacular and ecstatic aspects of the Isiac cults),[112] and a specific material agency, previously termed *Aegyptiaca Romana* or, more recently, "Egyptianized materiality".[113]

Egyptianism(s) in the Danubian provinces

The Danubian provinces, as a notion, is a modern historiographic construct from the 18th-19th century,[114] marking the territory of the *Publicum Portorii Illyrici,* often presented as the Lower and Upper Danubian provinces, Illyricum, and Großillyricum.[115] The arrival and spread of the Isiac cults in this area of the empire occurred during the Flavian, Antonine, and Severan periods,[116] and it also has specific, regional aspects.[117] Most studies focusing on the Isiac cults in this region present archaeological evidence in the light of classical, art-historical, and descriptive methodologies.[118] A reinterpretation of Egyptianized materiality of Roman religion through the methodology of religious studies is crucial for current scholarship.[119] This section examines particular cases from the western part of the Danubian provinces (*Illyricum*), in order to elucidate the role of agency in the Egyptianized materiality of Roman religion in space sacralisation and religious communication.

An appropriation of religion occurred between the 1st century BC and the first half of the 1st century AD in the *Regnum Noricum*. Due to the Amber Route and the intensification of Rome's military and economic presence in the late Republican period, the eastern part of the *Regnum Noricum* was in a living contact with the region of the Po.[120] The intense material connectivity along the Aquileia-Emona-Magdalensberg road is reflected not only in the ceramic and terracotta material, but also in the materiality of religious communication.[121] As I. Tóth highlighted, the Egyptianized material of Roman religion probably appeared in two waves in Illyria. The first phase occurred during the late Republican period due to the presence of religious entrepreneurs and providers whose influence was probably less significant and could not maintain the first religious groups in the long term.[122] The second wave was much more successful, reflecting the strong economic relationship between Noricum and Pannonia with the Po region, primarily in the area of the Amber Road. The mobility of some prominent Aquileian families and the rich economic bonds between Noreia and Aquileia mentioned by Pliny and Strabo suggest to some scholars that the introduction of Isis Noreia occurred in the late 1st century BC. This thesis was proposed by H. Kenner, based upon an analysis of the Roman bronzes from Magdalensberg and the cultural interaction between Delos, Aquielia, and Noricum.[123]

The reinterpretation of the iconography of Isis-Noreia by Julia Polleres[124] and the analysis of the archaeological context of the epigraphic and iconographic material from Hohenstein and the Frauenberg shrine[125] suggest that the hypothesis proposed by Kenner and Tóth is not plausible. Based upon the sporadic literary, iconographic, and epigraphic sources, it is difficult to reconstruct when and how the divine agency of Isis Noreia was formed; however, the association of an exotic, Egyptianized divinity with the most important female divinity of the Norican Kingdom demonstrates the influence of religious entrepreneurs and the popularity of Isis. How much Egyptianism, as an attractive feature in Roman religious communication, played in this story is hard to tell, especially given the lack of certain iconographic elements in the features of Isis Noreia. The recently suggested Middle and Neoplatonic phase of Egyptianism during the Principate, which promoted an exotic façade of "Egyptian wisdom", can be interpreted as a reinvented religious tradition by the Roman elite, often associated in local contexts with pre-Roman female divinities.[126]

Egyptianized materiality and other Egyptianisms, such as Egyptian behaviour (spectacles and Isiac festivals), played a much more important role after the Marcommanic Wars.[127] As a turning point in Roman religious communication too, the Marcommanic Wars

---

[107] Gordon 2017a.

[108] On the formation of small group religions during the Principate, see: Rebillard, Rüpke 2015; Lichterman et al. 2017. On the notion of religious bricolage and exoticism, see: Altglas 2014.

[109] Rüpke 2018, 11-13. See also: Gasparini, Gordon 2018, 578-587.

[110] On space sacralisation, see: Szabó 2018b, 2-5.

[111] Gordon, Gasparini 2014.

[112] Gasparini 2018.

[113] Mol 2017; Versluys 2018, Gasparini, Gordon 2018, 587-603.

[114] Alföldy 2004; Szabó 2018c, 480.

[115] Szabó 2020.

[116] Tóth 2015.

[117] See the studies of Bricault/Deac/Piso and Ruscu in this volume.

[118] The best introduction to the material from this area of the Empire is still the *RICIS* and the *Atlas* established by L. Bricault: Bricault 2001. See also: *http://ricis.huma-num.fr/carte.html.*

[119] Szabó 2018c.

[120] Tóth 2015, 27.

[121] Tóth 2015, 29-30.

[122] Kenner 1958, 57; Tóth 2015, 44.

[123] Kenner 1958.

[124] Polleres 2007.

[125] Schrettle 2012; Schrettle 2016, 192.

[126] Gasparini, Gordon 2018, 585-586.

[127] Tóth 1976. See also: Kovács 2017.

(e.g., Arnuphis and the rain miracle)[128] and the Antonine Plague helped these exoticisms to flourish in the religious narratives and visual languages of small group religions in the late 2nd century AD.[129] The last phase of the temple of Isis Noreia in Hohenstein and the rich Egyptianized material evidence from Celeia shows that objects imported directly from Egypt played an important role in maintaining these sacred spaces. The small religious groups, mostly in urban environments, where the visibility and competition of religious groups was much stronger.[130] Bronze statuettes of Egyptian divinities have been found at Lauriacum, Hallstatt, Seewalchen, Lentia, Celeia, and Steyr.[131] Faïence amulets with Egyptian divinities were discovered in Zeiselmauer.[132]

The provinces of Pannoniae are also very rich in Egyptianized material.[133] Since the systematic excavation of the Iseum of Savaria, the study of the Isiac cults has changed its focus too **(Fig. 8.1)**.[134] The paradigmatic work of István Tóth from 2005 (published posthumously in 2015) highlighted the importance of the correlation between the literary and archaeological sources.[135] Tóth tried to reconstruct the major elements of Roman religious communication within the sacred space of the Iseum of Savaria based on the text of Apuleius.[136] Although his interpretation was probably too textual,[137] his study illustrated the importance of Egyptianisms as exotic elements in the successful maintenance of a sacred space and their religious providers. The Iseum of Savaria has a rich Egyptianized materiality used during indoor and outdoor religious festivals and processions, creating and maintaining a specific sense-scape, which downplayed the exoticism of the sacred place. The well-excavated sanctuary and its rich archaeological material need to be analysed in the future from the perspective of the Lived Ancient Religion approach, with a focus on the role of agency of materiality in religious communication, the archaeology of Isea, and the exoticism of the objects.[138]

Pannonia provides splendid examples of Egyptianisms **(Fig. 8.2)**. Imported objects directly from Egypt (the most beautiful example being the vases from Egyed),[139] pseudo-hieroglyphic objects,[140] bronze statuettes used as votive offerings or religious souvenirs, musical instruments evoking a specific Egyptianized soundscape,[141] architectural features evoking and reconstructing the landscape and geography of Egypt (or the memory of it), natural elements – such as the Nile's water,[142] springs, specific vestments of the religious providers, vegetal motifs on wall paintings, and Egyptianized theophoric personal names are just a few of the exotic elements that played a role in the Egyptianized façade of these cults.

The case of Savaria and the Isiac sanctuaries on the Amber Road were not only local sanctuaries. In fact, they became regional destinations for pilgrimage.[143] Economic mobility and urbanism played an essential role in the dynamism of small group religions. The case of the Aquileian families from Noricum and Pannonia and the case of Salona highlights the importance of the merchants and the staff of the *Publicum Portorii Illyrici* in the maintenance of these small group religions.

In Salona, two types of Egyptianized materials are well documented: bronze statuettes imported from Egypt and ushebti (shabti) statuettes.[144] These miniature or small statuettes from Salona were, unfortunately, recovered from undocumented contexts. Some of them were part of the Carrara-Bratanic-Marovic collection, others are labelled as "from Split" or "from Dalmatia". Many of them date to the Late Ptolemaic period, but there are also Roman copies (suggested by Petar Selem). A more detailed analysis of the older, 18-19th century, literature might help to understand the provenance of the unusually large number of these objects. Selem presumed that these Egyptianized objects indicate the presence of an ethnic Egyptian community. Viewing these objects, such as the small statuettes of Artemis Ephesia, as ethnic markers or agents of religious individuation was recently proposed by Ias Elsner.[145] A small number of these objects, unearthed in documented contexts, shows that they were not necessarily used in domestic contexts, but were mobile objects, probably serving as religious souvenirs from a regional pilgrimage site.

Objects termed as Egyptianized materiality of Roman religious communication clearly played an important role in attracting human agents and to maintain the exotic façade of these small group religions.[146] Similarly, exotic features as religious agents and strategies of communication with divine agents contributed toward the successful creation and maintenance of the Isiac or Egyptianized cults during the Principate.[147] Some of these cults, such as those of Isis and Mithras, may have even competed with the larger urban centres.[148]

---

[128] AÉ 1934, 245.

[129] Jones 2005; Tóth 2015, 116.

[130] Scherrer 2007; Lazar 2011.

[131] Fleischer 1967, 136.

[132] Alföldy 1974, 342, footnote nr. 209.

[133] Mráv 2016.

[134] Sosztarits et al. 2013. See also: Sosztarits 1998; Gabler 2015.

[135] Tóth 2015. For a detailed review, see: Szabó 2018d.

[136] Tóth 2001; Hódi 2012.

[137] Tóth 2015, 134. The texts do not always correspond with the archaeological material; for example, his *ad literam* interpretation of the *ex visu* inscription from Siscia.

[138] Andringa 2018; Gasparini, Gordon 2018.

[139] Mráv, Giumlia-Mair 2014.

[140] Tóth 2015, 30 and 145.

[141] Sosztarits et al. 2013.

[142] Sosztarits 2013.

[143] For the Scarbantia Iseum see: Mráv, Gabrieli 2011.

[144] For the most recent catalogue of finds, see: ROMIS.

[145] Elsner 2007, 229-231. See also: Szabó et al. 2016, 232-233.

[146] On the maintenance of small group religions, see: Gordon 2017b.

[147] Lichtermann et al. 2017. See also: Beck 1996 on the formation of small group religions.

[148] In Savaria the mithraeum was recently identified, but it had less of a relationship with the Iseum compared to the Dolichenum from Savaria: Kiss 2011.

Fig. 8.1. The Iseum of Savaria (photo by the author in November 2012).

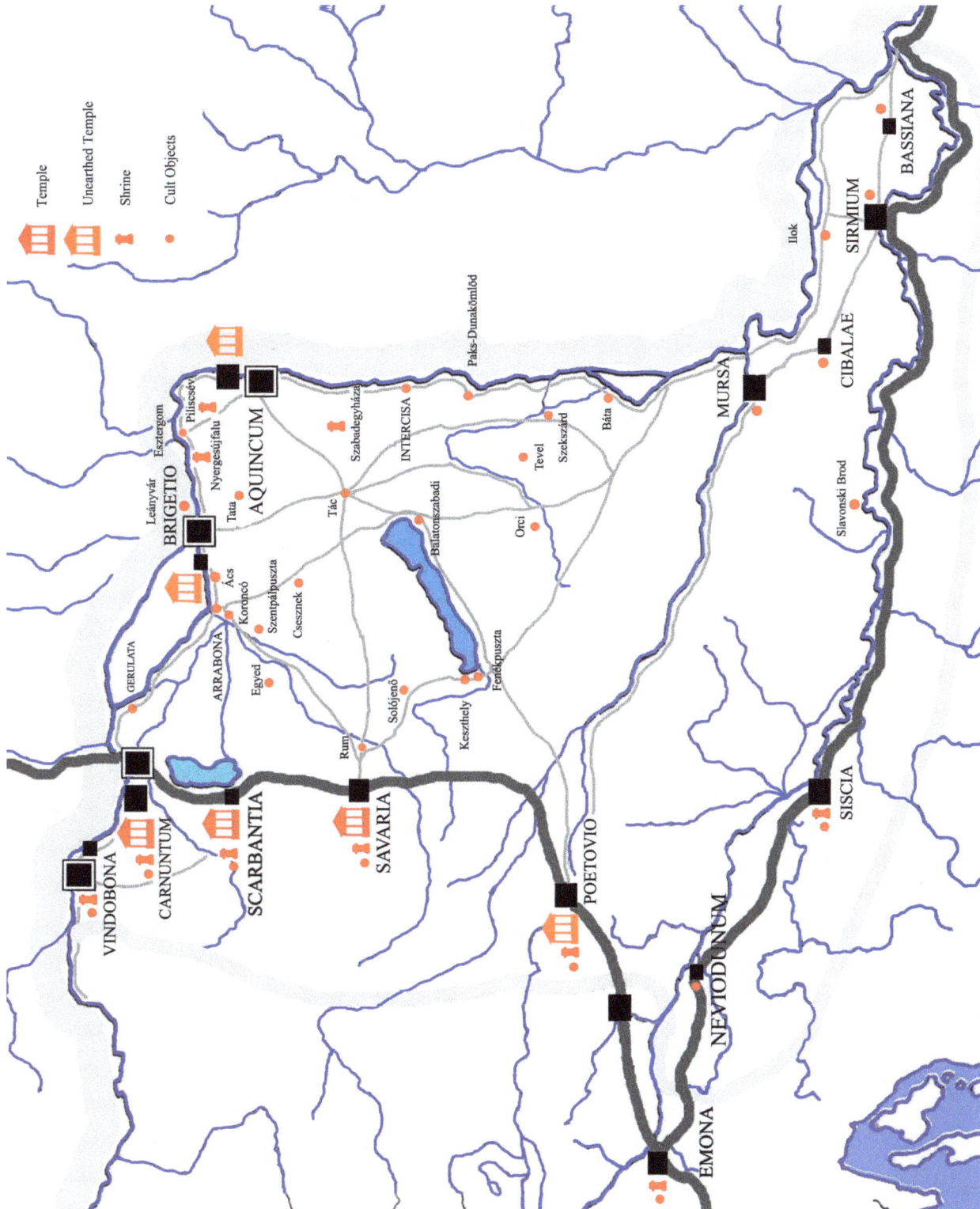

Fig. 8.2. The Egyptian Gods in Pannonia (after Zsolt Mráv).

The "Africanism" of Roman Egypt: varieties of exoticisms

My last question concerns the Africanism of the Egyptianized cults: how much, if at all, were Isis, Serapis, Osiris, and other divinities considered African? How much was Egypt, itself, "African" during the Principate?

The Africanism of Egypt is not a self-evident notion today. The modern semantic network of Egypt does not contain the notion of Africa.[149] The modern state of Egypt, as a prominent member of Pan-Africanism, only became part of contemporary political and cultural narratives in the last few decades.[150] The association of the word Africa with "black Africa" as an ethnic or cultural marker is a result of ancient and modern colonialism. Cultural elements from central and southern Africa were already considered exotic and odd during the reign of Pepi II, a perspective that continued into the Ptolemaic period.[151] Even the 25th Dynasty from Meroe is considered "unusual" or "non-Egyptian" by contemporary historians.[152]

To understand the possible Africanism of ancient Egypt as a geographic and cultural space, we need to rely upon literary sources from Republican and Imperial times. First, the geographic treatises of antiquity interpret Egypt as a part of the same land as Aethiopia and Libya. Strabo, in his Geography (book XVI, chapter 4), claims that: *Since, in my description of Arabia, I have also included the gulfs which pinch it and make it a peninsula, I mean the Persian and Arabian Gulfs, and at the same time have gone the rounds of certain parts both of Aegypt and of Aethiopia, I mean the countries of the Troglodytes and the peoples situated in order thereafter as far as the Cinnamon-bearing country, I must now set forth the remaining parts that are continuous with these tribes, that is, the parts in the neighbourhood of the Nile; and after this I shall traverse Libya, which is the last remaining subject of my whole geography.[153]* In one of his epistles, Seneca speaks about Egypt as bordering the sands of Africa, but still interprets them as two different cultural entities (ep. moral. 115.26: *Aegyptiis harenis sive ex Africae solitudinibus advectae*).[154] Columella also considers Egypt as a different area from Africa (De Re Rustica II.11: *sunt enim regionum propria munera, sicut Aegypti et Africae*).[155] Sallust even identifies the border between Africa and Egypt (Iug. 19.3: *ad Catabathmon, qui locus Aegyptum ab Africa dividit*).[156] The literary sources also emphasize the anthropological differences between Africans and Egyptians. Africanism (in linguistics *Africitas*), however, remained a similar exotic element, often used together with Egypt in literary analogies.

The case of Africa is best described by Apuleius, when he focuses upon local appropriations of the *Africitas*.[157] Apuleius, in contrast with Plutarch, presents Isis and Egypt, not as a Greek or Hellenistic cultural transfer, but as having an ancient, foreign, and mystical heritage, emphasizing the exotic Egyptianism of the Isiac cults. In Apuleius' work, the *Africitas* of Egypt is already present and is probably related to his personal background. We can easily observe in his work the intensification of cultural exchanges between the Punic, Libyan, and Egyptian religions in North Africa. This phenomenon, as far as I know, was not transported beyond this region; therefore, we cannot really speak about an African Egyptianism in the Danubian provinces. A particular example of the cohesion of African and Egyptian culture under Roman rule is the great tomb in the necropolis of Ghirza. The monument is an extraordinary example of cross-cultural dialects of Libyan, Egyptian, Roman, and Punic art and architecture.[158] These cultural transfers and appropriations occurred naturally in North Africa during the Hellenistic and Roman periods, but outside the continent, they were used as exotic tools and agents in human or human-divine communication strategies.

Final remarks

Egyptianism, similar to other ancient exoticisms, such as Persianism or Africanism, became an important cultural and religious marker, an agent in religious communication which not only contributed toward the creation of a small religious group, but also maintained the sacred spaces of these groups for more than a generation.[159] Interpreting the materiality of Isiac cults from this perspective in the western part of Illyricum, the traditional notions and contemporary denominations marking geographic units and entities (e.g., Egyptian cults or Alexandrian cults) or exclusive divine agents (e.g., the Isis-Serapis cult) can be replaced by a more complex approach to Roman religion, where exotic materiality, texts, narratives, and visual languages are used as tools and agents in group formation, space sacralisation, and other facets of Roman religious communication. From this point of view, Egyptianism is not only a cultural and geographic marker, two elements whose importance was always present in Roman antiquity, but also a successful religious agent. Analysing them in the context of the Danubian provinces, an area of the empire which was radically different climatically, culturally, and geographically, opens new avenues of research. An interesting concept in the maintenance of small group religions in the Danubian provinces is the religious interference and intra-connectivity between exoticisms: how Persianism alternated with Egyptianism, or when and

[149] Mol 2017, 175.
[150] Tawfik 2016.
[151] Kozma 2010, 274-275.
[152] Redford 2004.
[153] Strabo, *Geography*. English translation, Loeb Classical Library volume VII, 1932. Public Domain: http://penelope.uchicago.edu/Thayer/E/Roman/Texts/Strabo/home.
[154] Reynolds 1965, 115.
[155] Schneider 1828, 476.
[156] Richardson 2008, 98.
[157] Mattiacci 2014.
[158] Selden 2014, 223-225.
[159] Altglas 2014 as a vivid introduction in religious exoticism, as tool in religious communication.

where Africanism also became Egyptianism. Moreover, how can we prove these temporary or flexible cultural identities in individual case studies?

Studying Roman religion today means focusing on individual agency,[160] facets or religious communication,[161] strategies in the sacralisation of space,[162] and, less prominently, the role of materiality of religion in communication and ritualisation.[163] Other important topics, however, such as belief, divine agency, and polis religion, seem to be marginalized.[164]

Exoticisms, as tools and even agents in religious communication, played an important role not only in creating small religious groups and sacred spaces, but also in constantly shaping the visual representation of gods, divine agents, and their nature, indirectly influencing the very personal beliefs of ancient people. [165]

Ancient Sources

Strabo, Geography: *Loeb Classical Library*, 8 volumes (Greek texts with facing English translation by H. L. Jones). Harvard (1917 thru 1932).

Bibliography

Albrecht et al. 2018: J. Albrecht, Ch. Degelmann, V. Gasparini, R. Gordon, M. Patzelt, G. Petridou, R. Raja, A. K. Rieger, J. Rüpke, A. Sippel, E. R. Urciuoli, L. Weiss, *Religion in the making: the Lived Ancient Religion approach*, Religion Journal. Open Access: https://doi.org/10.1080/0048721X.2018.1450305.

Alföldy 1974: G. Alföldy, *Noricum*. London (1974).

Alföldy 2004: G. Alföldy, „Die 'illyrischen' Provinzen Roms: von der Vielfalt zu der Einheit". In *Dall'Adriatico al Danubio. L'Illirico nell'età greca e romana. Atti del convegno internazionale Cividale del Friuli, 25-27 settembre 2003 (I Convegni della Fondazione Niccolò Canussio 3)*, G. Urso (ed.). Pisa (2004): 207-220.

Altglas 2014: V. Altglas, *From Yoga to Kabbalah: Religious Exoticism and the Logics of Bricolage*. Oxford (2014).

Alvar 2008; J. Alvar, *Romanising oriental gods: Myth, salvation and ethics in the cults of Cybele, Isis and Mithras*. Leiden/Boston (2008).

Andringa 2018: W. von Andringa, "Archéologie des Isea: sur la difficile reconnaissance des pratiques isiaques". In *Individuals and Materials in the Greco-Roman Cults of Isis. Agents, Images and Practices. Proceedings of the VIth International Conference of Isis Studies (Erfurt, May 6-8 – Liège, September 23-24, 2013)*, V. Gasparini, R. Veymiers (eds.). RGRW 187, vol. II. Leiden/Boston (2018): 571-583.

Beck 1996: R. Beck, „The mysteries of Mithras". In *Voluntary Associations in the Ancient World*, J. Kloppenborg, G. Wilson (eds.). London (1996): 176-185.

Belayche, Mastrocinque 2013: N. Belayche, A. Mastrocinque (eds.), *Reédition critique a Franz Cumont, Les Mystéres á Mithra*. Bibliotheca Cumontiana, Scripta Maiora 3. Rome (2013).

Bricault 2000: L. Bricault, "Études isiaques: perspectives". In *De Memphis a Rome. Actes du Ier Colloque International sur les etudes isiaques Poitiers-Futuroscope, 8-10 avril 1999*, L. Bricault (ed.). Leiden/Boston/New York (2000): 189-210.

Bricault 2001: L. Bricault, *Atlas de la diffusion des cultes isiaques*. Paris (2001).

Bricault, Bonnet 2013: L. Bricault, C. Bonnet (eds.), *Panthée: Religious Transformations in the Graeco-Roman Empire*. Leiden/Boston (2013).

Bricault 2015: L. Bricault, "Cultes orientaux, égyptiens, alexandrins, osiriens, isiaques…: identités plurielles et interpretationes variae". In *Romanising Oriental Gods? Religious transformations in the Balkan provinces in the Roman period. New finds and novel perspectives*, S. Müskens, A. Nikolovska (eds.). Skopje (2015): 19-33.

Elsner 2007: I. Elsner, *Roman Eyes: Visuality and Subjectivity in Art and Text*. Princeton (2007).

Fleischer 1967: R. Fleischer, *Die römischen Bronzen aus Österreich*. Mainz (1967).

Gabler 2015: D. Gabler, "Le questioni cronologiche del tempio di Iside a Savaria". In *Culti e Religiosità nelle Province Danubiane*, L. Zerbini (ed.). Bologna (2015): 247-266.

Gasparini 2016: V. Gasparini, "Listening stones. Cultural appropriation, resonance, and memory in the Isiac cults". In *Vestigia. Miscellanea di studi storico-religiosi in onore di Filippo Coarelli nel suo 80° anniversario (PAwB LV)*, V. Gasparini (ed.). Stuttgart (2016): 555-574.

Gasparini 2018: V. Gasparini, "Les acteurs sur scène. Théâtre et théâtralisation dans les cultes isiaques". In *Individuals and Materials in the Greco-Roman Cults of Isis. Agents, Images and Practices*, V. Gasparini, R. Veymiers (eds.). RGRW 187, vol. II. Leiden/Boston (2017): 714-746.

Gasparini, Gordon 2018: V. Gasparini, R. Gordon, „Egyptianism Appropriating 'Egypt' in the 'Isiac Cults' of the Graeco-Roman World", *Acta Antiqua Academiae Scientiarum Hungaricae*, 58 /1-4. 2018: 571-606.

---

[160] Rüpke 2015.
[161] Rüpke 2018.
[162] Szabó 2018a.
[163] Raja, Rüpke 2015. See also: Meier, Tillesen 2014.
[164] Bremmer 2018.
[165] This study was supported by the Postdoctoral Research Grant PD NKFI-8 nr. 127948 by the National Research, Development and Innovation Office of Hungary (2018-2021). See also the Digital Atlas of Sanctuaries in the Danubian provinces: *https://danubianreligion.com/atlas-of-roman-sanctuaries-in-the-danubian-provinces/*.

Gordon 2007: R. Gordon, „Institutionalised religious options: Mithraism". In *The Companion of Roman Religion*, J. Rüpke (ed.). Oxford (2007): 392-405.

Gordon, Gasparini 2014: R. Gordon, V. Gasparini, "Looking for Isis 'the Magician' (ḥkȝy.t) in the Graeco-Roman World". In *Bibliotheca Isiaca III*, L. Bricault, R. Veymiers (eds.). Bordeaux (2014): 39-53.

Gordon 2017a: R. Gordon, „Persae in spelaeis Solem colunt: Mithra(s) between Persia and Rome". In *Persianism in Antiquity*, R. Strootman, M. J. Versluys (eds.). Stuttgart (2017): 289-326.

Gordon 2017b: R. Gordon, „Projects, performance and charisma: Managing small religious groups in the Roman Empire". In *Beyond Priesthood: Interacting with Religious Professionals and Appropropriating Traditions in the Imperial Period*, R. Gordon, G. Petridou, J. Rüpke (eds.). Berlin (2017): 277-316.

Hódi 2012: A. Hódi, "Apuleius Savariensis II", *Ókor* 4. 2012: 63-68.

Jones 2005: C. P. Jones, "Ten dedications 'To the gods and goddesses' and the Antonine Plague". *Journal of Roman Archaeology* 18. 2005: 293-301.

Kenner 1958: H. Kenner, „Die Götterwelt der Austria Romana". *JÖAI* 43. 1958: 57–100.

Kiss 2011: P. Kiss, "Mithras altäre aus Savaria". In *Religion in public and private sphere. Acts of the 4ᵗʰ International Colloquium The Autonomous Towns of Noricum and Pannonia*, I. Lazar (ed.). Koper (2011): 183-192.

Kovács 2017: P. Kovács, "Marcus Aurelius' rain miracle: when and where?". *Študijné zvesti Archeologického ústavu* 62. 2017: 101-111.

Kozma 2010: Ch. Kozma, "Genetic disorders in Ancient Egypt". In *Genetic Disorders Among Arab Populations*, A. Teebi, (ed.). New York (2010): 273-296.

Lazar 2011: I. Lazar, "The World of Gods and Religious Life in Roman Celeia". In *Religion in public and private sphere. Acts of the 4ᵗʰ International Colloquium The Autonomous Towns of Noricum and Pannonia*, I. Lazar (ed.). Koper (2011): 23-38.

Leclant 2000: J. Leclant, "40 ans d'études isiaques : un bilan". In *De Memphis a Rome. Actes du Ier Colloque International sur les etudes isiaques Poitiers-Futuroscope, 8-10 avril 1999*, L. Bricault (ed.). Leiden/Boston/New York (2000): 19-25.

Lichterman et al. 2017: P. Lichterman, R. Raja, A. K. Rieger, J. Rüpke, „Grouping Together in Lived Ancient Religion", *Religion in the Roman Empire* 3/1. 2017: 3–10.

Mastrocinque 2017: A. Mastrocinque, *The mysteries of Mithras. A different account.* Tübingen (2017).

Mattiacci 2014: S. Mattiacci, "Apuleius and Africitas". In *Apuleius and Africa*, B.T. Lee, E. Finkelpearl, L. Graverini (eds.). New York/London (2014): 87-111.

Meier, Tillesen 2014: Th. Meier, P. Tillessen, "Archaeological imaginations of religion: an introduction from an Anglo-German perspective". In *Archaeological imaginations of religion*, Th. Meier, P. Tillessen (eds.). Budapest (2014): 11-247.

Mol 2017: E. Mol, "Object ontology and cultural taxonomies. Examining the agency of style, material and objects in classification through Egyptian material culture in Pompeii and Rome". In *Materialising Roman Histories*, A. Van Oyen, M. Pitts (eds.). Oxford (2017): 169-190.

Mráv 2016: Zs. Mráv, The "Alexandrian Gods". In *Saint Martin and Pannonia. Christianity on the frontiers of the Roman World*, E. Tóth, T. Vida, I. Takács (eds.). Szombathely (2016): 29-34.

Mráv, Gabrieli 2011: Zs. Mráv, G. Gabrieli, „A scarbantiai Iseum és feliratos kőemlékei (The Iseum of Scarbantia and its inscriptions)". *Arrabona* 49/1. 2011: 201-238.

Mráv, Giulia-Mair 2014: Zs. Mráv, A. Giulia-Mair, "The aes Corinthium vessels from Egyed, Hungary". *Folia Archaeologica* 56. 2014: 73-102.

Mráv, Szabó 2016: Zs. Mráv, A. Szabó, "Aegyptiaca in the Hungarian National Museum. Exhibition in chamber gallery for the honour of the Vth. Aegyptus et Pannonia symposium Lapidarium, 15th October – 31. December 2008". *Aegyptus et Pannonia V. Acta Symposii anno 2008.* Budapest (2016).

Polleres 2007: J. Polleres, „Isis-Noreia. Ägiptisch-einheimischer Synkretismus in der Provinz Noricum". In *Götterwelten. Tempel-Riten-Religionen in Noricum*, H. Dolenz, F. Leitner (eds.). Klagenfurt (2007): 61-66.

Rebillard, Rüpke 2015: E. Rebillard, J. Rüpke, "Introduction: groups, individuals and religious identity". In *Group Identity and Religious Individuality in Late Antiquity*, E. Rebillard, J. Rüpke (eds.). Washington (2015): 1-13.

Redford 2004: D. Redford, *From Slave to Pharaoh: The Black Experience of Ancient Egypt.* Baltimore (2004).

Reynolds 1965: Seneca, *Ad Lucilium Epistulae Morales*, Translation and comments: L. D. Reynolds. Oxford (1965).

Richardson 2008: J. Richardson, *The Language of Empire: Rome and the Idea of Empire from the Third Century BC to the Second Century AD.* Cambridge (2008).

Rüpke 2015: J. Rüpke, „Individual choices and individuality in the archaeology of religion". In *A Companion to the Archaeology of Religion in the ancient World*, R. Raja, J. Rüpke (eds.). Leiden/Boston (2015): 437-451.

Rüpke 2018: J. Rüpke, *Pantheon. A new history of Roman religion.* Princeton (2018).

Scherrer 2007: P. Scherrer, „Noreia - Prähistorisch-gallorömische Muttergottheit oder Provinzpersonifikation". In *Auf den Spuren keltischer Götterverehrung: Akten des 5. F.E.R.C.AN.-Workshop, Graz 9.-12. Oktober 2003*, M. Hainzmann (ed.). Wien (2007): 207-241.

Schneider 1828: J. G. Schneider (ed.), *Scriptores Rei Rusticae.* Augustae Taurinorum (1828).

Schrettle 2012: B. Schrettle, „Walter Modrijans Ausgrabung im Tempelbezirk auf dem Frauenberg und das so genannte Heiligtum der Isis Noreia". *Schild von Steier* 25. 2012: 144-153.

Schrettle 2016: B. Schrettle, „Das Heiligtum Frauenberg. Vom latènezeitlichen Zentralort zum kaiserzeitlichen Zempelberg". In *Zentralort und Tempelberg. Siedlungs- und Kultentwicklung am Frauenberg bei Leibnitz im Vergleich*, M. Lehner, B. Schrettle (eds.). Wien (2016): 185–196.

Selden 2014: D. Selden, "Apuleius and Afroasiatic Poetics". In *Apuleius and Africa*, B.T. Lee, E. Finkelpearl, L. Graverini (eds.). New York/London (2014): 205-270.

Sosztarits 1998: O. Sosztarits, "The Isis Sanctuary and the Relics of Egyptian Cults in Savaria". In *Egyptian Renaissance. Archaism and the Sense of History in Ancient Egypt*, F. Tiradritti (ed.). Budapest (1998): 129-207.

Sosztarits et al. 2013: O. Sosztarits, P. Balázs, A. Csapláros (eds.), *A savariai Iseum.* Szombathely (2013).

Szabó et al. 2016: Cs. Szabó, R. Ota, M. Ciută, „Artemis Ephesia in Apulum. Notes on a new bronze statuette". *Acta Archaeologica Hungarica*, 67/2. 2016: 231-243.

Szabó 2018a: Cs. Szabó, "Reinterpreting Mithras. A very different account". *Acta Archaeologica Academiae Scientiarum Hungaricae* 69. 2018: 211–216.

Szabó 2018b: Cs. Szabó, *Sanctuaries in Roman Dacia. Materiality and religious experience.* Oxford (2018).

Szabó 2018c: Cs. Szabó, "Review: Zerbini, Livio (ed.): Culti e Religiosità nelle Province Danubiane. Atti del II Convegno Internazionale Ferrara 20-22 Novembre 2013. I libri di Emil, Bologna, 2015". *Acta Archaeologica Academiae Scientiarum Hungaricae* 67. 2018: 480-483.

Szabó 2018d: Cs. Szabó, "Pannonian religion or religions of Roman Pannonia? Review article: Tóth I., Pannóniai vallástörténet, Pécs/Budapest, 2015". *Journal of Roman Archaeology* 31. 2018: 883-890.

Szabó 2020: Cs. Szabó, "Danubian provinces. History of a notion". *Transilvania* 6. 2020: 88-96.

Tawfik 2016: R. Tawfik, "Egypt and the Transformations of the Pan-African Movement: The Challenge of Adaptation". *African Studies* 75. 2016: 297-315.

Tomorad 2016: M. Tomorad, "The phases of penetration and diffusion of Egyptian artifacts and cults in the region of Istria and Illyricum (from the 7th c. B.C. to the 4th c. A.D.)". In *Aegyptus et Pannonia V,* H. Győry (ed.). Budapest (2016): 185-226.

Tóth 1976: I. Tóth, "Marcus Aurelius esőcsodája és az egyiptomi kultuszok. Das Regenwunder von Marc Aurel und die ägyptischen Kulte". *Antik Tanulmányok* 23. 1976: 45-51.

Tóth 2001: I. Tóth, "Apuleius Savariensis". *Savaria* 25/3. 2000 (2001): 191-201.

Tóth 2015: I. Tóth, *Pannóniai vallástörténet.* Pécs/Budapest (2015).

Versulys 2010: M. J. Versluys, "Understanding Egypt in Egypt and beyond". In *Isis on the Nile. Egyptian Gods in Hellenistic and Roman Egypt. Proceedings of the 4th International conference of Isis Studies, Liege, 27-29th November 2009,* L. Bricault, M. J. Versluys (eds.). Leiden/Boston (2010): 7-38.

Versluys 2013: M. J. Versluys, „Orientalising Roman Gods". In *Panthée: religious transformations in the Graeco-Roman Empire*, L. Bricault, C. Bonnet (eds.). Leiden (2013): 239-259.

Versluys 2018: M. J. Versluys, "Egypt and/ in / as Rome". In *Beyond the Nile: Egypt and the Classical World,* J. Spier, S. Cole (eds.). Los Angeles (2018): 230-237.

9

Gods of Egyptian Origin at Dierna (Orşova, Romania): Methodology, Assemblage, Influences and Interpretations

Ştefana Cristea
(National Museum of Banat Timişoara; Center for studies on the Middle East and the Mediterranean, Babeş-Bolyai University, Cluj-Napoca)

Călin Timoc
(National Museum of Banat Timişoara)

Abstract: As the title suggests, this article does not only intend to discuss the artifacts related to the deities of Egyptian origin discovered in the Roman city of Dierna (Orşova, Romania). It aims to fill an inconsistency in the research of Dierna and of Roman Dacia, from the perspective of religious life. We have established a methodology, integrated religious manifestations into the archaeological assemblage represented by the city/province, and we provide some interpretations to the artifacts that serve as the main topic of the article. We anchor our research in a few key concepts, such as "lived ancient religion" and "resilience theory" in archaeology, megatheism, religions of Roman Empire, and the gods of Egyptian origin. In the 2nd and 3rd centuries AD the Egyptian influence in the religious and spiritual life of the Roman Empire was intertwined with the Jewish one and comprised the gods of Egyptian origin, Graeco-Egyptian magic, some aspects of Gnosticism and early Christianity. We believe that this influence reached Dierna through the Greek colonies from the western coast of the Black Sea, as a consequence of the military and commercial navigation on the Danube River. Research on the religions of the Roman Empire should consider the environmental and social changes with consequences in the economy, political, and religious fields, as well as the emergence of the coping mecanisms and the building of new emotional beliefs, in order to find a way to thrive.

Keywords: Dierna, Roman Dacia, religions of Roman Empire, gods of Egyptian origin, lived ancient religion, resilience theory in archaeology, megatheism.

Methodology and Terms

The study of the religions from the Roman Empire can be approached in different ways, and in this paper we rely primarily on the archaeological sources discovered in the Roman provinces of Dacia and Moesia, as well as in Egypt or Lycia. We hypothesize that Graeco-Egyptian influences reached Dierna by means of the Danube river, with the main propagation point along the western coast of the Black Sea, especially the Greek colonies of Tomis and Callatis. The agents were the naval personnel of the *Classis Moesica* as well as Alexandrian traders. From this point of view, Dierna's case seems similar to that of Potaissa; however, at Potaissa, the primary agents that helped to spread Graeco-Egyptian influence were soldiers of the *legio V Macedonica*, which was stationed in the area of the western coast of the Black Sea for a long time. Archaeological exploration of both cities has yielded unique objects, which demonstrate Dacia's direct connection with Egypt.

We also incorporate in the article some ancient written sources: Apuleius' *Metamorphoses* (2nd century AD), Plutarch's *De Iside et Osiride* (late 1st century - early 2nd century AD), the aretalogies of the goddess Isis, the oracular inscription of Apollo from Oenoanda (around 200 AD), *The Book of Wisdom* of Pseudo-Solomon (late 1st century BC – 1st century AD), and the texts of Zosimos of Panopolis (late 3rd – early 4th century AD). And, even though the time frame to which we refer is that of the 2nd and 3rd centuries AD, we will also employ evidence from earlier periods in order to shape our arguments and interpretations. Using the museum's inventory records, as well as documents from the museum's archive regarding Imre Pongrácz' collection and the theft that occurred in 1990, we managed to identify a total of five objects that belong or belonged at one point to the National Museum of Banat Timişoara, which attests the worship of the gods of Egyptian origin in the ancient Dierna (Orşova, Romania). The brief presentation of the city and its importance on the Danubian limes was made based on epigraphic, archaeological and cartographic sources.

In recent decades, researchers have developed a series of terms, expressions and theories to help explore the complex topic of religions from the Roman Empire as deeply as possible. Given the multitude of approaches that have been used by researchers over time regarding this field of research, we want to briefly present the theories and key-concepts considered in this article. We are aware, as Greg Woolf noted, that "ordering was never an innocent procedure"[166], or that "to define is to limit" as Oscar Wild said, and that none of these concepts are without their flaws.

Today, the archaeological evidence relating to religions, religious spaces, or religious rituals, are regarded as reliable sources by researchers in the field of "History of Religion". Despite the fact that, in some cases, archaeologists resort to "religion" and "ritual" when no other explanation seems viable, archaeological data, combined with other types of sources, can successfully contribute to the understanding of ancient religious life, in its complexity. In this context we encounter the concept of "archaeology of religion".[167] As researchers, we can deal with small objects, such as amulets, statuettes, jewellery, musical instruments, or other objects used in rituals, with larger items such as altars, inscriptions, cult statues, and even architectural structures. Naturally, in order to achieve the most accurate interpretation possible, we must consider the archaeological objects within the context in which they were discovered. This allows us to establish the relationship between objects and human actions.

A relatively new concept that has made a strong impression on the study of the religions of the Roman Empire is "lived ancient religion". This concept was first employed for the study of contemporary religion, using a methodology originating in anthropology and sociology.[168] More recently, the concept has been transmuted into the field of ancient religion by Jörg Rüpke and his colleagues. Rüpke defines this concept as "a set of experiences, of practices addressed to, and conceptions of the divine, which are appropriated, expressed, and shared by individuals in diverse social spaces."[169] In 2015, he refined this notion even more as "everyday experience, practices, expressions, and interactions that could be related to "religion". Such "religion" is understood as a spectrum of experiences, actions, and beliefs (…)."[170] It focuses upon cultural appropriation as well as the different degrees of religiosity of the inhabitants of the Roman Empire[171] and the different ways of expressing it. "Lived ancient religion" has had a profound impact on scholars because it offers a way forward in the study of religion that allows the most diverse interdisciplinary approaches, with specific methods that enable us to glimpse into the mechanisms of its "making". Communication plays a crucial role in the structure of this

concept, with the implication of materiality ("archaeology of religious experience"[172]), actions, gestures, and bodily movements as expressions of the human dimension.[173] The adoption of concepts such as "habitus"[174] can also build a more nuanced understanding of the religious life of the inhabitants of the Roman Empire.

Votive practices were at the very core of Roman religiosity and denote the practical spirit that the Romans infused in all aspects of their lives. Official and civic religion, individual religion, and all types of cults share the notion of votive practices, which represent the materiality of the contract between the believer and the gods, represented by temples, altars, inscriptions, and images in a wide variety of sizes, shapes and materials.[175] In fact, four of the artifacts discussed in this article pertain to the category of "gifts for the gods".

Even if we chose the city of Dierna as a recognizable archaeological assemblage[176] in which to perform our inquiry, the reader should be aware that it was not the "city" but the "people"[177] who operated as an ordinal element (constructive or restrictive) of religious manifestations, whatever background or gender they had. Considering how people worshipped the gods of Egyptian origin, the term "Isiac cults"[178] is the most suitable because it expresses the existence of several types of religious manifestations, as well as several deities to whom they are addressed, while emphasizing the dominant role played by the goddess Isis[179]. This term focuses on the deities rather than their place of origin, as phrases such as "Egyptian cults" or "Alexandrian cults" imply.

We must, however, highlight the fact that we refer to the way in which the Isiac cults manifested in the place of origin, without the emphasis falling on the place, but rather on the characteristics related to a certain moment as part of the narrative. Moreover, terms like "religions of the Roman Empire" (instead of "Roman Religion"[180]) leave

---

[166] Woolf 1997, 71-72.
[167] Raja, Rüpke 2015, 1-25.
[168] Gasparini et al.2020, 1.
[169] Rüpke 2011, 191.
[170] Raja, Rüpke 2015, 4.
[171] Gasparini et al. 2020, 1.
[172] Raja, Rüpke 2015.
[173] Gasparini *et al.* 2020, 2-3.
[174] Asimaki, Koustourakis 2014.
[175] Nemeti, Nemeti 2019, 284.
[176] Hamilakis, Jones 2017.
[177] For Rüpke people are "the grammar of sentences used in many narratives" (Rüpke 2018a, 145).
[178] Preferred by Malaise 2007, 19-22.
[179] "Dans son emploi moderne, l'expression « cultes isiaques » doit s'appliquer à ce qui concerne le culte hors d'Égypte, entre la fin du IVe siècle av. J.-C. et la fin du IVe siècle apr. J.-C., d'une douzaine de divinités, plus ou moins hellénisées, appartenant à un même cercle mythique, cultuel et liturgique, originaires de la vallée du Nil. Ces déités sont Isis, son époux Osiris ou Sérapis, leur fils Harpocrate, leur compagnon Anubis/Hermanubis, le faucon Horus, Boubastis, l'ancienne Bastet, le taureau Apis, Hydreios, forme hydriaque d'Osiris, Nephthys, la sœur d'Isis, et dans une certaine mesure Neilos." (Malaise 2007, 21)
[180] Rüpke 2018 a, 143-144. Richard Gordon, under the influence of the anthropologist A. F. C. Wallace, notice: "the religion of any society is not an internally coherent set of rituals and beliefs practised and held by all its members, but rather a loose federation of beliefs only partly expressed in a series of cult institutions". (Gordon 1972, 92) Gordon's conclusions are even more valid within the Roman Empire, with a society so complex and diverse, and constantly changing, moreover being justified the use of the expression religion of the Roman Empire vs. Roman religion.

room for exceptions, local adaptations, personal choices, and the individual as the main actor. At the same time, we prefer to make reference to the "gods of Egyptian origin", rather than "Egyptian gods", since, after leaving Egypt, they penetrated into the Greek and then the Roman world, where they intermingled with other ways of thinking and other gods. The gods of Egyptian origin underwent a series of cultural appropriations, transmutations, associations, amalgamations, and conversions, which practically transformed them into different gods. They may have had the same names (e.g. Isis, Osiris), but their images changed, as well as their specific *paraphernalia*, or the message they sent[181].

As a highly male-dominated society with the army as its driving force, the Roman Empire was action oriented and people took the most practical approach in their lives. Thus, Clifford Ando's point of view seems appropriate: "Romans did not need faith; they had an orthopraxy."[182] Researching the intimate mechanism of the changes that emerged within the religions of the Roman Empire shows us that "Roman orthopraxy was invested not in rituals that did not change, but in correct performance per se. What is more, the correctness of any given performance was subject to empirical verification, and the results of that testing could and occasionally did provoke not merely an exact repetition of a performance but changes in the ritual itself."[183] Therefore, as is the case of the gods of Egyptian origin and Isiac cults, for the reality of the Roman Empire, the dawn of religious manifestations in which they were involved are important only as a part of the succession of the amendments applied to these manifestations. Most of the time, the amendments do not follow a chronological thread, but they are formed, as Rüpke states, as a narrative[184] that develops both in time and concurrent on several levels. The starting and ending points of the narrative are important, but the concept it is more focused on the process, as most of the terms and concepts we use in this article. In this context, we can understand the transformation suffered by the Isiac cults as a result of a "habitus" shaped over a long period of time as a product of the amalgamation of a personal and collective history with the fixed structures of the institutions[185].

The religious changes that occurred within the Roman Empire, including the Roman province of Dacia in the 2nd-3rd centuries AD, cannot be understood without considering the influences of Gnosticism and Hermeticism in the presence of the indisputable increase of henotheistic / megatheistic[186] tendencies. Henotheism, as H.S. Versnel defines it, is a modern expression based on the acclamation

"one is (the) god" who "does not (necessarily) entail monotheistic notions ("there is no other god except this god"), although this connotation may creep in from time to time. It denotes a personal devotion to one god ("there is no other god like this god") without involving rejection or neglect of other gods"[187]. Nevertheless, we prefer the term megatheism[188] considering that, while "henotheism" seems to be an immutable truth, megatheism gives the sensation of becoming and, by its very definition, implies the competitive characteristic of the imperial period which takes different forms, as Chaniotis pointed out.

A concept first introduced in the context of archaeology and more recently in the study of urban religion is "resilience theory"[189]. This theory was initially used in the study of materials, economy, and psychology.[190] By 2008-2009, this concept became an important part of research in city management and urban planning, overlapping with terms such as sustainability and stability. "Resilience theory" in archaeology is not only important for understanding past societies but can also help us to understand our own relationship with the environment and, perhaps, to discover in the past solutions for current issues[191]. Archaeology can provide knowledge about past cycles of dynamics inside socio-ecological systems, identifying the patterns, the key moments, and the inevitable stages important for systems resilience. This may help us to develop new directions in global management to diminish the risks in our existence and increase social resilience[192]. The interactions between human societies and the environment encapsulated in archaeological contexts reveal the way in which human strategies sometimes led not only to the disappearance of some elements from the environment, but also to the collapse of those societies[193]. For some communities, archaeology can contribute toward gaining a better understanding of human behaviour and social dynamics, from a plurality of angles, in specific circumstances[194]. It is very easy to link archaeological "resilience theory" to the problem of climate change and to the coping mechanisms of human beings dealing with disasters. In the logical interconnection of these concepts, religion, seen as the sum of religious practices and rituals, favours such resilience. This is why we have included the concept of "resilience" and "resilience theory" in our research.

---

181 We are in debt to Prof. Laurent Bricault for the fruitful discussions in structuring our ideas in this regard, had during the conference.
182 Ando 2008, X-XII.
183 Ando 2008, XIV.
184 Rüpke 2018 a, 140-143.
185 Asimaki, Koustourakis 2014, 126-127.
186 As the very definition of Versnel pointed out, "henotheism" is more closely connected to monotheism then "megatheism", expression used and defined by Angelos Chaniotis (Chaniotis 2010).

187 Versnel 1998, 35-38.
188 Angelos Chaniotis use "megatheism" as "an expression of piety which was based on a personal experience of the presence of god, represented one particular god as somehow superior to others, and was expressed through oral performances (praise, acclamations, hymns) accompanying, but not replacing, ritual actions. That the existence of such a god was a concern in the Imperial period is directly attested through an oracle quoted in the Theosophia Tubingensis, a response to someone who asked Apollo is there is another god with a superior power".(Chaniotis 2010, 113)
189 Rüpke 2019.
190 Bradtmöller *et al.* 2017, 1; Rüpke 2019, 2.
191 Rüpke 2019, 2-3; Rüpke 2020, 116; Redman 2005, 70.
192 Redman 2005, 70.
193 Redman 2005, 71.
194 Redman 2005, 71.

Municipium Septimium Diernense

Located on the left bank of the Danube, on the narrow terrace between the Grațca and Schela valleys, the archaeological site at Orșova (**Fig. 9.1**) was not well-known until the 1970s when the hydroelectric dam at the Iron Gates was put into use[195]. Chance discoveries and isolated instances of archaeological research were conducted during the re-development of Orșova during the period of Austro-Hungarian dualism. A local priest, Antal Boleszny, and a teacher, Sandor Mihalik, were among those who made efforts to preserve the Roman remains.[196] Larger archaeological campaigns were undertaken east of the city, where the barracks of the Honvéd Infantry Regiment were built in the mid-19th century. The barracks partially overlapped the periphery of the ancient civil settlement and part of the eastern necropolis of the ancient city. The site has never been systematically investigated, however, when the hydrotechnical project at the Iron Gates of the Danube was constructed, rescue excavations were carried out in several locations in Orșova, between 1966-1969. The Roman fort and the late Roman fortification, the central urban area of Dierna, and the eastern necropolis were the primary focus. The results of these archaeological investigations were published only to a certain degree or very briefly.[197]

Doina Benea synthesized the results of the archaeological excavations undertaken in the context of the hydrotechnical project and highlighted the fact that only a Roman city existed in this place with no trace of a prior settlement.[198] Despite this, the toponym seems to be of Dacian origin and is mentioned in several forms in the ancient geographical sources: Tierna, Tsierna, and Zerna.[199]

Because of its strategic position along important communication routes, including the eastern Iron Gates section of the Danube, Dierna was transformed into a river port and a mandatory stop for any ship that navigated the middle Danube. The city played an important role in directing navigation on the Danube River and in supporting the ships that used the Sipp channel located a few kilometres to the east.[200] The town was also a good place to cross the Danube from the left bank of the river. In fact, a settlement with a fortification similar to Dierna, called suggestively Transdierna in the late Roman era, was a common point for crossing the river ever since the Dacian-Roman wars.[201] Therefore, this was one of the "gates" consecrated for entry into the province of Dacia. From this point began the imperial road that climbed along the Cerna and Timiș rivers to Tibiscum.[202]

According to the historical tradition, the Roman city of Dierna was founded by Emperor Trajan. A small number of inscriptions referring to the settlement, which is situated near the confluence of the rivers Cerna and Danube, demonstrate that the rank of municipality was acquired only during the reign of Septimius Severus.[203] The Roman fort, constructed in the late 1st or early 2nd century AD, was likely abandoned after the conquest of the Decebal's kingdom by the emperor Trajan. The *quadriburgium* appears to have been built in the late 3rd century AD, when the city was integrated into the border of the Roman Empire.[204]

Doina Benea demonstrated that Dierna had a large port equipped with warehouses and that the history of the settlement, as well as that of the fortification, can be discussed in the context of two broad periods of time: an early phase represented by an economic boom during the time of the province of Roman Dacia, and another, perhaps as prosperous as the previous one, during the Tetrarchy and the Constantinian dynasty.[205] The analysis of tiles discovered here supports a strong second phase, since the units of the late Roman army were involved in the construction of the settlement.[206] The impressive quantity of ceramic material of various shapes and types, including amphorae, *mortaria*, small cups, and simple *paterae* made of kaolin, found at Dierna clearly indicates that the city was connected to fluvial and interprovincial commerce.

Based upon a Roman inscription discovered in Serbia, Radu Ardevan demonstrated that within the city council (*ordo decurionum*) was a *quinquenalis portus*, a port administrator. This is a magistracy that is not found in other similar Roman cities, reinforcing the special place of Dierna in the regional economy.[207] At the same time, important discoveries in the city's necropolis (e.g., tombs in cists, lead and stone sarcophagi, gold pieces and rare jewels) reveal information about the population of Dierna and their economic status.[208] The impressive number of stamped military bricks discovered here, bearing the names of the legion *VII Claudia* as well as the legions of *Dacia Ripensis*, *XIII Gemina,* and *V Macedonia*, demonstrate that, when Dierna was an active part of the Roman limes, it played a very important role in the defensive system of the Roman Empire.[209]

Information about the city planning of Dierna is scarce. The late 19th century excavations in the gardens of the inhabitants of Orșova revealed the remains of imposing buildings (quarry stone walls with mortar), some of which had a porch with columns and an inner courtyard. During the same period, archaeologists working along the road to

[195] Benea 1975, 91-92; Florescu 1978, 143.
[196] Timoc 2006, 58-59.
[197] Bujor 1974.
[198] Benea 2016, 72, 142-143.
[199] Poenaru Bordea 1996, 54.
[200] Zotović, Kondić 1978, 195; Timoc 1996, 249-250.
[201] Mirkovic 2007, 36.
[202] Fodorean 2006, 232-233.

[203] Ardevan 1998, 72-73.
[204] Benea 2013, 152; Benea 2016, 311-312.
[205] Benea 2001a, 129-130; Benea 2001b, 149-150.
[206] Piso, Ardeț, Timoc 2019, 130-131.
[207] Ardevan 1998, 134.
[208] Benea 2008, 113-114.
[209] IDR III/1, 63-65; Gudea 1997, 31; Gudea 2001, 74; Bondoc 2009, 53-56.

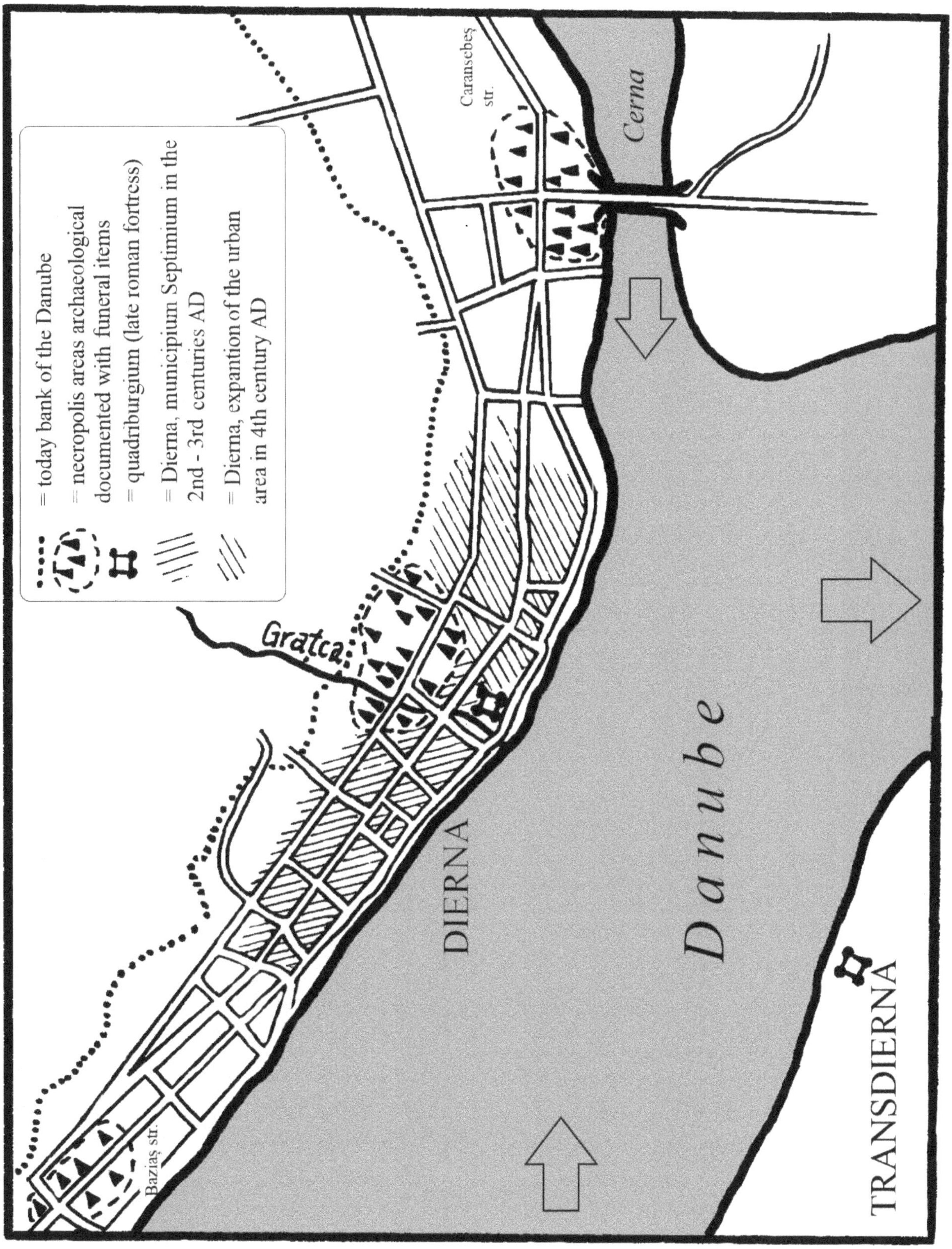
= today bank of the Danube
= necropolis areas archaeological documented with funeral items
= quadriburgium (late roman fortress)
= Dierna, municipium Septimium in the 2nd - 3rd centuries AD
= Dierna, expantion of the urban area in 4th century AD
Caransebeş str.
Cerna
Gratca
DIERNA
Danube
TRANSDIERNA
Baziaş str.

Fig. 9.1. Dierna (drawing - Călin Timoc)

Baziaş (Caraş-Severin county, Romania) discovered life-size marble statues of *togati*, as well as several statuettes of Greco-Roman deities.[210] Religious dedication to Jupiter,[211] Hercules,[212] Venus,[213] Mithras,[214] and Dolichenus[215] as well as Thanatos[216] are attested in Orşova. From the agricultural hinterland of Dierna, a *villa suburbana* in Jupalnic (Mehedinţi county, Romania) and some rural settlements near Eşelniţa (Mehedinţi county, Romania) are known.[217]

Due to the poor excavation techniques of the late 1960s, we do not understand Dierna's stratigraphy very well, but it can be concluded from the analysis of coins that, until the period of military anarchy, the commercial life of Dierna's inhabitants was not affected. The heyday of the region was followed by a period of anxiety and disturbance that ceased between the reigns of Gallienus (253-268 AD) and Aurelian (270-275 AD), when a new phase of the city's existence began as a result of Aurelian's withdrawal of the administration and military forces from Dacia (271 AD). For a brief period of time, Dierna was home to refugees and Roman citizens who wanted to remain under the protection of the Empire. By the end of the 3rd century AD, probably during the reign of emperor Diocletian (284-305 AD), the urban area was extended, and it is likely that the port was reinforced.[218] Being a military and urban centre in the new province of *Dacia Ripensis*, life under the influence of the Roman Empire continued in Dierna until the early 5th century AD, when the fortifications were devastated by the Goths or the Huns.[219] Procopius of Caesarea counts it among the active Byzantine cities along the Danube until 565 AD. The fortifications were probably rebuilt at the beginning of the 6th century, as they were in Drobeta, in order to defend the Balkan provinces of Byzantium from Avaro-Slavic incursions.[220]

Gods of Egyptian origin at Dierna

Investigating the presence of the gods of Egyptian origins in this Roman city is not an easy task. On the one hand, archaeological excavations conducted within this ancient port were few and we are unable to undertake new excavations given that most of the ancient city was flooded as a result of the hydroelectric project. On the other hand, the archaeological artifacts from Dierna were collected from these excavations up to the 1960s according to the criteria and with methods accessible at that time. Many objects entered into museum collections through private antiquarians, such as Imre Pongrácz (former commander of the Orşova port at the end of the 19th century, from which the Banat Museum obtained about 6000 objects), without

having a clear archaeological context. Moreover, some of the artifacts have been lost or are difficult to identify due to the two World Wars and the repeated movement of the museum's heritage.[221] We are aware of at least ten objects from Dierna and its environs that reflect gods of Egyptian origin, 5 of which are discussed here. The small number of artifacts should not be viewed as evidence that the gods of Egyptian origin were not important at Dierna. Instead, this is simply a result of the poor archaeological techniques and the fact that many objects and information about them disappeared through theft or negligence.

1. Osiris

Among the total of 6000 artifacts acquired by the Banat Museum after Pongrácz's death, there were five statuettes representing the god Osiris:[222] three of the statuettes were made of bronze (6 cm, 7 cm, and 12 cm, respectively in height) and represent the god as he appears traditionally, standing, in the form of a mummy, holding in his hands the symbols of power (*heka* and *nekhakha*) and wearing the *atef* crown; the fourth only represent the head of Osiris placed on a bronze support (12 cm); the fifth is recorded as being of marble (14 cm). In the drawings made at the beginning of the 20th century of the artifacts from the collection, there are two representations of these bronze statuettes: one measuring 6 cm, and another measuring 7 cm (**Fig. 9.2**). Neither of them was discovered in Dierna, as can be seen from the notes made in Hungarian, at the bottom of the page.

A police statement from 1990 regarding the theft of 31 items from the museum, describes one artifact as a bronze statuette of Osiris. The statuette of Osiris noted in the museum register (no. 1569) measures 6 cm, while in the database of the National Institute of Heritage, the Department of Mobile, Intangible and Digital Heritage, among the items stolen from the Banat Museum is a statuette of Osiris, accompanied by a photo.[223] From this photo one can determine the height of the statuette, 12 cm to which is added the base in the form of a truncated cone with a height of 4 cm. It is possible that this statuette is the same as the one mentioned in the Pongrácz collection (the one of 12 cm high), but we cannot be certain given the fact that a drawing of this artifact is not preserved (a few pages with the drawings of the items from the collection have been lost over time, making their identification quite difficult).

What completes the already existing information is the fact that, one of the older registers of the museum documents

[210] Milleker 1912, 239.
[211] Isac 1971, 112-113.
[212] Timoc 2004, 448-449.
[213] Poenaru Bordea 1996, 54.
[214] Milleker 1899, 52.
[215] Pribac 1999, 205; Timoc 2004, 447-448.
[216] Oanţă-Mărghitu 2013, 486-487, no.118 (Dorel Bondoc).
[217] Juan Petroi 2003, 7.
[218] Timoc 2009, 286-287.
[219] Madgearu 2008, 85; Madgearu 2010, 83.
[220] Davidescu 1980, 227.

[221] Vasile Rămneanţu (2000) discusses the fate of cultural objects requisitioned at the end of WWI by Serbian troops at the time of Banat's evacuation, goods that have been subject of diplomatic negotiations since 1932. From the list drawn up on June 18, 1919, attached to the article, there are no objects dated to the Roman period or related to ancient Egypt.
[222] Berkeszi 1908, 206.
[223] http://furate.cimec.ro/detaliu.asp?tit=Statueta--Zeul-Osiris&k=18842B4F8048461CB44DB9356E5999B1

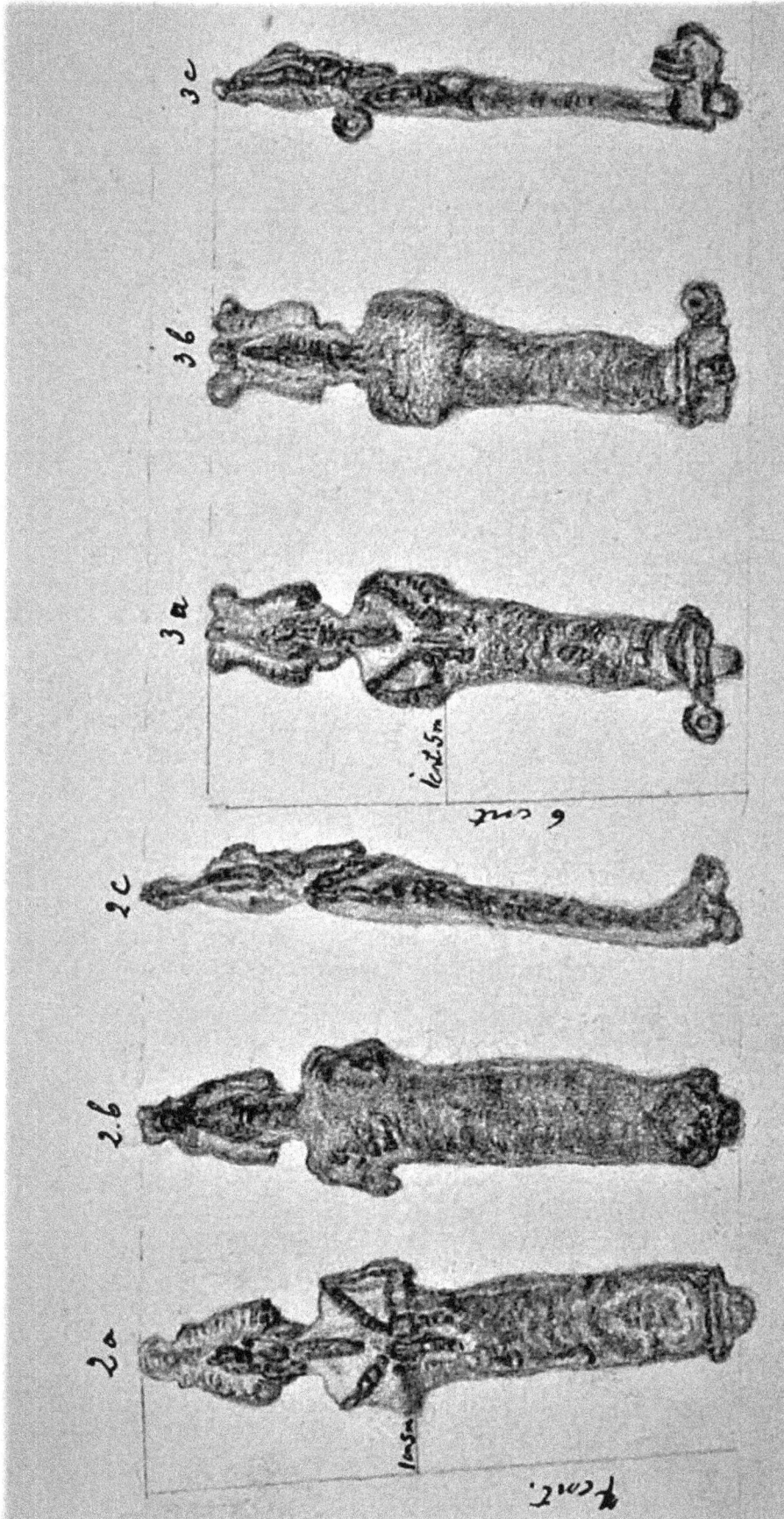

Fig. 9.2. Osiris (bronze?) statuettes - Imre Pongrácz drawings (National Museum of Banat Timişoara)

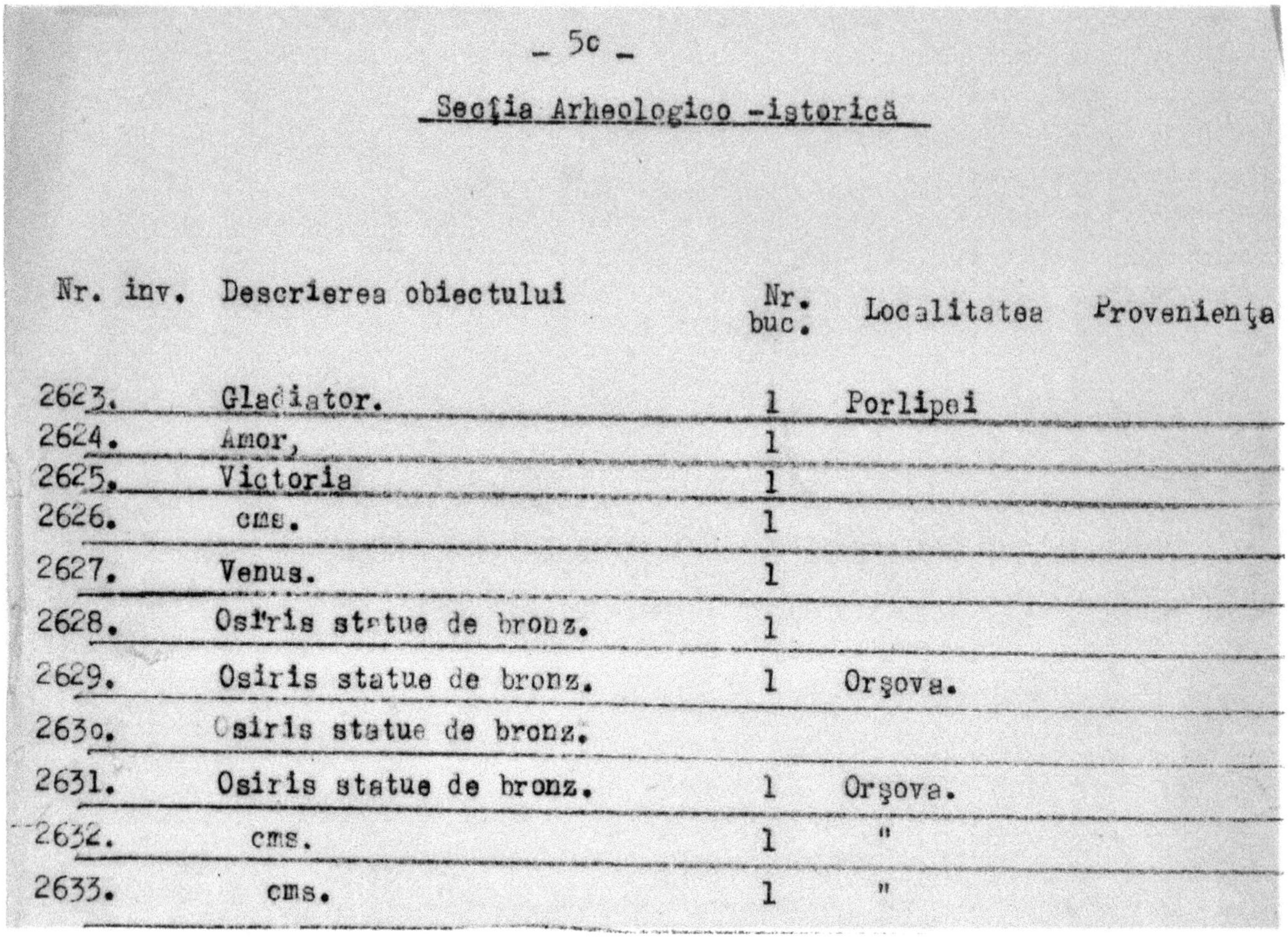

_ 5c _

Secţia Arheologico -istorică

Nr. inv.	Descrierea obiectului	Nr. buc.	Localitatea	Provenienţa
2623.	Gladiator.	1	Porlipei	
2624.	Amor,	1		
2625.	Victoria	1		
2626.	cms.	1		
2627.	Venus.	1		
2628.	Osiris statue de bronz.	1		
2629.	Osiris statue de bronz.	1	Orşova.	
2630.	Osiris statue de bronz.	1		
2631.	Osiris statue de bronz.	1	Orşova.	
2632.	cms.	1	"	
2633.	cms.	1	"	

Fig. 9.3. Page from an old inventory register in which one can observe that there should have been six bronze statuettes representing Osiris, four of them from Orşova (Dierna) (National Museum of Banat Timişoara)

six statuettes representing the god Osiris, four of which are described as originating from Orşova (Dierna). It is possible, however, that the place of discovery was assigned not because there was clear evidence, but because they were part of the Pongrácz collection (**Fig. 9.3**). Nevertheless, we believe that there were at least two statuettes discovered in Orşova: the one that was stolen and the only one that still exists in the museum's collection and which is probably the one described with the current register inventory number 1569 (no. 2628 in the older register). Although the artifact is corroded, most features are still visible (**Fig. 9.4**), including the symbols of power held in the hands of the god (sceptre and whip), the false beard, the *atef* crown; the *ureaus* on the front is barely recognizable. This item closely resembles one in a Pongrácz drawing, both having a height of 6 cm. Unlike the piece preserved in the museum, the one in the drawing has a side loop on the bottom left that probably allowed it to be fastened. Both have a pivot which probably served the same purpose, except that the one in the drawing is longer.

2. Serapis

Among the Imre Pongrácz drawings, is a statuette representing the bust of a mature male deity that is not well preserved. The thin beard is rendered by unclear curls, while the hair reaches the figure's shoulders, also represented by a series of curls. Fortunately, the drawing depicts the rear of the statuette, which allows us to observe the presence of a possible *tenia*, a ribbon that seems to divide the hair into two registers. The key attribute of this statuette that permits us to identify the subject as Serapis is the dent on the crest of the head, which represents the place where a *calathos* was attached, the distinctive element of this god of Egyptian origin. It is possible that this iconographic element was manufactured separately and attached to the bust, similar to numerous other cases. The bust also incorporates a summary representation of the clothing of the god covering his chest.

The handwritten notes at the bottom of the drawing demonstrate that this artifact was discovered in Dierna (Orşova). There is no information, however, about the dimensions of this item, or about the material from which it was moulded, although we presume that it was made of bronze. In fact, the police statement mentioned above lists no. 31 of the stolen artifacts as a "bust of Serapis made of bronze". Unfortunately, the inventory number with which the item is identified in this paper (no. 1151) corresponds to another object in the museum, the basalt head of a pharaoh, an object stated to have been brought from Egypt.

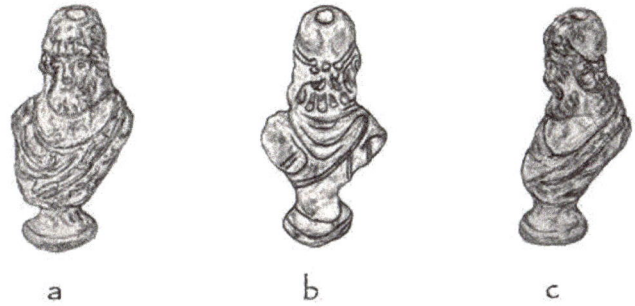

Fig. 9.5. Statuette of Serapis – Imre Pongrácz drawings (National Museum of Banat Timişoara); image processing – Ştefana Cristea

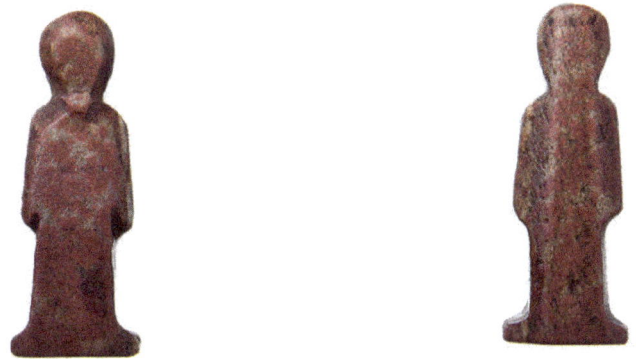

Fig. 9.6. The knot of Isis amulet, probably from Orşova (Dierna) (photo Milan Şepeţan – National Museum of Banat Timişoara)

3. The knot of Isis

Inventory number 1123 from the register of 1958 refers to a small figurine from Orşova composed of red marble. A section of an earlier register describes "ornaments, idols and amulets of bronze and iron" (inv. nos. 2782-2796). One small artifact (inv. no. 2794), measuring 1 x 3 cm, is an amulet that represents "the knot of Isis", also termed "the girdle of Isis" (*tjt, tyet, tiet, thet*) (**Fig. 9.6**). The amulet is manufactured from red jasper and is very similar to an *ankh* represented as a loop in the upper part with a protrusion in the area in which it narrows. From that area begins the proper body of the amulet, which is usually represented by two elongated loops towards the base; it continues with a flaring base. The artifact from the collection of the National Museum of Banat is schematically represented and slightly eroded, suggesting the figure of a man standing, which makes an identification of the type of amulet it represents difficult. Usually this type of amulet was red, representing the blood of the goddess Isis, and, the same as the *ankh*, symbolizes the

Fig. 9.4. Bronze statuette depicting Osiris, probably from Orşova (Dierna) (photo Milan Şepeţan – National Museum of Banat Timişoara)

We failed to identify the bust under another inventory number, or to find the physical object; therefore, the only information we have is from the Pongrácz drawing and a photo from Berkeszi's article (**Fig. 9.5**).[224]

---

[224] Berkeszi 1908, 205.

life force and creative powers of the goddess Isis. Such amulets can also be found in blue, green or gold.

4. Ra

In April 1896, Stăniştea Gavril found a marble statuette representing the god Ra in the Iron Gates area of the Danube river. The statuette was purchased by the museum on March 31, 1897 and was recorded in the first Hungarian register of the museum.[225] Unfortunately, we do not know the details related to its discovery. It is possible that the artifact was carried by water from the Orşova area, being the closest settlement located upstream from the discovery place. We are somewhat uncertain if the attribution of the deity is correct, as the details of the iconographic elements are not described and the dimensions are not provided.

5. Isis (?)

Alexandru Popa believes that a statuette representing Isis originates from the settlement of Dierna.[226] We can identify this statuette on the list accompanying the aforementioned police statement (no. 28), where it is defined as "a bronze statuette of Isis on a wooden base". The artifact (inv. no. 2876) is described in the register as a representation of the goddess Venus (many of the hand-written notes in the inventory register are incorrect). We were unable to locate a photograph of the statuette, now lost; however, it is documented among the Pongracz drawings (**Fig. 9.7**). The bust was most likely a metal element for furniture, since it has a fastening nail on the back.

Based upon the drawing, we note that the features of the face are not harmoniously crafted: the forehead is too high, the eyes are very close, the nose is large compared to the rest of the features, the big mouth has fleshy lips, and the chin is rather prominent. All the features are crammed into the central part of the face, giving a strange appearance to the goddess. On the other hand, the hair is nicely represented: the face of the deity is framed by two twisted strands that fall onto the shoulders; at the back, it is arranged in strands that overlap and give the hair an elegant and youthful look. The drawing indicates that the deity is depicted with a coiled snake around its neck. The snake's head is on the chest area of the goddess, but we cannot be sure that the person who made the drawing interpreted what he saw correctly. Whether or not there is actually a snake, no specific iconographic elements referring to Isis (Isiac knot, the *basileion*, the *sistrum*) are represented. This leads us to believe that the identification is not correct.

Our analysis of the notes at the bottom of the page indicate that the statuette was discovered in Serbia (Nagy Gradistye). Alexandru Popa probably did not have access to this information, nor to the image of the artifact and it, therefore, seems that he only assumed that the item was

Fig. 9.7. Statuette wrongly considered to represent Isis – Imre Pongrácz drawings (National Museum of Banat Timişoara); image processing – Ştefana Cristea

from Dierna and represented the goddess Isis. In fact, the description of Alexandru Popa, according to which the goddess appears emerging from a lotus flower, does not correspond to what we see in the drawing. The presence of the snake, however, as well as the appearance of the face of the goddess, lead us to speculate that this may represent a local interpretation of the Celtic goddess Sirona (normally this goddess had the snake wrapped around her hand while her hair is in a bun) or a local deity.

Magical context at Dierna

Evidence of the Graeco-Egyptian practice of magic and alchemy at Dierna with Gnostic and Jewish influences derives from a tomb and a workshop discovered at Orsova in the 1960's. Although this evidence does not pertain to the gods of Egyptian origin, it is still instructive to describe the discoveries in order to understand the complex reality of the moment, how the religious narrative developed at Dierna under the influence of Egypt in the 2nd and 3rd centuries AD, and how the gods of Egyptian origin were integrated in the archaeological assemblage represented by the Roman city of Dierna. We observe from these two examples that the imprint of Egyptian Gnosticism is undoubtedly visible and, at the same time, that the influence of magical practices and discoveries connected to the natural sciences as they develop in Egypt reached even the most distant areas of the Roman Empire. We must bear in mind that priests were not the only experts in religious and magical practices, but that there were also "itinerant ritual experts": *magoi, haruspices, augures, harioli, vates, coniectores.*[227]

---

[225] Adelković, Demian 2016, 115.
[226] Popa 1979, 20.

[227] Eidinow 2017, 260-264.

1. At the end of the 1960's, a brick sarcophagus discovered at Dierna have been dated to the 3rd or 4th centuries AD.[228] Inside the sarcophagus was a small lead coffin and four pots of red paste, two at the head and two at the feet of the deceased, broken by the discoverers. Inside the coffin were the remains of a child with funerary objects placed near the head, a small golden leaf, two golden medallions, and two gold earrings. One of the medallions incorporates a red jasper gem on which is a representation of Sol in a quadriga pulled by galloping horses. The god wears a crown with four rays; he holds the reins in his left hand and a whip in his right hand. There is also the wavy shape of a snake depicted. In a golden frame, identical to the previous one, there was a badly damaged silver coin that seems to be an imitation of a Republican coin. One side seems to bear a representation of Roma, while the other side probably depicts Luna in a chariot.[229] Gideon Bohak highlights the fact that when engraved gems and rings were used as seals in Jewish magic rituals, as described in the collection of spells, they usually borrowed non-Jewish images, such as Helios in a quadriga, Orpheus playing his lyre, or Hercules strangling the Nemean lion.[230] Therefore, researchers cannot always know what the intention was in choosing one motif or another on intaglios or amulets or to which ethnic group belongs the owner.

The folded golden leaf has a four-row incised text, from left to right. All researchers who have published this item consider that it represents an amulet with magical significance, a *phylacterion* or *Totenpaß*. The first two lines are written in a magical alphabet, *charakteres*, and some of the pearly signs seem to be inspired by Greek letters. Both Nicolae Vlassa, the first scholar to publish it, and Roy Kotansky, who included in his volume inscribed gold, silver, cooper and bronze *lamellae*, agreed that these signs are a sort of cypher for the divine name IAΩ AΘΩNAI.[231] *Charakteres*, as Frankfurter defines it, is "the general term for the small designs and figures found in lines or clusters on magical papyri and gems, having no apparent source in any known alphabet, and yet operating in such a way that a 'meaning' is implied.(...) The most common form of magical 'charakteres' consist of asterisks and straight lines with small circles or lobes on each end".[232] Due to their visual form, magical *charakteres* represent symbols, viewed as a sacred writing intimately interlinked with the nature of the substances invested with magical powers

(gold in our case) and the voicing of some magical spells. Moreover, in the case of the magical *charakteres* used in Greco-Roman, Greco-Egyptian, and Coptic magical texts and amulets, it can be concluded that they often represented improvisations, maintaining at the same time an impression of pursuing a precise purpose. In Late Antiquity, stories circulated throughout the Mediterranean about several heavenly books whose contents were only intelligible to deities, angels, or enlightened ones. In this regard, Frankfurter quotes the Egyptian Gnostic Gospel of Truth. Laurent Motte, however, has demonstrated that the 'heavenly letters' referred to in this text are Egyptian hieroglyphs. Frankfurter gives examples in which, the magical *charakteres* represent the names of some cosmic powers.[233]

Lines 3-4 have the following Greek inscription: IAΩ AΘΩNAI / IΩ. At first sight, the orthographic variant *Atonai* for *Adonai* is noted as well as the fact that all the names refer to the same god, *Iahveh*. The representation of *Sol* in association with the name *Iao Atonai* suggests that it designates a solar divinity. The invocation "Io" at the end is intended to summon the god for the salvation of the bearer and to hasten his emergence. As Joachim Sliwa noticed, magical papyri and amulets help us to understand the processes, in terms of beliefs, which unfolded between the 1st and 3rd centuries AD.[234] The magical *formulae* used in spells were written almost exclusively with Greek letters and, apart from their general purpose of protection from evil, often served to other, more specific, purposes: to heal diseases, to help in love affairs, and to operate in conjunction with concepts in Gnostic books.[235] In the 1st century BC, Diodorus of Sicily and Marcus Terentius Varro seem to have been acquainted with the Iao version of the Jewish god, most likely pronounced by the Greeks and Latins as it is written.[236] Flavius Josephus, however, notified his readers that, until the 1st century AD, there were Jews who knew how to pronounce it correctly, although, they were not encouraged to do so.[237] Some scholars consider that the name of the Highest God of the Jews was substituted in public readings by epithets or other appellation formulas which represent divine titles (Elohim, Adonai), wishing to preserve the sacred character of the name.[238] The practice of forbidding the pronunciation of the Tetragrammaton spread, especially, beginning in the 2nd century AD.[239] The Greek version of the Hebrew Tetragrammaton can occur as ιαεω, or ιαω much more frequently. The so-called *ιαεω – palindrome*, consisting of a succession of fifty-nine letters, is attested frequently in both magical papyri and gems. The translation of this magical formula is: "Iahweh is the bearer of the secret name, the lion of Re secure in his shrine".[240] The most

---

[228] Benea, Șchiopu 1974, 115-125.
[229] Giulia Sfameni Gasparro recalls one of the hymns dedicated to the goddess Isis, the aretalogy from Maroneia, in which Isis and Serapis are assimilated to the Sun and the Moon: "You took Serapis as your husband and after being joined in marriage, the world shone under your faces, you Helios and Selene, having opened your eyes", with the alternative translation of Grandjean ("Tu as pris Sérapis comme compagnon, et, après que vous eutes institué le mariage, le monde a resplendi sous vos visages, placé sous les regards d'Hélios et de Séléné".) and also Bricault's version (*RICIS* I, 177) ("Tu as pris Sérapis comme compagnon, et, après que vous vous soyez mariés, le monde a resplendi par vos visages, placé sous les regards d' Hélios et de Séléné".) (Sfameni Gasparro 2007, 40-41.)
[230] Bohak 2019, 39, 42-43.
[231] Vlassa 1974, 125-141; Kotansky 1994, 95-96.
[232] Frankfurter 1994, 205.

[233] Frankfurter 1994, 206-210.
[234] Śliwa 2017, 225.
[235] Śliwa 2017, 226.
[236] Vasileiadis 2013, 6-7.
[237] Vasileiadis 2013, 9-10.
[238] Vasileiadis 2013, 7.
[239] Vasileiadis 2013, 10.
[240] Śliwa 2017, 228.

common figures associated with this palindrome are solar deities: Isis with Harpocrates, Sarapis, Chnoubis, and Pantheos. Some researchers understand these objects to be love charms.[241] Pavlos D. Vasileiadis states that "two early identities of the deity named Ιαω are traceable. On the one hand, the name yhw was used as the theonym of the God of the Hebrews as he was conceived by Jewish-Egyptian communities like the colony at Elephantine during the sixth and fifth centuries BC. The further development of this theological notion behind the theonym Ιαω towards its utilization as a generally legible rendering of the four-letter name of the Biblical God — who was at the same time understood as the Highest God, the only true god who is universally worshiped — was a Hellenizing process. Indeed, this theological shift is discernible in the Septuagint Torah composed in Alexandria during the third century BC."[242]

2. In the summer of 1968, archaeological excavations were carried out in the yard of the "Ștefan Plavăț" High School. Part of a Roman construction was discovered, a construction that, based on the archaeological material, was considered to be a craft workshop.[243] It is possible that this building had a previous wooden phase, as suggested by the discovery of decomposed wood, nails, and coal, under the foundation of the stone walls a) and d). Archaeologists unearthed a large quantity of ceramics, traces of metalworking, iron dross, pieces of coal, fragments of crucibles and glass paste, vitrified pearls, small lumps and lead rolls, various bronze objects, tools, *fibulae*, and coins from the 1st to the 3rd or 4th centuries AD[244]. A golden leaf identified here was tightly rolled, and after scrolling it has a rectangular shape with slightly rounded corners, measuring 7.1 x 2.4 cm. Its surface is covered with small wrinkles, due to the rolling, and very small graphic signs (3 mm maximum), which implies difficulty both in writing and reading. The magical inscription consists of three distinct parts. The letters to the left can be interpreted as Greek vowels: ωι /υυυυ /ιωδ να; in the middle there is a drawing, which probably represents the demon to be sent to Iulia Cyrilla with a rectangular head and schematically represented limbs.[245] The text is that of a *defixio*, and, to the right, can be read as follows: "Demon menacing here, menace on my behalf now, now, at the house of Iulia Cyrilla".[246] The common verb *immineo*, as Kotansky read it, can carry a wide range of meanings: 'be at hand', 'threaten', 'be impending', 'strive for', or 'be eager for'. Here, it refers to a demon sent to menace, or sexually harass Iulia Cyrilla, in the form of an apparition or dream.[247] The duplication of *iam, iam* in Latin magical texts is not unusual and expresses the urge for the demon's fulfilment of the request for which he was invoked. The preposition *aput*, as a variant of *apud*, means 'in the presence of' or

'at the house of'.[248] As a demotic spell from the *Greek Magical Papyri in Translation* suggests, the gold lamellae may have been placed under the owner's pillow so that the demon summoned by the magic invocation would read the text and go to the house of Iulia Cyrilla.[249] It is possible that the spell from Dierna aimed at binding Iulia Cyrilla for sexual benefit, although it could also have been aimed at punishing her or separating a couple she was part of.

If we look at the entire archaeological assemblage of the building, we could consider the hypothesis of an alchemical workshop, in which case alchemy represents the study of nature and the exploitation of the knowledge acquired from this study.[250] Zosimos of Panopolis describe two types of ancient alchemy: one based on the established rhythms of nature, in which the processes are allowed to happen without being influenced or hurried, and another that calls for demonic help, even if the demons are also considered to be part of nature.[251] The presence of worked metals, glass, tools made of metal or bone, a small metal anvil (a rare and still unpublished find) and the large number of ceramic fragments from a great variety of vessels, the traces of furnaces and charcoal pieces, as well as the proof of the knowledge and use of demonic forces, lead us to hypothesize that this workshop was, in fact, an alchemical one. However, there is also the possibility that the golden leaf was found here in a secondary position, so the confirmation or denial of our hypothesis will be based upon future research on the archaeological material discovered here, and from other similar workshops.

The Way

Archaeological and epigraphic evidence suggests a strong influence from the western Black Sea coast to the cities on the Danube river (Troesmis (Iglița), Durostorum (Silistra), Novae (Svištov), Sucidava (Celei), Oescus (Gigen), Dubovan, Viden, Drobeta (Drobeta Turnu Severin), Dierna (Orșova), Viminacium (Kličevac), Montana) in terms of the spread of the deities of Egyptian origin. The dissemination of the Isiac religious manifestations seems to have reached the western coast of the Black Sea quite early, already by the 3rd century BC. Whether this was the result of the direct political-religious influence of the Ptolemies (as argued Fr. Cumont) or based exclusively on the humanity of the Greeks, some of whom were seduced by the radiance of the Egyptian gods (as Fraser argues)[252] is an unresolved question. L. Bricault demonstrates that the problem of the Isiac diffusion is a complex one and that multiple elements which defined and influenced it must be taken into account. From the Greek colonies in Crimea (3rd century BC) we have evidence attesting to the presence of the Isiacs, the most spectacular being a polychrome fresco from a Nymphaeum, where one of the ships pictured bears

[241] Śliwa 2017, 228.
[242] Vasileiadis 2017, 23.
[243] Bodor, Winkler 1979, 141-155.
[244] Stoicovici 1978, 245-250.
[245] Kotansky 1994, 97.
[246] Kotansky 1994, 98-99.
[247] Kotansky 1994, 99.

[248] Kotansky 1994, 100.
[249] Kotansky 1994, 100.
[250] Fraser 2004, 125-147.
[251] Fraser 2007, 33-54.
[252] Bricault 2007, 246.

the name of the goddess Isis.[253] L. Bricault links this reality to Arsinoe II who identified herself with the goddess and who was also the protector of the Lagide fleet (Arsinoe *Euploia*).[254] In Moesia Inferior, on the border of the Black Sea, most archaeological evidence has been discovered at Tomis (Constanţa);[255] however, artifacts related to deities of Egyptian origin have also been discovered at Callatis (Mangalia)[256], Dionysopolis (Balcic)[257], Istrus (Histria)[258], Odessus (Varna)[259], and Marcianopolis (Devnja),[260] the worshipers often forming *collegia.*[261]

In 160 BC, a group of Alexandrians in Tomis was placed under the protection of Serapis.[262] Religious manifestations addressed to the gods of Egyptian origin is also attested among the local population. Tacheva-Hitova believes that Tomis was "the centre of worship and religious influence of the Egyptian cults in Lower Moesia" during the Roman period.[263] The discoveries seem to support the perpetuation of the Hellenistic tradition, based on inscriptions and coins, until Philip the Arab, while figurative representations of these gods can be traced from the Flavian period into Late Antiquity. The presence of Alexandrian seafarers and traders is epigraphically attested at Tomis as a true ethnic community, doubled by a religious community with priests serving the temples and altars of the gods of Egyptian origin.[264] Bricault notes an inscription from the 3rd century AD: "hiéronautes réunis en collège sont mentionnés dans une inscription en compagnie de pastophores. Il est probable que ces fidèles sont à associer d'une façon ou d'une autre à Isis marine."[265] An exceptional discovery is the stone door of a funerary hypogeum on which deities and landscapes are represented schematically: Isis, Harpocrates, an Egyptian landscape, a goddess considered to be Venus with Amor, and a nude male character, perhaps Hercules.[266] Bricault highlights a temple that included a statue of Serapis, attested numismatically, which dates to the middle Severan period (Caracalla to Elagabalus).[267] In these centres of Isiac cults, representations of Serapis

deviate from the original Egyptian model, in order to suit Graeco-Roman spaces and population. Pluto-Serapis with Cerberus, Zeus-Serapis, Zeus-Sol-Serapis, Capitoline Zeus-Serapis, identified during the late Antonine and Severan periods by the name of *Theos Megas*, have been discovered in Odessos, Istros, Callatis and Dionysopolis.[268] Starting with Septimius Severus, *Theos Megas* from Odessos, understood as a Hades-Pluto, was assimilated with Serapis and represented on coins with a *patera* and a *cornucopia* in his hands and a *calathos* on his head.[269] As a local variant, on a certain type of coin discovered at Istrus, Callatis and Marcianopolis, Serapis appears in the form of the Thracian knight. Beginning with Commodus he is depicted with a *calathos* on his head, while in the early Severan period he has both a *calathos* and a crown of rays.[270] Among the coins discovered at Tomis, with representations of Serapis (Severus Alexander and Gordian III), is one with the bust of the god above the eagle, a version found only in Bithynia, and which Bricault considers to be taken from Alexandrian coins.[271] The latest coins from Tomis on which the god is depicted, are those from the reign of Philip II or Philip the Younger (238–249) in which the god and Philip II are depicted face to face. It is a type of coin issued during the reigns of Gordian III and Philip II in Moesia Inferior and Thrace, where the emperor considers himself an equal of the god, sharing the same divine sphere. The Alexandrian presence in Tomis continued until the 6th century AD, attested by a fragment of a funeral inscription which mentions a wine merchant from Alexandria.[272]

The Egyptian influence exerted on the inhabitants of Roman Dacia can be observed along the Danube, in Drobeta and Dierna, but also in Potaissa, among others.[273] If, in the case of the two ports, Drobeta and Dierna, the agents who introduced the deities of Egyptian origin and Graeco-Egyptian magic were the navigating soldiers enrolled in the *classis Flavia Moesica* and Alexandrian traders, in the case of Potaissa, the decisive role was played by the V legion Macedonica. And, although the gods of Egyptian origin (mainly Isis, Serapis, Osiris and Harpocrates) are also found in other settlements in the province of Dacia, a number of unique artifacts have been recovered at Potaissa and Dierna, attesting a close contact with the Egyptian world.

Contact between the V legion Macedonica and the East is attested around the year AD 66 in Judea, when it occupied the garrison of Ptolemais.[274] Information on the participation of this legion in the Jewish war and the

[253] Bricault 2001, 50; Bricault 2005, 115/0401
[254] Bricault 2007, 246-247; Bricault 2020, 39-40.
[255] Bricault 2001, 28-31.
[256] A funerary stela of an Isiac (2nd – 3rd centuries AD), coins with the image of Serapis and Isis sailing (3rd century AD), as well as a statuette discovered in a tomb representing Isis or a worshiper of her, along with other items (Bricault 2001, 30).
[257] A temple of Serapis (1st century BC), a public priest of the same god (1st century BC), coins with the image of Serapis (3rd century AD), a ceramic vessel with a possible image of the god Ra (3rd – 2nd century BC) (Bricault 2001, 30).
[258] An inscription proposing to bring the cult of Serapis in the city (3rd century BC), the head of a terracotta statuette representing Serapis, coins with the image of Serapis as a rider (3rd century AD) (Bricault 2001, 30).
[259] Coins with the image of the god Serapis (2nd- 3rd centuries AD), bronze statuettes of Isis (2nd- 3rd centuries AD) (Bricault 2001, 30-31).
[260] Temple of Serapis on the coins of Caracalla (211-217 AD) and Gordian III (238-244 AD), coins with the image of Serapis (3rd century AD) and a bronze statuette of Serapis (Bricault 2001, 31).
[261] Bricault 2014, 37-45.
[262] Bricault 2005, 618/1005; Tacheva-Hitova 1983, 12-13 n° I.17; Bricault 2007, 251; Bricault 2008, 206.
[263] Tacheva-Hitova 1983, 59.
[264] Tacheva-Hitova 1983, 59.
[265] Bricault 2007, 253.
[266] Barnea 1972, 257-260.
[267] Bricault 2007, 255.

[268] Bricault 2007, 257-258. Susan Guettel Cole, in her book from 1984, consider the possibility that this god is actually one of the *Theoi Megaloi* of Samothrace, but there is no evidence in this regard. However, in these Greek colonies there are attested temples of the gods of Samothrace and their mystai. (see Guettel Cole 184, 70-74.)
[269] Bricault 2008, 208-211.
[270] Bricault 2008, 212-213.
[271] Bricault 2008, 207.
[272] Barnea 1972, 261-262.
[273] Budischovsky 2004.
[274] Matei-Popescu 2010, 40.

conquest of Jerusalem are reported by Flavius Josephus. However, the legion did not return immediately to Moesia, at Oescus, where it had been previously quartered. Instead, the legion "followed Titus at Zeugma together with XV legion (Apollinaris) in order to meet the Parthian king Vologaeses and then southwards, to Alexandria. From there it was sent back to Moesia by sea, no sooner than the summer of 71."[275] The whole history of this legion is very interesting; however, it was stationed for a long time in the Lower Danube area, as well as in Dobrogea, and afterwards in Potaissa.[276] Deities and customs were clearly brought from Egypt to Potaissa by this legion, attested by epigraphic and archaeological evidence, which includes the presence of an Isiac *collegium*, a pseudo-obelisk covered with writing that imitates Egyptian hieroglyphs, a statuette representing a pharaoh in the position of veneration of a god, *shabti*, and a ring with a gem engraved with a bust of the god Serapis.[277] This hypothesis does not exclude the possibility that the gods of Egyptian origin were introduced to Potaissa by other means.

Meeting sailors of Graeco-Oriental or Egyptian origin in the naval troops of the Roman Empire was not an unusual situation. Mladen Tomorad analysed the demographics of *classis Ravennas* and *classis Misensis*, concluding that, "around 28% of the sailors in classis Misensis and 43% of the sailors in classis Ravennas came from Southeastern Europe and with the sailors from Egypt and the Hellenistic East they made up more than 60% of the entire number of the sailors in these two fleets. In the Misene fleet inhabitants from Dalmatia, Pannonia and Egypt usually served in the same units"[278]. There was also a *classis Pontica*, naval forces created as a result of the increasing interest of the empire in the Pontic area (*bellum Mithridaticum* or *bellum Bosporanum*); however, it rarely occurs in the epigraphic sources.[279] Wheeler pointed out that "the *classis Pontica*'s sphere of operations was trans-provincial and thus not part of a single governor's charge."[280] The role of these naval troops was also to remove the Pontic area from the influence of pirates, as Josephus states.[281] Epigraphic evidence of "the only praetorian fleet in the Black Sea", *classis Pontica*, disappears completely after the time of the Severans[282]. From inscription, can be conclude that vexillations of legions, auxiliary troops and the fleet of Moesia Inferior atested at Tyras, Olbia, Chersonesus "were quartered inside the cities and only

later, the military quarters separated by walls, forming real citadels"[283], therefore the interaction between the civilian population and the military is carried out openly including at the religious level.

The Interpretation

In order to make a relevant interpretation of the five artifacts from Dierna, there are several issues to consider: how the presence of the god Osiris evolved in the Roman Empire and what god should we actually see under this name; how the Isis/Serapis pair unfolded in the 2nd-3rd centuries AD and what is hidden behind these names; the extent to which Gnosticism can be noticed in the province of Dacia; the process of transforming the classical gods into messengers of an ineffable, inaccessible, omnipotent god of the classical gods, and the references in some inscriptions of the 3rd century AD, explicitly, to their supernatural power (*numen*), which shows us that they had begun to be considered as demigods rather than gods; as well as of the phenomenon defined as "lived ancient religion", reflecting the fear of the gods and hope in their help. Although we have tried to structure these concepts for a more logical approach, it is obvious that, in reality, it cannot be divided so strictly. They intertwine, overlap, and complement each other, finally forming the narrative of the religious life of the ancient city of Dierna in the 2nd and 3rd centuries.

Several statuettes representing the god Osiris are attested in the territory of Roman Dacia. Their number is not very high and, moreover, their discoveries were accidental, without an archaeological context.[284] In these conditions, it is difficult to determine how they were used and, if they were related to provincial funeral practices, whether they were involved in some Isiac or Graeco-Egyptian magical manifestations. A correspondence between Osiris or Osiris-Apis and Serapis (the first inscriptions in this regard dated to the reign of Ptolemy III Euergetes) should not be overlooked[285]. For the identification of Osiris with Serapis, during the reign of Ptolemy V Epyphanes (204-180 BC), an inscription discovered near Alexandria is instructive. The reading of the Greek text is controversial: Ὀσόρωι τε καὶ Σαράπιδι is translated as "to Osiris who is also Sarapis" by some scholars, or "to both Osiris and Sarapis" by others[286]. Mark Smith presents another Ptolemaic inscription (Greek, hieroglyphic, and demotic) to support the equivalence of the Egyptian Osiris with the Greek Serapis.[287] The situation

[275] Matei-Popescu 2010, 40; Wheeler 2012, 137-138.
[276] For the extended history of the legio V Macedonica, Prosopography included, see Matei-Popescu 2010, 35-76.
[277] Bricault 2005, 725-726; for the inscription attesting the existence of a *collegium Isidi* see CIL III, 882, Ardevan 1998, 426, no. 428; for shabti see Deac 2017, 249-251; for the statue with a representation of a pharaoh see Deac 2011; for Bes at Potaissa see Cristea 2016; for the pseudo-obelisk see Deac 2014.
[278] Tomorad 2003, 447. Moreover, Tomorad gives the example of three navigators - Petroni Celeris (*natione Alexandrinus*), Bato Scenorarbi (*natione Dalmata*) and Tiberio Marco (*natione Musiaticis*) - who served on the trireme and wore the name of the goddess Isis.
[279] Wheeler 2012, 123, 126-127, 130.
[280] Wheeler 2012, 131.
[281] Wheeler 2012, 131-134.
[282] Wheeler 2012, 147.

[283] Matei-Popescu 2010.
[284] Nemeti 2003, 280-281 knows only three of the statuettes; Nemeti 2010 presents seven such items, not all with a known place of discovery. Neither of them includes the two statuettes from Dierna.
[285] Smith 2017, 395-398.
[286] "On behalf of King Ptolemy and Queen Cleopatra, the manifest and beneficent gods: to Osiris who is also Sarapis (Ὀσόρωι τε καὶ Σαράπιδι), to Isis, to Anubis, and to all deities, male and female" (Smith 2017, 398)
[287] "The Greek dedication is to 'Sarapis the great god', but the hieroglyphic and demotic inscriptions refer instead to 'Osiris of Coptos, foremost in the house of gold'". (Smith 2017, 398). As for the name of the dedicator and his father, it is evident once again the equivalence of the two gods: 'Pamin the son of Psenosiris' (son of Osiris), in the demotic

was maintained through the Roman period, when such evidence is even more numerous, including inscriptions in which a correspondence is made with both Osiris and Osiris-Apis as well as figural representations.[288] Regarding the inscriptions, Smith discusses two stone monuments as examples, one from Kom Abu Billu, where the god is named Osiris-Apis in the demotic text and Serapis in the Greek text and one from Abydos (1st century BC or 1st century AD) in which the correspondence is made between "'Osiris the great god and lord of Abydos'" from the demotic text and "the lord (κύριος) Serapis" from the Greek text[289]. In terms of artistic representations, a series of *stelae* from Abydos represent Osiris, along with his specific iconographic elements, sitting or standing, usually with Isis next to him. The text that accompanies the images calls the god 'the lord Sarapis', 'Sarapis who is in Abydos', 'the lord Sarapis who is in Abydos', 'Sarapis the greatest god', or 'Sarapis the greatest god who is in Abydos'[290].

Important for the correspondence between Osiris and Serapis, but also for Serapis's assuming the role of the ruler of the Underworld, is the case of a *stela* from Middle Egypt, now in the Louvre, in which we receive information about the beliefs of navigators of Egyptian origin. The three navigators are represented in front of Osiris, with his usual appearance (mummiform, with the sceptre and whip in the hands placed over the chest and wearing the *atef* crown) after they were led by Anubis who is represented behind them. The Greek text begins with the phrase "Come to our aid, lord Sarapis" and gives us knowledge about the occupation of the three, as well as the circumstances of their death, all three bearing Egyptian names[291]. As Smith notes, it is relevant that Serapis is mentioned in the context of the afterlife, even if the image is still that of Osiris[292]. An analysis of human names from Roman Egypt derived from the name of Serapis helps to demonstrate the spread of religious manifestations related to this god which peaked in the 2nd-3rd centuries and decreased between the 4th and 7th centuries.[293] It is interesting that we encounter such names, especially among the Greek-speaking population and less among the population bearing traditional Egyptian names.[294] There is no undeniable confirmation that this is true for the other provinces of the empire, including Moesia Inferior and Dacia, but we have no reason to believe otherwise.

In the province of Dacia there is no archaeological evidence of any burial that obviously involved rituals of Egyptian origin. In one grave from Callatis a substantial amount of resin was observed suggesting that the deceased person was mummified, while an object resembling a *sistrum* was discovered among the funerary offerings[295]. The objects from this tomb give us clues to the practices of burial rituals similar to the Egyptian ones, in which an image of Osiris might have been involved, as well as on the influences it may have had on the ports on the Danube banks. It should be noted, however, that the god Osiris dissemination throughout the Roman Empire is achieved as a funerary deity, as well as Osiris Hydreios[296].

Normally, the *tyet*, an amulet representing the "knot of Isis", was related to protection provided by Isis during the journey of the dead to the underworld and one can find it in Spell 156 from the *Book of the Dead*. The type and colour of stone used to manufacture these amulets,[297] were important because their role was to transfer certain magical powers or qualities to those who wore them.[298] As Geraldine Pinch pointed out, the *tyet* amulet is "normally made in a red stone such as carnelian or jasper" and "may be linked to menstrual blood and its place in the creation of human life"[299]. Budge considers that the form of the amulet represents the genital organs of the goddess Isis and that it was probably intended to protect not only the dead, but also the living[300]. The spell specifies that the amulet will be placed on the neck area of the deceased and that the sap of a certain plant will be used in the ritual[301]. In order to ensure that the spell contains knowledge involving powerful forces destined only for a small number of initiates, it is forbidden to divulge the content of the spell and guarantee its effectiveness[302].

What role could such an amulet have played in the lives of the inhabitants of Dierna? Since there is no indication to suggest burials involving rituals specific to Egypt, we can assume that the amulet was brought from Egypt by a sailor (merchant or military) as a protective amulet, or as a reminder of his place of origin or ethnic heritage. In fact, the paucity of archaeological discoveries in the immediate vicinity of Dierna connected with the Isiac cults (e.g. statuettes, inscriptions, gems) only allows us to speculate.

Starting with the Hellenistic period and continuing in the Roman imperial period, the popularity of Isis increased. She no longer belonged to a population or an area, because

---

inscription and 'Paniskos the son of Sarapion' (son of Serapis) in the Greek inscription (Smith 2017, 299).

[288] Smith 2017, 399-403.
[289] Smith 2017, 399-400.
[290] Smith 2017, 400.
[291] Smith 2017, 401. Mark Smith offers further other examples from Roman Egypt: Greek graffiti from the temple of Seti I in Abydos, Greek papyri in which the celebrations of the two gods are overlapped (Smith 2017, 401).
[292] Smith 2017, 402.
[293] "A total of 33 persons with a Sarapis-related name are attested in sources of the third century BC, 123 in those of the second century BC, 99 in those of the first century BC, 423 in those of the first century AD, 2137 in those of the second century AD, 1297 in those of the third century AD, and 485 in those of the fourth century AD" (Smith 2017, 402)
[294] Smith 2017, 403.

[295] Deac 2013, 184.
[296] Malaise 1972, 203-207.
[297] About how the Egyptians perceived and described in their texts the main colours (white, black, red, green, blue, yellow) see Schenkel 2019.
[298] Pinch 1994, 108; Budge 2001, 133; most of the Egyptian funerary amulets were produced from various red materials or gold (Budge 2001, 135-149).
[299] Pinch 1994, 116; Budge add to these materials also wood, glass, faience, agate, carnelian, all red, as well as gilded stones or solid gold (Budge 2001, 137).
[300] Budge 2001, 137.
[301] Pinch 1994, 116.
[302] Pinch 1994, 116.

she absorbed a sum of classical Graeco-Roman deities (Isis-Venus/Aphrodite, Isis-Ceres/Demeter, Isis-Tyche/Fortuna) and the names of many goddesses became local epithets of her name. Isis no longer acted exclusively as the protector of procreation and births, but, like Serapis, performed miracles, saving people from great danger or even death. Together with Serapis, she healed, sometimes through direct intervention such as by apparitions or dreams, which is why we often find them associated with Aesculapius and Hygia, either in inscriptions or in figural representations. These remarkable acts were made known by the priests and worshipers of the two gods through inscriptions and hymns inscribed in stone and recited in public[303]. The way Isis is defined in the hymns dedicated to her (aretalogies) spread with some necessary changes in the Graeco-Roman world. In a hymn, Isidorus addresses the goddess: "Mighty One, I shall not cease to sing of Your great Power, / Deathless saviour, many-named, mightiest Isis, / Saving from war, cities and all their citizens: / Men, their wives, possessions, and children. / As many as are bound fast in prison, in the power of death, / as many as are in pain through long, anguished, sleepless nights, / All who are wanderers in a foreign land, / And as many as sail on the Great sea in winter / When men may be destroyed and their ships wrecked and sunk.../ All (these) are saved if they pray that You be present to help./ Hear my prayers, O One Whose Name has great Power; / Prove Yourself merciful to me and free me from all distress."[304]

In the aretalogy of Isis from Maronea (ca. 120 BC), it is evident that distancing from Memphite roots occurred in order to be as accessible as possible to the Greek population. In this context, Osiris is sometimes replaced by Serapis, and Isis is presented as a Greek goddess, rather than an Egyptian one. The text from Maronea becomes, as L. Bricault pointed out, "une véritable interpretatio graeca du texte arétalogique originel, sans aucun doute connu de l'auteur, destinée à présenter de la manière la plus compréhensible qui soit la personnalité d'Isis à un public non familier de l'Égypte."[305] Versnel noticed, that this aretalogy is "the first explicit identification of Greek Demeter and Egyptian Isis". However, he also observes an obvious "Egyptian flavour" in the text and gives clear examples in this regard[306]. In the arethalogy from Kume, the goddess defines herself as being so powerful that everything she wants will be done[307]. A very important aspect of Isis, as perceived in the Greek and the Roman worlds, is that of the protector of navigation and sailors; thus, March 5th celebrated the re-start of the navigable season (*Ploiaphesia / Navigium Isidis*)[308]. She is furthermore the powerful mistress of the waters[309].

It was in the power of Isis of the aretalogies to provide to her devotees' security, fortune, knowledge, health, and immortality. Notwithstanding that the aretalogies, representations, and epithets she receives, transform Isis into *summa numinum, dea summas, una quae es omnia,*[310] the personification of the power of the nature,[311] the mentality of Roman society did not allow her to occupy such a place alone[312]. Therefore, a male god, Osiris or Serapis, had to be incorporated. We believe that this is why Apuleius places Osiris next to her as "père suprême des dieux, l'invincible Osiris",[313] not to take from her the status of supreme god. However, in the end, Isis is the one to whom destiny complies[314].

Both in the written and in the epigraphic sources a paradoxical phenomenon can be observed: on the one hand Isis is considered a Supreme Being, multifarious and with countless names, who creates everything that exists and to which everyone submits, including Destiny, while on the other hand, the saviour Isis, approaches mortals directly and has the characteristics of an angel/demon (in the sense of lesser divinity). Robert Turcan focuses on the feminine henotheist/megatheist aspect of the goddess, defining it as a reaction to the crisis taking place in the 2nd century AD. In Addition to the henotheistic facet of the gods, Valentino Gasparini discusses the demonic feature that Isis and Osiris/Serapis receive in the context of the theological crisis that the author suggestively calls the "Age of Anxiety",[315] which originated in the Hellenistic heritage. To perform this analysis, he uses as main sources Apuleius' *Metamorphoses* (noting the merit of Nicole Méthy in observing the way in which Isis is presented as Supreme Being in this source) and an inscription from Thessalonica. According to Apuleius, Isis can no longer be invoked with a single name and cannot be recognized due to a single face. In other texts of Apuleius (*De deo Socratis* and *De dogmate Platonis*) she became *ineffabilis* and *indicta et innominabilis,* and people's access to this Supreme Being was limited. Nevertheless, in *Metamorphoses*, Isis is not only eager to listen to the difficulties Lucius is going through, but intervenes directly in his aid, acting as a lower deity, a messenger of the central god.

Meanwhile, the hymns dedicated to the goddess present a different, opposite reality. Paraskevi Martzavou considers that Isis aretalogies can be divided into two types that correspond to two different moments staged as parts of the initiation process, placed in dedicated spaces from the sanctuaries: the "I-am-Isis", and the "You-are-Isis" type and he identifies in the text of Apuleius two episodes that are very similar to the two types of aretalogies. Martzavou

---

[303] Vesnel 1998, 39.
[304] Sfameni Gasparro 2007, 56.
[305] Bricault 2007, 251-252.
[306] Versnel 1998, 42-43.
[307] "What pleases me, that shall be finished; for me everything makes way" (Versnel, 44).
[308] Bricault 2007, 253. For Isis *Pelagia* and for Serapis and his connection with the Sea see Bricault 2006; Bricault 2020.
[309] "I soothe the sea and make it wave", "I make the navigable unnavigable whenever it pleases me" (Versnel, 43).

[310] Turcan 2007, 73, 84.
[311] Turcan 2007, 77-81.
[312] I am in debt to Jörg Rüpke who, through the generous discussions we had in Newcastle in 2019, spotlight this issue.
[313] Turcan 2007, 75; Gasparini 2011, 707.
[314] Turcan 2007, 76; "I overcome Fate, Fate harkens to me" (Versnel 1998, 45).
[315] Gasparini 2011, 697-701.

argues, based on *Metamorphoses*, that the aretalogies were part of the Isiac initiation and "had a performative role"[316]. It is clear that the apparition of Isis in the narration of Lucius has a striking impact on all his senses and create a strong emotional attachment to the goddess[317]. The aretalogies inscribed in stone may have served as a reminder of this emotion, lived during the initiation process, and of the strong bond with the goddess and the community of initiates with a periodic reinforcement[318]. The hymns themselves were designed to address the emotional side of the audience, by the solemn tone, the implied funerary character, and the surprising information about the powers of the goddess, some of which have clear Egyptian origin[319]. The inhabitants of Roman Dacia are no strangers to such hymns, and one of them, originate in Ulpia Traiana Sarmizegetusa, is analyzed in the article signed by L. Bricault, D. Deac and I. Piso, in this volume. The sounds of musical instruments, which certainly accompanied the recitation of the text, also heightened the emotions. Paraskevi Martzavou lists some of the emotions felt by the audience, the same emotions underlined by Chaniotis as ingredients from which gods are made of: admiration and gratitude, fear, hope, and piety[320].

An explanation for this discrepancy is sought and, in this regard, Valentino Gasparini consider the information provided by Plutarch's *De Iside et Osiride*: "Isis and Osiris first were not even divine, but demigods (demons), and only later they were promoted to the rank of gods"[321]. The Platonic interpretation of the demons is important for Plutarch and Apuleius: "lower divinities, souls of the deceased, intermediate and guardian spirits. Demons share both the divine status (they are superior and eternal beings) and the human one (they have corporeal, or semi-corporeal, intellectual and emotional characteristics). As an intermediate ring between the two worlds, they often become messengers between heaven and earth: only the demons, among the superior beings, intervene repeatedly and directly and in detail in human life, in order to play a saving role with their interventions, normally carried out through dreams." To these ideas overlap Gnostic, Orphic, and Stoic influences. Gasparini notice the existence in the text of *Metamorphoses* of both denomination *dea* and *numen*, which refer to Isis, and this reflect the religious context of the 1st - 3rd centuries AD.

This situation is also found in the inscriptions of the province of Dacia, without necessarily being related to the goddess of Egyptian origin, but rather to a wide spectrum of gods: Aesculapius and Hygia, Apollo, Serapis, Liber, Bonus Puer, Caelestis, Dolichenus, Hierobolus, and Saturnus. It is possible that they were deities who initially had the status of demigods, being later raised among the gods (as Plutarch says about Isis and Osiris) or, on the contrary, gods who lost their importance in the context of the increasing power of megatheism[322]. Isis is not the only deity on whom this paradox hovers. A similar situation can be observed in the case of Theos Hypsistos who is included in the category of the *epekoos* gods (like Isis), but who is an ineffable god, with many names, a god who cannot be seen, but who sees everything, who is served by lesser gods named angels (like the supreme Orphic god)[323]. Inscriptions dating from the 2nd century BC onward, prove that the tendency to consider Isis as the universal and creative power as Supreme Being is not specific to the period between 2nd - 3rd centuries AD, even if an enhancement of this phenomenon can be observed during this period[324]. But what can be said about the demonic dimension of Isis and Osiris? Gasparini introduces the inscription from Thessalonica (late 2nd century BC) which contains information similar to Plutarch's text[325]. Damaios' poem alludes to the myth of Isis and Osiris, and the two gods are invoked as saving deities, with direct references to the invention of navigation. Osiris is directly defined here as a demon (in the sense of a minor deity) in the same way as in Plutarch's text. Gasparini proposes Manetho, high priest of Heliopolis, as the source of the two texts. These helped to forge new directions in the Hellenistic Isiac cults by introducing some elements promoted by Plato's philosophy (like demonology)[326].

In the oracular inscription of Apollo from Oenoanda[327] (late 2nd - early 3rd centuries AD), using terms of Orphic influence, the *Aether* is stated to be the true god, and the one who wants to pray to him must face the sun at dawn. The Olympian classical gods are nothing but *angeloi* of this megatheistic god, messengers between men and god and, at the same time, part of him. The same divine hierarchy can be found at Lactantius (around 308 AD) and in the *Theosophy of Tübingen* (late 5th century AD)[328] and also

---

[316] Martzavou 2012, 270-280.

[317] Martzavou 2012, 274.

[318] Martzavou 2012, 278.

[319] Martzavou 2012, 180-181.

[320] Martzavou 2012, 283; Chaniotis 2011; Chaniotis 2012.

[321] Gasparini 2011, 702-706.

[322] In Mihai Barbulescu's article about *numen* in the votive inscriptions from Dacia, the author makes a distinction between two situations: the one in which *numen* in the dative is followed by the name of the divinity / divinities in the genitive, when *numen* represents the divine power of the respective god and the one in which *numen* in the dative is followed by the name of the divinity / divinities in the dative, in which case *numen* would designate a demigod or a deity inferior to *deus*. Bărbulescu remarks that almost all the inscriptions from the province of Dacia in which *numen* receives the meaning of demigod are dated in the 3rd century AD. (Bărbulescu 2005)

[323] Chaniotis 2010, 116-117.

[324] Bricault 1996; Gasparini 2011, 709-710.

[325] "For you, Osiris the demon, [Phylakides] built this enclosure and, inside of it, the well-carved coffin, carried by the drift of the current where you bring your periplus to fruition in the starry night and make Isis charming during celebrations. Indeed, first you yourself assembled the boards of the ship and made your way with polished oars. But rise, and may you allow to Phylakides and his children the good present of the fame, keeping them healthy so that everyone, by seeing all this, will stir his heart to never forget the Gods. [Poem] of Damaios." (*RICIS* 113/0506, trans. V. Gasparini); Gasparini 2011, 710-714.

[326] Gasparini 2011, 714.

[327] "Self-generated, untaught, without-mother, un-moveable,
not using a name, many-named, in-fire-dwelling,
this is God. We angels [angeloi] are a small part of God.
This [reply] to those who inquired about God, who he actually is:
All-Seeing Aether is God, [the oracle] said, looking to him
at dawn, pray, gazing towards the east." (Cline 2011, 20)

[328] Cline 2011, 19-22, 26-30.

at the Middle Platonists and Neoplatonists. Consequently, the 2nd - 3rd centuries AD represent a moment when the old, classical gods coexist with megatheistic tendencies and beliefs and with the beginning of Christianity. The solar gods became very popular, and gods who until now did not have this dimension, such as Serapis, absorbed these solar gods as an aspect of their personality. The change that took place in the religions of the Roman Empire can be noticed in the tendency of creating a universal but inaccessible god, many-named (as Isis), and also in the loss of power and influence of the classical Greco-Roman gods and their transformation into angels / demons (but not in a strict Christian sense). Lactantius uses the term *daemones* with a negative connotation, as a Christian term, referring to another oracular text of Apollo. However, the oracle used the concept of *daemon* in a neutral way, as a less important divinity[329]. For the Late-Antique philosophers the concepts of *angelus* and *daemon* are interchangeable, as Cline observes, representing "a particular sort of divine intermediary"[330].

Therefore, are the gods of Egyptian origin identified at Dierna Supreme Beings or minor deities? Based on the evidence and the more general religious and social phenomena acknowledged throughout the empire, we believe they are both and even more. What characterized the deities originating in the eastern part of the Roman Empire and especially in Egypt, is a high degree of adaptability and fluidity of appearance and meaning. Therefore, we do not believe that the double role played by the divine pair would have appeared in some way paradoxical or contradictory for the worshippers of Isiac cults. Moreover, although the magical dimension of the personality of the gods Isis, Osiris, Harpocrates/Horus, and Nephthys[331] was perpetuated only to a very small extent in the Grec and Roman world, the discovery of the "knot of Isis" amulet at Dierna, once again, supports the perception of the gods of Egyptian origin in a way much closer to their origins, than in other cities of the province of Dacia. Concurrent we are aware that this may well be just a particular case. Frankfurter sees the demonization and the division of certain gods in Late Antiquity as a consequence of the collapse of the temples as a space of ritual preservation, providing as an example Osiris, who was associated with the demon Akephalos in the 5th – 6th centuries AD[332]. The inhabitants of Dierna had to have a strong motivation to choose a religion based on the assembling of the durable emotional beliefs[333]. Recently, an effective and compelling tool, "resilience theory", has been used by archaeologists to investigate the dynamics of the socio-ecological systems, in which behaviour adjusts

to environmental changes in order to endure and thrive[334]. In this regard, reactions to climatic changes, coping mechanisms following disasters, and the anticipation of future feelings are important aspects to consider. Jörg Rüpke applied the notions of this theory in the urban space of Rome and other cities, emphasizing the relationship between humans and the space in which they live through the analysis of religious practices (*fasti*, the demographic dynamic, plagues and other disasters, the idea of a city and its survival), understanding the resilience as a process that develop in time[335]. Since Dierna is submerged, we can only make comparisons with other ports on the Danube, such as Drobeta, for which we have similar chronologies, environmental characteristics, and external influences.

We welcome the idea that catastrophic moments, such as climatic change, earthquakes, volcanic eruptions, epidemic plagues, and barbarian attacks, represent decisive factors that prompted changes in the religious experiences of Romans[336]. Jan Dietrich defines a catastrophe as "a process in the framework of the essentially interconnected link between nature and culture which leads to an event in a vulnerable community that destroys the essential foundations of this community and is perceived as comprehensive calamity"[337]. A catastrophic event will be perceived like that only by humans, because a natural shift, even a dramatic one, it is not a catastrophe *per se*, but only from a cultural perspective. "This is why disasters never occur in nature, but only in culture; even if their origin is to be found in the interdependency between nature and culture."[338] And what emphasizes a catastrophe is not only the risk or threat it entails, but also the human experience perceived by the survivors of such an event, as well as coping mechanisms of catastrophes. At a practical level, drought and famine lead to the digging of new wells or building cisterns, dislocation of populations, reorientation towards more resistant cultures; earthquakes generate new architectural solutions and floods lead to building canals, stilling basins and dams[339]. In the case of wars and epidemics, we can observe archaeologically practical methods of dealing with events, such as building stronger walls and tunnels, water basins and storerooms, improving weapons and military strategies, or moving settlements from an infected area to a new one[340]. For the geographical area of Dierna, in the period between the reigns of Gordian III (238-244 AD) and Trebonianus Gallus (251-253 AD), the borders of the empire were under the pressure exerted by the Goths, Sarmatians and Carps. As a coping mechanism, the Romans reconstructed some military camps, such as those at Ravna or Boljetin, in order to consolidate the border[341]. Disasters play an important

---

[329] Cline 2011, 29-30.
[330] Cline 2011, 30.
[331] For the magical implication of Isis and other "Isiac deities" in the Roman Empire see Gordon, Gasparini 2014.
[332] Frankfurter 2018, 68.
[333] The religious context of Dierna is only partially known. A cosmopolitan port like Dierna, must have had a diverse set of deities and an amalgamation of religious manifestations in which the deities of Egyptian origin were only one element, albeit an important one.

[334] Bradtmöller et al. 2017, 1.
[335] Rüpke 2020, 114-144.
[336] Grattan 2006.
[337] Dietrich 2015, 153.
[338] Dietrich 2015, 153.
[339] Dietrich 2015, 153-154.
[340] Dietrich 2015, 154-155.
[341] A hoard consisting of 193 coins from the time of Maximinus Thrax (235-238 AD), probably buried during the expedition undertaken by the emperor against the Sarmatians or Dacians, was discovered at Ravna

role in individual and social self-definition, creating what Chaniotis calls an "emotional community" around a deity, in which all members feel the same fear, hope, piety, and pride, strengthened by rituals[342]. It represents a personalised relation of human beings with the world, a relation in which there is no place for meaningless events[343]. As long as they can give a face and a name to the disaster, it can be limited in its complexity and possible to tame until the level of acceptance and can be integrated into the world. The rituals performed in times of great distress help members of a community to channel the fear born from feeling of powerless vulnerability in order to develop a collective effort to overcome the disaster[344]. The shift that resulted in defining deities in the 2nd - 3rd centuries AD derives from a multitude of gods with limited powers to an omnipotent god that controls everything and to whom all the powers of the world submit, including Destiny, which further reduces the complexity of the disasters and causes a decrease in anxiety. Moreover, the association of emperors such as Gordian III, Philip I (Philip the Arab) or Philip II (Philip the Younger) with a compelling god (Serapis), in a time of deep social, political, economic and military instability of the empire and even before, is thought to be not only a political legitimation of the actions of the emperor as an equal of the god, but also as an act of propaganda[345].

Conclusion

As the title of the paper suggests, we did not limit ourselves to presenting some artifacts related to the religious manifestations centred on the gods of Egyptian origin in Dierna. Rather, we wanted to expand the discussion into other aspects related to the study of the religions of the Roman Empire: methodology, assemblage, influences, and interpretations. We have listed and defined the terms and concepts used in the text or which have influenced our approach, and it is easy to observe that all these terms have a dynamic dimension and refer to the religions of the Roman Empire as a process and as a narrative, and not only as a static reality. At the same time, we stressed the fact that a religious manifestation from a certain place is part of a more complex dynamic which involves various aspects of life, some specific to a particular moment (e.g., a harsh winter, a plague, or a war) and some specific to broader trend (e.g., the spread of Christianity or the function of magic in the Roman Empire). The materiality of the Isiac cults is just one aspect of the assemblage represented in the Roman city of Dierna, an assemblage in which the socio-ecological dynamic, the coping mechanisms of changes, disasters, and fears were important elements to consider.

Lifeways in Dierna cannot be investigated without considering the influences that made their mark on this Roman city: the proximity of the Danube river, its location in a border area, the presence of the Roman military and commercial navigation to and from the Greek colonies on the western coast of the Black Sea. In the propagation of certain religious practices the external factors which generate anxiety and fear are important. There were also specific internal factors, that captivated an audience by creating an emotional connection with the gods in a manner that led to new emotional beliefs which represented the basis of motivation in choosing those gods. The hymns (aretalogies) and rituals dedicated to the gods of Egyptian origin, as well as fragments appropriated from mythology, possess a deep emotional charge. The gods were presented as extremely powerful, but at the same time had certain human characteristics which made them trustworthy, as suggested by the written sources.

The central point of the article is represented by the five items from Dierna and its environs, related to the Isiac cults (two statuettes with the representation of the god Osiris, a bust of the god Serapis, a statuette with the image of the god Ra and an amulet representing the "knot of Isis"), whose specific archaeological contexts are unknown. Wishing to offer an interpretation of these artifacts, we have emphasised the general direction of the dissemination of these gods, which could have been applied in the case of Dierna. In the study of this Roman port, we encountered several difficulties and limitations: the archaeological excavations were made in the 1960's with the methodologies, techniques, and knowledge from that moment; the Roman city was flooded and, therefore, archaeological excavations can no longer be achieved in the Roman Dierna; insufficient study of the archaeological material resulting from the excavations and their summary publication.

We are confident that a re-examination of the archaeological material collected from this area and the documentation of the archaeological excavations, a comparison with other ports on the Danube River, as well as the undertaking of new archaeological excavations in areas still accessible will enrich the image we have of this border city of the Roman Empire. In this way the role played by the gods of Egyptian origin that reached Dierna from the Black Sea through the Danube will be much clearer. A more detailed analysis of the archaeological material will help us to find new elements that will cause a better understanding of the religious and social changes that occur in the 2nd - 3rd centuries AD.

Bibliography

Andelković, Demian 2016: Andelković, B. and Demian, N., *Colecţia de antichităţi egiptene a Muzeului Banatului din Timişoara*. Timişoara (2016).

Ando 2008: Ando, C., *The Matter of the Gods*. Berkeley/ Los Angeles/London (2008).

(Zotović, Kondić 1978, 196); the fort at Boljetin was probably rebuilt as a measure against the bellicose activity of Carpi, perceived as a serious threat in the Iron Gates area (Zotović, Kondić 1978, 197).

[342] Chaniotis 2011, 265.

[343] Dietrich 2015, 156-157.

[344] "We can differentiate between typically apotropaic rituals, mourning and fasting rituals, elimination and substitution rituals, atonement rituals and evocation rituals for protection against and coping with collective disaster. Quite often, several types were used simultaneously." (Dietrich 2015, 162.)

[345] Christodoulou 2015.

Ardevan 1996: Ardevan, R., "Dierna – toponyme et histoire". In *Roman Limes on the Middle and Lower Danube*, P. Petrović (ed.). Belgrad (1996): 243-246.

Ardevan 1998: R. Ardevan, *Viaţa municipală în Dacia Romană*, Timişoara, 1998.

Asimaki, Koustourakis 2014: Asimaki, A. and Koustourakis, G., "Habitus: An attempt at a thorough analysis of a controversial concept in Pierre Bourdieu's theory of practice", *Social Sciences* 3(4) (2014): 121-131.

Avram 2018: Avram, Al., "Sur les pastophores de Tomis". In *La Dacie et l'Empire romain. Mélanges d'épigraphie et d'archéologie offerts à Constantin C. Petolescu*, M. Popescu, I. Achim, F. Matei-Popescu (eds.). Bucarest (2018): 121-126.

Barnea 1972: Barnea, I., "Relaţiile Provinciei Scythia Minor cu Asia Mică, Siria şi Egiptul", *Pontica* V (1972): 251-265.

Bărbulescu 2005: Bărbulescu, M., "*Numen* în inscripţiile votive din Dacia". In *Corona Laurea. Studii în onoarea Luciei Ţeposu Marinescu*, C. Muşeţeanu, M. Bărbulescu, D. Benea (eds.). Bucureşti (2005): 85-89.

Benea 1975: Benea, D., "Observaţii cu privire la topografia Diernei în epoca romană". *Banatica* III (1975): 91-98.

Benea 1978: Benea, D., "Die V. Makedonische Legion auf den nördlichen Donaulimes im 3. - 4. Jahrhundert". *Acta Musei Napocensis* XV (1978): 235-244.

Benea 1979: Benea, D., "Opaiţe romano-bizantine în colecţia Muzeului Banatului". *Sargetia* XIV (1979): 219-224.

Benea 1996: Benea, D., *Dacia sud-vestică în secolele III-IV*. vol. 1. Timişoara (1996).

Benea 2001a: Benea, D., "Les fouilles de Dierna (I). Le secteur D". In *Die Archäologie und Geschichte der Region des Eisernen Tores zwischen 106-275 n.Chr.*, M. Zahariade (ed.). Bucureşti (2001): 129-148.

Benea 2001b: Benea, D., "Archäologische Forschungsarbeiten bei Dierna (II)". In *Die Archäologie und Geschichte der Region des Eisernen Tores zwischen 106-275 n.Chr.*, M. Zahariade (ed.). Bucureşti (2001): 149-160.

Benea 2013: Benea, D., *Istoria Banatului în Antichitate*. Timişoara (2013).

Benea 2016: Benea, D., *Istoria Banatului. Antichitatea*. Bucureşti (2016).

Benea, Şchiopu 1974: Benea, D. and Şchiopu, A., "Un mormînt gnostic de la Dierna". *Acta Musei Napocensis* XI (1974): 115-124.

Bennett 2014: Bennett, Z., "What's in a name? Transforming our Perception of the Function of Demonic Entities in the Ancient Egyptian Book of Two Ways". *Rosetta* 15.5 (2014): 1-18.

Beretta 2004: Beretta, M., *When glass matters. Studies in the history of science and art from graeco-roman antiquity to early modern era.* Firenze (2004).

Beretta 2009: Beretta, M., *The Alchemy of Glass. Counterfeit, Imitation and Transmutation in Ancient Glassmaking.* Sagamore Beach (2009).

Berkeszi 1908: Berkeszi, I., "A Délmagyarországi Történelmi és Régészeti Múzeum Temesvárott". *Muzeumi Közlemények*. Budapest (1908): 198-212.

Bodor, Winkler 1979: Bodor, A. and Winkler, I., "Un atelier de artizanat la Dierna (Orşova)". *Acta Musei Napocensis* XVI (1979): 141-155.

Bohak 2016: Bohak, G., "The Diffusion of the Graeco-Egyptian Magical Tradition in Late Antiquity". In *Graeco-Egyptian Interactions: Literature Translation and Culture 500 BC-AD 300*, I. Rutherford (ed.). Oxford (2016): 357-381.

Bohak 2019: Bohak, G., "The Use of Engraved Gems and Rings in Ancient Jewish Magic". In *Magical Gems in their Contexts*, K. Endreffy, Á. M. Nagy, J. Spier (eds.). Budapest (2019): 37-45.

Bondoc 2009: Bondoc, D., *The Roman Rule to the North of the Lower Danube during the Late Roman and Early Byzantine Period.* Cluj-Napoca (2009).

Bounegru, Zahariade 1997: Bounegru, O. and Zahariade, M., *Les Forces Navales du Bas Danube et de la Mer Noir aux Ier-VIe Siècles.* Oxford (1997).

Bradtmöller et al. 2017: Bradtmöller, M. and Grimm, S. and Riel-Salvatore, J., "Resilience theory in archaeological practice – An annotated review". *Quaternary International* XXX. (March 2017): 1-14.

Bricault 2001: Bricault, L., *Atlas de la diffusion des cultes isiaques (IV e av. J.-C. – IV e s. apr. J.C.).* Mémoires de l'Académie des Inscriptions et Belles-Lettres, Tome XXIII. Paris (2001).

Bricault 2005 (RICIS): Bricault, L., *Recueil des inscriptions concernant les cultes isiaques (RICIS)*, Vol. I-II - Corpus, Vol. III – Planches. Mémoires de l'Académie des Inscriptions et Belles-Lettres, Tome XXXI. Paris (2005).

Bricault 2006: Bricault, L., "Isis, Dame des flots". *Ægyptiaca Leodiensia* 7. Liège (2006).

Bricault 2007: Bricault, L., "La diffusion isiaque en Mésie Inférieure et en Thrace: Politique, commerce et religion". In *Nile into Tiber. Egypt in the Roman World. Proceedings of the IIIrd International Conference of Isis Studies, Leiden, May 11-14-2005*, L. Bricault, M. J. Versluys, P. G.P. Meyboom (eds.). Leiden/Boston (2007): 245-266.

Bricault 2008: Bricault, L., "Les Monnaies à types ou marques isiaques de la mort de Sévére Alexandre à la prise du pouvoir par Dioclétien (235-284 apr. J.-C.)". In *Sylloge Nummorum Religionis Isiacae et Serapiacae*

(SNRIS), L. Bricault (ed.). Mémoires de l'Académie des Inscriptions et Belles-Lettres, Tome XXXVIII. Paris (2008): 246-247.

Bricault 2014: Bricault, L., "Les Sarapiastes". In *Le myrte et la rose. Mélanges offerts à Françoise Dunand par ses élèves, collègues et amis*, G. Tallet, Ch. Zivie-Coche (eds.). Montpellier (2014): 41-49.

Bricault 2020: Bricault, L., *Isis Pelagia: Images, Names and Cults of a Goddess of the Seas*. Leide/Boston (2020).

Budge 2001: W. Budge, E. A., *Amulets and Magic*. London/New York (2001).

Budischovsky 2004: Budischovsky, M.-Ch., "Témoignages isiaques en Dacie (106 - 271 ap. J.-C.): Cultes et Romanisation". In *Nile into Tiber. Egypt in the Roman World. Proceedings of the IIIrd International Conference of Isis Studies, Leiden, May 11-14, 2005*, L. Bricault (ed.). Leiden/ Boston (2007): 267-288.

Chaniotis 2010: Chaniotis, A., "Megatheism: The Search for the Almighty God and the Competition of Cults". In *One God: Pagan Monotheism in the Roman Empire*, S. Mitchell and P. van Nuffelen (eds.). Cambridge (2010): 112-140.

Chaniotis 2011: Chaniotis, A., "Emotional Community through Ritual. Initiates, Citizens, and Pilgrims as Emotional Communities in the Greek World". In *Ritual Dynamics in the Ancient Mediterranean: Agency, Emotion, Gender, Representation*, A. Chaniotis (ed.). Stuttgart (2011): 264-290.

Christodoulou 2015: Christodoulou, P., "Isis, Serapis and the Emperor". In *Romanising Oriental Gods? Religious transformations in the Balkan provinces in the Roman period. New finds and novel perspectives. Proceedings of the International Symposium, Skopje, 18-21 September 2013*, A. Nikoloska, S. Müskens (eds). Skopje (2015): 167–211.

Cline 2011: Cline, R., *Ancient Angels. Conceptualizing Angeloi in the Roman Empire*. (RGRW 172). Leiden/ Boston (2011).

Cristea 2016: Cristea, Ş., "An Image of the god Bes in Potaissa". *Aegyptus et Pannonia* 15 (2016): 37-49.

Deac 2011: Deac, D., "A Pharaoh Depiction in Roman Dacia", *Ephemeris Napocensis* XXI (2011): 111-114.

Deac 2013: Deac, D., "Comunitatea isiacă din Callatis". In *Atheovest I. In Memoriam Liviu Măruia. Interdisciplinaritate în Arheologie şi Istorie. Timişoara, 7 Decembrie 2013*, A. Stavilă, D. Micle, A. Cîntar, C. Floca, S. Forţiu (eds.). Szeged (2013): 183-189.

Deac 2014: Deac, D., "Imitating the Egyptian Hieroglyphic Script in the Roman Era. The Case from Potaissa". *Zeitschrift für ägyptische Sprache und Altertumskunde* 141 (2014): 34-38.

Deac 2017: Deac, D., "Shabtis and Pseudo-Shabtis from the Roman Provinces of Pannonia, Dacia and Moesia. An Overview". In *Egypt 2015: Perspectives of Research. Proceedings of the Seventh European Conference of Egyptologists. 2nd-7th June 2015, Zagreb, Croatia*, Egyptology 18, M. Tomorad, J. Popielska-Grzybowska (eds.). Oxford (2017): 241-256.

Dietrich 2015: Dietrich, J., "Coping with Disasters in Antiquity and the Bible: Practical and Mental Strategies". In *Past Vulnerability: volcanic eruptions and human vulnerability in traditional societies past and present*, F. Riede (ed.). Aarhus (2015): 151-167.

Düringer 2014: Düringer, E.-M., *Evaluating emotions*. London (2014).

Eidinow 2017: Eidinow, E., "In search of the "beggar-priest". In *Beyond Priesthood Religious Entrepreneurs and Innovators in the Roman Empire*, R. Gordon, G. Petridou, J. Rüpke (eds.). Religionsgeschichtliche Versuche und Vorarbeiten 66. Berlin (2017): 255-276.

Florescu 1978: Florescu, R., "Epoca romană". In *Comori arheologice în regiunea Porţile de Fier*, E. Florescu, R. Florescu, I. Opriş, S. Perisic, J. Rankov, D. Putnik (eds.). Bucureşti (1978): 143-147.

Fodorean 2006: Fodorean, Fl., *Drumurile din Dacia romană*. Cluj-Napoca (2006).

Frankfurter 1994: Frankfurter, D., "The Magic of Writing and the Writing of Magic: the Power of the Word in Egyptian and Greek Traditions". *Helios* vol. 21/2 (1994): 189-221.

Frankfurter 2018: Frankfurter, D., "The Threat of Headless Beings: Constructing the Demonic in Christian Egypt". In *Fairies, Demons, and Nature Spirit. "Small Gods" at the Margins of Christendom*, M. Ostling (ed.). London (2018): 57-78.

Fraser 2004: Fraser, K. A., "Zosimos of Panopolis and the Book of Enoch: alchemy as forbidden knowledge". *ARIES* Vol. 4/ 2 (2004): 125-147.

Fraser 2007: Fraser, K. A., "Baptised in Gnôsis: The Spiritual Alchemy of Zosimos of Panopolis". *Dyonisius* Vol. XXV (2007): 33-54.

Gasparini 2011: Gasparini, V., "Isis and Osiris: Demonology vs. Henotheism?". *Numen* 58 (2011): 697-728.

Gasparini et al. 2020: Gasparini, V., Patzelt, M., Raja, R., Rieger, A.-K., Rüpke, J. and Urciuoli, E. R., "Pursuing lived ancient religion". In *Lived Religion in the Ancient Mediterranean World*, V. Gasparini, M. Patzelt, R. Raja, A.-K. Rieger, J. Rüpke, E. R. Urciuoli (eds.). Berlin/Boston (2020): 1-8.

Gordon 1972: Gordon, R., "Mithraism and Roman Society: Social factors in the explanation of religious change in the Roman Empire". *Religion* 2:2 (1972): 92-121.

Gordon, Gasparini 2014: Gordon, R. and Gasparini, V., "Looking for Isis 'the Magician' (ḥkȝy.t) in the Graeco-Roman World". In *Bibliotheca Isiaca*, III, L. Bricault, R. Veymiers (eds.). Bordeaux (2014): 39-53.

Grattan 2006: Grattan, J., "Aspects of Armageddon: An exploration of the role of volcanic eruptions in human history and civilization". *Quaternary International* 151 (2006): 10-18.

Grimes 2006: Grimes, S. L., *Zosimus of Panopolis: Alchemy, Nature, and Religion in Late Antiquity.* Dissertation. Syracuse University (2006).

Grimes 2018: Grimes, S. L., "Secrets of the God makers: re-thinking the origins of Greco-Egyptian alchemy". *SYLLECTA CLASSICA* 29 (2018): 67–89.

Gudea 2001: Gudea, N., "Die Nordgrenze der römischen Provinz Obermoesien. Materialien zu ihrer Geschichte (86-275 n.Chr.)". *Jahrbuch des Römisch-Germanischen Zentralmuseums Mainz* 48 (2001) Sonderdruck.

Guettel Cole 1984: Guettel Cole, S., *Theoi Megaloi: The Cult of the Great Gods of Samothrace.* Leiden (1984).

Hamilakis, Jones 2017: Hamilakis, Y. and Jones, A. M., "Archaeology and Assemblage". *Cambridge Archaeological Journal* 27 (01) (2017): 77-84.

Hommel *et al.* 2017: Hommel, B., Moors, A., Sander, D. and Deonna, J., "Emotion Meets Action: Towards an Integration of Research and Theory". *Emotion Review* vol. 9 / 4 (October 2017): 295-298.

IDR III/1: Russu, I. I. (ed.), *Inscripţiile Daciei Romane*, Vol. III: Dacia Superior, 1 (Zona de Sud-Vest: teritoriul dintre Dunăre, Tisa şi Mureş). Bucureşti (1977).

Kotansky 1994: Kotansky, R., "Greek Magical Amulets. The Inscribed Gold, Silver, Cooper, and Bronze *Lamellae*. Part I – Published Texts of Known Provenance". *Papyrologica Coloniensia* XXII/I (1994).

Juan Petroi 2001: Juan Petroi, C., "Centre istorice ale unor oraşe dunărene din Banat. Evoluţie, perspective". *Historia Urbana* tom. IX / 1-2 (2001): 29-49.

Malaise 2007: Malaise, M., "La diffusion des cultes isiaques: un problème de terminologie et des critiques". In *Nile into Tiber. Egypt in the Roman World. Proceedings of the IIIrd International Conference of Isis Studies, Leiden, May 11-14-2005*, L. Bricault, M. J. Versluys, P. G.P. Meyboom (eds.). Leiden/Boston (2007): 19-39.

Martzavou 2012: Martzavou, P., "Isis Aretalogies, Initiations and Emotions: the Isis Aretalogies as a source for the study of emotions". In *Unveiling Emotions: Sources and Methods for the Study of Emotions in the Greek World*, A. Chaniotis (ed). Stuttgart (2012): 267-291.

Matei-Popescu 2010: Matei-Popescu, Fl., *The Roman Army in Moesia Inferior.* Bucharest (2010).

Medeleţ, Toma 1997: Medeleţ, Fl. and Toma, N., *Muzeul Banatului. File de cronică. I. 1872-1918.* Timişoara (1997).

Mirković 2007: Mirković, M., *Moesia Superior. Eine Provinz an der mittleren Donau.* Mainz am Rhein (2007).

Nemeti 2003: Nemeti, S., "Stăpânii lumii de dincolo". In *Funeraria Dacoromana. Arheologia Funerară a Daciei Romane*, M. Bărbulescu (ed.). Cluj (2003): 251-281.

Nemeti 2005: Nemeti, I., "Isis din colecţia Botár". In *Corona Laurea. Studii în onoarea Luciei Ţeposu Marinescu*, C. Muşeţeanu, M. Bărbulescu, D. Benea (ed.). Bucureşti (2005): 349 – 355.

Nemeti 2009: Nemeti, S., "Scythicum frigus. Repères pour une histoire du climat au Bas-Danube (Ier siècle apr. J.-C.)". In *Société et climats dans l'Empire romain. Pour une perspective historique et systémique de la gestion de ressources en eau dans l'Empire romain*, E. Hermon (ed.). Napoli (2009): 411-427.

Nemeti 2010: Nemeti, I., "Osiris în Dacia". In *Antiquitas Istro - Pontica. Mélanges d'archéologie et d'histoire ancienne offerts à Alexandru Suceveanu*, M. V. Angelescu, I. Achim, A. Bâltâc, V. Bolindeţ, V. Bottez (eds.). Cluj-Napoca (2010): 279-283.

Nemeti 2013: Nemeti, S., "Magical Practices in Dacia and Moesia Inferior". In *Jupiter on your side. Gods and Humans in Antiquity in the Lower Danube Area (Accompanying publication for the thematic exibitions in Bucharest, Alba Iulia and Constanţa – May-September 2013)*, C.-G. Alexandrescu (ed.). Bucharest (2013): 143-156.

Nemeti, Nemeti 2019: Nemeti, S. and Nemeti, I., "Votive practices and self-representation in Potaissa (Dacia)". In *Akten des 15. Internationalen Kolloquiums zum Provinzialrömischen Kunstschaffen. Der Stifter und sein Monument Gesellschaft – Ikonographie – Chronologie 14. bis 20. Juni 2017 Graz / Austria*, B. Porod, P. Scherred (eds.). Graz (2019): 284-296.

Oanţă-Mărghitu 2013: Oanţă-Mărghitu, R., *Aurul şi argintul antic al României (catalog de expoziţie).* Bucureşti (2013).

Peter 2008: Peter, U., "Mésie et Thrace". In *Sylloge Nummorum Religionis Isiacae et Serapiacae (SNRIS)*, L. Bricault (ed.). Mémoires de l'Académie des Inscriptions et Belles-Lettres, Tome XXXVIII. Paris (2008): 201-219.

Pinch 1994: Pinch, G., *Magic in Ancient Egypt.* London (1994).

Piso *et al.* 2019: Piso, I., Ardeţ, A. and Timoc, C., *Inscriptiones Daciae Romanae. Apendix III: Inscriptiones laterum museorum Banatus Temesiensis.* Cluj-Napoca (2019).

Poenaru Bordea 1996: Poenaru Bordea, Gh., "Dierna". In *Enciclopedia Arheologiei şi Istoriei Vechi a Românei*, C. Preda (ed.), vol. II (D-L). Bucureşti (1996): 54-55.

Popa 1979: Popa, Al., *Cultele egiptene şi microasiatice în Dacia romană*. PhD thesis. ms. (Universitatea Babeş-Bolyai). Cluj-Napoca (1979).

Radu *et al.* 2013: Radu, M., Gherasim, C., Huzui, A. and Stoiculescu, R., "The Reflection of Orşova City Evolution". *Cartographic Materials* vol. 7 / 2 (2013): 205-214.

Raja, Rüpke 2015: Raja, R. and Rüpke, J., "Archaeology of Religion, Material Religion, and the Ancient World". In *A Companion to the Archaeology of Religion in the Ancient World*, R. Raja, J. Rüpke (eds.). Boston (2015): 1-25.

Rămneanţu 2000: Rămneanţu, V., "Demersurile diplomaţiei româneşti pentru recuperarea bunurilor de patrimoniu ridicate de trupele sârbesti din Banat în 1919", *Analele Banatului* (SN) VII-VIII (1999-2000): 679-686.

Redman 2005: Redman, C. L., "Resilience Theory in Archaeology", *American Anthropoligist* vol.107 / 1 (Mar., 2005): 70-77.

Rüpke 2011: Rüpke, J., "Lived Ancient Religion: Questioning "Cults" and "Polis Religion"", *Mythos* (NS) 5 (2011): 191-204.

Rüpke 2018a: Rüpke, J., "Reflecting on Dealing with Religious Change", *Religion on the Roman Empire (RRE)* volume 4 / 1. Tübingen (2018): 132-154.

Rüpke 2018b: Rüpke, J., *Pantheon. A New History of Roman Religion*. Princeton (2018).

Rüpke 2019: Rüpke, J., "Urban Time and Rome's Resilience: Steeling Oneself against Disaster in Religious Practices". *NVMEN* 67 (2019): 1-28.

Rüpke 2020: Rüpke, J., *Urban Religion. A Historical Approach to Urban Growth and Religious Change*. Berlin/Boston (2020).

Sfameni Gasparro 2007: Sfameni Gasparro, G., "The Hellenistic Face of Isis: Cosmic and Saviour Goddess". In *Nile into Tiber. Egypt in the Roman World. Proceedings of the IIIrd International Conference of Isis Studies, Leiden, May 11-14-2005*, L. Bricault, M. J. Versluys, P. G.P. Meyboom (eds.). Leiden/Boston (2007): 40-72.

Siard 2007: Siard, H., "L'hydreion du Sarapieion C de Délos : la divinisation de l'eau dans un sanctuaire isiaque". In *Nile into Tiber. Egypt in the Roman World. Proceedings of the IIIrd International Conference of Isis Studies, Leiden, May 11-14-2005*, L. Bricault, M. J. Versluys, P. G.P. Meyboom (eds.). Leiden/Boston (2007): 417-447.

Śliwa 2017: Śliwa, J., "From the world of gnostic spells. The ιαεω-palindrome". In *Within the Circle of Ancient Ideas and Virtues. Studies in Honour of Professor Maria Dzielska*, K. Twardowska, M. Salamon, S. Sprawski, M. Stachura, S. Turlej (eds.). Krakow (2014): 225-231.

Smith 2017: Smith, M., *Following Osiris. Perspectives on the Osirian Afterlife from Four Millennia*. Oxford (2017).

Stoicovici 1978: Stoicovici, E., "Atelier de sticlă rubin de la Dierna (Orşova)", *Acta Musei Napocensis* XV (1978): 245-250.

Tacheva-Hitova 1983: Tacheva-Hitova, M., *Eastern Cults in Moesia Inferior and Thracia (5th century BC – 4th century AD)*. Leiden (1983).

Timoc 2006: Timoc, C., "Cercetări arheologice austro-ungare inedite la castrul roman de la Dierna-Orşova". *Patrimonium Banaticum* V (2006): 57-60.

Timoc 2008-2009: Timoc, C., "Despre topografia portului antic al Orşovei (Dierna)". *Studii de Istorie a Banatului* XXXII-XXXIII (2008-2009): 285-287.

Timoc 2016: Timoc, C., "Câteva sarcofage din piatră de la Dierna (Orşova) din Lapidariul Muzeului Naţional al Banatului". *Analele Banatului* (SN) XXIV (2016): 283-290.

Turcan 2007: Turcan, R., "Isis Gréco-Romaine et l'Hénothéisme Féminin". In *Nile into Tiber. Egypt in the Roman World. Proceedings of the IIIrd International Conference of Isis Studies, Leiden, May 11-14-2005*, L. Bricault, M. J. Versluys, P. G.P. Meyboom (eds.). Leiden/Boston (2007): 73-88.

Urbanová 2018: Urbanová, D., *Latin Curse Tablets of the Roman Empire*. Innsbruck (2018).

Vasileiadis 2013: Vasileiadis, P. D., "The Pronunciation of the Sacred Tetragrammaton: An Overview of a Nomen Revelatus that Became a Nomen Absconditus". *Judaica Ukrainica* vol. 2 (2013): 5–20.

Vasileiadis 2017: Vasileiadis, P. D., "The god Iao and his connection with the Biblical God, with special emphasis on the manuscript 4QpapLXXLevb". *Vetus Testamentum et Hellas* vol. 4 (2017): 21–51.

Versnel 1998: Versnel, H. S., *Inconsistencies in Greek and Roman Religion. 1, Ter Unus: Isis, Dionysos, Hermes, Three Studies in Henotheism*. Leiden/Boston/Köln (1998).

Vlassa 1974: Vlassa, N., "Interpretarea plăcuţei de aur de la Dierna". *Acta Musei Napocensis* XI (1974): 125-141.

Wheeler 2012: Wheeler, E. L., "Roman Fleets on the Black Sea: Mysteries of the Classis Pontica". *Acta Classica* LV (2011): 119-154.

Woolf 1997: Woolf, G., "Polis-Religion and its Alternatives in the Roman Provinces". In *Römi-sche Reichsreligion und Provinzial-religion*, H. Cancik, J. Rüpke (eds.). Tübingen (1997): 71–84.

Zotović, Kondić 1978: Zotović, L. and Kondić, V., "Fortificații romane și bizantine timpurii la Porțile de Fier". In *Comori arheologice în regiunea Porțile de Fier*, E. Florescu, R. Florescu, I. Opriș, S. Perisic, J. Rankov, D. Putnik (eds.). București (1978): 193-202.

www.ingramcontent.com/pod-product-compliance
Lightning Source LLC
Chambersburg PA
CBHW061300270326
41932CB00029B/3420